# The German Crocodile

A LITERARY
MEMOIR

Originally published in German in 2017 as *Das Deutsche Krokodil* by
Rowohlt Verlag GmbH, Reinbek bei Hamburg

First published in English in 2021 by DAS Editions.
A publishing imprint of Afropolitan Digital Limited
Salatin House 19 Cedar Road Sutton, Surrey SM2 5DA UK

The views expressed in this memoir are solely those of the author.
While some names have been changed to protect the identity of certain parties,
all the events in this memoir are true to the best of the author's memory.

A CIP catalogue record for this book is available from the British library.

ISBN:   978-1-8382215-0-8
eISBN:  978-1-8382215-1-5

Ayor font copyright ©2021 Duah Francis Boafo.
AYOR was inspired by NSIBIDI, a system of symbols indigenous to what
is now southeastern Nigeria.

Design and Typeset in the UK by Sheer Design and Typesetting
Printed and bound in Great Britain by Clays Ltd, Elcograf S.p.A

The translation of this work has been supported
by a grant from the Goethe-Institut.

This book has been selected to receive financial assistance
from English PEN's PEN Translates programme,
supported by Arts Council England. English PEN exists
to promote literature and our understanding of it, to
uphold writers' freedoms around the world, to campaign
against the persecution and imprisonment of writers
for stating their views, and to promote the friendly
co-operation of writers and the free exchange of ideas.
www.englishpen.org

Praise for *The German Crocodile*

'Much more than a personal story, this is a portrait of our society and epoch in miniature. (...) A mixture of reportage and *Bildungsroman* that simply had to be written.'

Kristina Maidt-Zinke, *Süddeutsche Zeitung*

'It is, among many other things, the most beautiful and moving ode to a mother that you can imagine.'

Jan Wiele, *Frankfurter Allgemeine Zeitung*

'The rise of the black Reich-Ranicki (...) A book that will make you laugh and cry (...) A must-read!'

Alexander von Schönburg, *Bild*

'Smart, reflective (...) It reads like literary fiction: I was gripped, often moved to emotion.'

Claudius Seidl, *Frankfurter Allgemeine Sonntagszeitung*

# The German Crocodile

## A LITERARY MEMOIR

IJOMA MANGOLD

*Translated from the German by*
*Ruth Ahmedzai Kemp*

**DAS EDITIONS**

A publishing imprint of Afropolitan Digital Limited

*For my mother*

# Contents

"Madness, madness. Everywhere, madness!"

Hans Sachs in *The Master-Singers of Nuremberg*

# PART I

# The Boy

Whenever the boy answers the phone, he always gives his full name. Some people who call to speak to his mother find this amusing and mimic him, as though the boy's naively narcissistic way of answering the phone merited an affectionate echo. When he pronounces his full name, it comes to nine syllables. The sounds and the rhythm pulse like a wave. But that's not the reason why he answers with such a tongue twister; no, this is his attempt to mitigate his fate. His middle name is his hope of tempering the exoticism of his first name: Ijoma Alexander Mangold.

When you look at it like this, it's actually 2-1 to Germany. But only when he manages to remind the person he's talking to of the existence of his middle name.

For all his attempts, it doesn't really work. Although his middle name appears on official documents like sports certificates, it isn't really given the same weight as his first name. The grown-ups clearly can't be dissuaded from the assumption that Ijoma is the name that best describes the boy, even though they always trip up when they say it. The way people stumble over his name is a source of grave embarrassment for the boy. It doesn't seem to bother anyone else. They even seem to derive a certain enjoyment when they praise its uncommon beauty; the logical conclusion is that he should count himself lucky he wasn't a run-of-the-mill Matthias, Andreas or Oliver.

He sees it differently, but he doesn't say so. He senses a great pressure to identify with his first name. His mother has told him several times he can call himself Alexander in kindergarten or at school if he wants to, but he can't imagine really going to the effort of changing it. It's not easy to tell people that from now on they should call you by a different name. 'What's wrong with you?' they would ask. 'Why would you want to get rid of your beautiful first name?' He doesn't want to go that far.

His mother says he was named Alexander after his great-great-grandfather, who was a tailor in Berlin. He could listen to the stories about his great-great-grandfather over and over; he never tires of hearing about him. He's grateful for his Berlin ancestor whose protective hand hovers over his middle name. Whenever his middle name is pushed aside, he can defend it by invoking his great-great-grandfather.

His first name is his father's legacy.

It seems a rather disproportionate intervention, given that his father has been completely absent from his life. All he knows about his father is that he studied medicine in Heidelberg and then went back to Nigeria soon after his son was born. There are only a few photos. In one, his father stands next to his grandmother, holding his son in his arms, wearing a suit and tie. In the background are vineyards, the Odenwald. The boy isn't particularly interested in the photos, but whenever his mother gets the album out – he can't exactly stop her – he's always amazed by the sheer joy on his grandmother's face. Isn't she at all bothered by this stranger holding her grandchild, he wonders. Why doesn't she look annoyed or uncomfortable? Doesn't it seem wrong to her that this stranger is taking up so much space in the family photo? Unlike his mother, who can't be relied on to react to things in any normal way, Grandma is usually more reliable. If it had been up to him, this photo and others like it would have been filtered out by now. He wouldn't mind if the picture were cropped. After all, if you're not around in life, why should there be a place for you in the photos?

The boy doesn't resent his father, but he doesn't miss him either. He has no memory of him, so he can see no reason for him to show up in the photo albums.

His mother sees it differently. She's always singing his praises. The boy can see through it: she just wants to establish an endearing image of a likeable father. She doesn't want her son to think badly of him just because he isn't there. She doesn't want her son to feel abandoned. Now and then she tells him the story about how his father came to Germany to study medicine, supported by his village. He had always assumed that he would go back home with the skills he acquired in this country, with his specialism in paediatric surgery. And on the other hand, she, his mother, couldn't imagine them going to Africa to live there. Much as she loves Africa, she felt too German for that. She and his father separated amicably; there was no reason to blame him or hold anything against him.

The boy is wary of these conversations about his absent father. His mother extols his virtues and tries to make it sound like everything is as it should be, but the fact remains that he – unlike all his friends – doesn't have a dad. And why should he listen to stories about a person who for him doesn't even exist?

To his relief, these conversations don't come up too often.

The good thing is that his father now has his own family in Nigeria. To avoid giving his wife any cause for jealousy or jeopardising the blessing of the household, his mother explains, they decided not to stay in touch. The boy is reassured by the potentially jealous wife; at least his father won't suddenly turn up at their door, in his suit and tie. The boy can do without any surprises like that. The absent father is a gap, a flaw, but as long as no one brings it up, it's an absence you can forget about. When his mother remarks that the boy has the same beautiful pianist hands as his father, he rolls his eyes. It's not the absence of his father that's the problem, it's the trail he left behind, the markers that point to him. But it's in the boy's first name that his father is most present. Whenever he tells someone his name, it inevitably leads to questions and it's the answers to those questions that draw people's attention to what is unusual about the boy's circumstances. 'Oh, so you have your father's first name and your mother's family name?' For some reason, people expect it to be the other way around.

These conversations are bearable enough; they're usually over quite quickly. But if only his mother didn't make such a fuss over his name! She never stops going on about how beautiful and unusual it sounds; that it means 'a stroke of luck'; that it isn't at all exotic in Nigeria; how nice it sounds when a name has three different vowels in it. This name – which the boy sees as a weakness, a flaw – is, in his mother's eyes, a cause for pride. This is what upsets him most. But the boy never says anything.

In any case, it seems to him that his first name has less to do with his father, than with his mother and her desire to be contrary, to do things differently. To choose a Nigerian to father her child – only his mother would have that idea. To raise a child without a father – who else would choose such a thing? And then to give your child a name that does the precise opposite of camouflage – that's the embodiment of her dauntless character!

———•——

Fortunately, there's Dossenheim near Heidelberg, a place so orderly and predictable that it effortlessly cocoons the boy and his unusual circumstances. When his mother is working, the boy is looked after by Tatie and Pfeifer-Papa. They're native Dossenheimers, with four children of their own who are already grown up. Everything is different at theirs, sometimes even unnervingly so, but there's a calming sense of order. Pfeifer-Papa's left arm ends above the elbow. He was hit by a bullet during the war, and his forearm had to be amputated. The boy doesn't know which war that was, but it stands to reason that you might lose your arm in one. He knows that much. He has an uncle you can't really talk to. He always glares at you suspiciously, as though he's about to say that something or other isn't allowed, or like he's about to catch you doing something forbidden. But his aunt says he only stares like that because his hearing is bad, because of the shelling during the war. Pfeifer-Papa with his arm stump is much nicer. He never stares at you in that fierce way. The worst you get with him is a mournful look when he talks about the suffering in the world. But it's so impressive when you see how dexterous he is with his arm stump, opening a can by clamping it between his upper arm and chest, operating the can opener with his hand. Pfeifer-Papa only wears his prosthesis on Sundays, along with his tie, to go to church. This reminds the boy of Grandma, who only puts her dentures in when she's expecting visitors. When the doorbell rings, she disappears into the bathroom and comes back with a facial expression that's so completely different, the boy is never absolutely certain that she's still the same Grandma: her cheeks are no longer sunken, but filled out; her lips, which normally droop inwards, now bulge outwards; there's something festive about the glimpse of dazzling white teeth you get when she laughs. But then the boy misses the mischievous intimacy that he normally associates with her.

There are three things in Pfeifer-Papa's apartment that make him uneasy. He looks at them from a respectful distance and avoids asking any silly questions about them. One is the photo of Eintracht Frankfurt football team; it's in a glass frame, and all the players have signed their names with a black marker pen at leg height. The club's flag hangs above the photo. Since football plays no role in the boy's home whatsoever, it seems a strange thing to hang on a wall; if Pfeifer-Papa's wall had a scalp hanging on it, it would hardly have been any stranger. Pfeifer-Papa is easily moved to emotion and gets teary when he talks about how rotten the world is and about the goodness of exceptional individuals, so there's clearly no place for wisecracks when it comes to this photo.

This is true of another picture, also framed, not only because it hangs in immediate proximity, but also because of a very curious-looking man who the boy finds unsettling, in spite of his friendly smile. Maybe it's the funny white robe he's wearing? He has mischievous eyes and a white cap on top of his ring of silver hair. He doesn't look stern at all. The boy doesn't know what it is about him, although Pfeifer-Papa occasionally praises his extraordinarily kind heart. Then sometimes his eyes well up with tears again.

The man in the photo remains a mystery, but the boy is confident it won't be long until he has the answer. It's surely just a matter of putting one and one together to get two. Because there's also a picture above the bed in the bedroom, a fairly large picture of an old man, but one whose smile isn't so friendly; whenever the boy sneaks into the bedroom on his own, his unruly beard sends a shiver down his spine. The old man only has a head and upper body; his lower half dissolves into a puff of clouds. The picture is so creepy he only lets himself glance quickly at it, fleeting glimpses that aren't long enough even to work out whether it's a photo or a painting.

And even though he can't say who the cloud man in the bedroom is or the smiling man in the white robe, he feels sure there must be some connection between them. But what? At some point he gets to the bottom of it. It turns out the man in the clouds is God-the-Father and the man in the white robe is the Pope, which, as Pfeifer-Papa explains to him, also means 'father'. The robe man is the cloud man's representative here on earth.

---

The boy is four when Tatie dies. It's his first time at a funeral. He knows something awful has happened, but he does not sense this within himself, he only sees this in other people's faces. Pfeifer-Papa is all alone now. People say, 'he's a widower'. The double bed stays in the same place under the picture of God and the clouds. Does Pfeifer-Papa still sleep on the same side of the bed, or does he swap sides? Well, one thing's for sure, he's reorganised the pictures in his shrine. A photo of Tatie now takes centre stage. Whenever the boy visits, Pfeifer-Papa takes him over to the sideboard where the framed photo has pride of place, held up by a stand that folds out from the back. Then he says that he goes to her grave every day and talks to her. This idea makes the boy a little uneasy, but he nods, with a guilty conscience, in anticipation of the five Deutschmarks he'll soon be given.

Pfeifer-Papa's evening strolls take him past the house where the boy lives with his mother. He smokes a big cigar as he walks. Whenever he bumps into the boy, he says, 'Don't need nuffin' else. Mama's grave an' me cigars is all I need.' The boy looks intently at the smouldering cigar; he inherits the empty boxes for his Lego bricks or Airfix. The boxes are very useful but he particularly loves them because they have the word *Fehlfarben* on them – *non-standard colours*. The boy is mesmerised by unfamilar words and phrases like this. When he's watching the lottery numbers being drawn with his grandmother (unlike his mother, she has a television), they always say *ohne Gewähr* – *subject to change*. The less he understands a word, the more official it sounds. As though all the threads of the invisible power that rules the world come together in that word. *Ohne Gewähr* is not an expression that would ever pass his lips. It was something people only said on television in the ceremonial announcement of the lottery numbers. It is a similar thing with the most important book in the boy's possession, the Marklin catalogue, which lists every toy he ever hopes to own. The crucial information, however, is what you need to pay for the 103 series (the brownish-red IC locomotive) or the German Crocodile 196 series (not quite as long as the Swiss Crocodile, but still) and here again – how else could it be with such important information? – it is packaged in words as enigmatic as a magical spell: *recommended retail price*. A phrase as smooth as a sheer cliff face with nothing to grip onto. And on the Bundesbahn poster on the wall in his bedroom, with the same locomotive, 103 series, it says: *Every hour, every class.* At least as enigmatic and unintelligible as that Christmas carol with the rose springing from the Virgin.

———

The boy is always glad when he runs into Pfeifer-Papa on his evening stroll, only this changes over the years. Pfeifer-Papa talks a lot, too often for the boy's taste, about the poor children in Africa who have nothing to eat. It makes the boy feel uncomfortable because he's not really sure whether he's somehow one of the children in Africa, too, if one were being very precise about it. Pfeifer-Papa doesn't seem to think about that, but all the same, the boy is left with a bad feeling. As the years go by, this otherwise inconsequential lament becomes more pointed. One day, Pfeifer-Papa expresses his disbelief that millions of fireworks are let off here in Germany on New Year's Eve while the children are starving in Africa! The boy finds such arguments difficult to refute. But all the same, he's determined not to go without his bangers and rockets. And this time he's pleasantly surprised by his mother. Although he knows she also has some kind of connection to Africa, she dispels his pangs of conscience and insists he needn't worry, and anyway you can't set one thing off against the other like that. The boy is only too pleased to accept this explanation, even though he suspects his mother is probably standing on shaky ground. He's been in church with Pfeifer-Papa often enough to know what the collection's there for.

The boy takes almost everything for granted: everything seems to make sense, everything's in the right place. The only thing he has doubts about is his mother. It's obvious that she doesn't respect the natural order of things. His mother seems anomalous, somehow. He's always looking at her in astonishment. Sometimes, for example, she speaks strangely, as if she wants to pronounce the words differently to everyone else: she elongates the syllables so much you'd think she had a foreign accent. When he's with his grandmother, he never has to fear that they'll stand out awkwardly. It's the opposite with his mother: with her, you never know what might happen next. She never says that thing that Grandma's always saying: 'Think of what people will say!' He personally has no problem with those words. With his mother, he sometimes feels naked, while everyone else is wearing their confirmation suit. His mother didn't have him baptised, either, although she herself likes to read the Bible. She even underlines entire sentences, noting keywords in the margin. He should decide about baptism for himself later, she insists.

The way she sings loudly while doing chores around the apartment is pretty strange, too. It's actually really embarrassing, but the boy knows you can't forbid people from singing without coming across as uptight. What's absolutely unbearable, though, is when she starts dancing around when she's singing. Her exuberance in general makes him cringe. Are her clothes flamboyant? Hard to say. Perhaps a bit, but he likes them. She wears clothes from Marimekko, a Finnish clothes brand. Her favourite thing to wear is Marimekko dresses, she says. They're so light and airy. She praises everything that comes from Scandinavia. His mother dyes her hair with henna. It shimmers like chestnuts in autumn.

The main source of embarrassment is undoubtedly the frank and direct way she addresses people, probing their feelings, memories, wishes and dreams. But he can't deny the astonishing fact that people sometimes respond by pouring out their hearts. It's as if a dam has been broken and their innermost thoughts start to flow freely.

One time, he's standing at the front door with a playmate. While they're waiting for his mother to open the door, his friend pulls a cheeky face. The friend waits boldly at the door where his mother is about to appear, his hands splayed at his temples, his tongue out. He knows this amounts to an act of grave contempt for his mother, but he doesn't have the strength to stop him; he feels disheartened that someone might even think of being so rude towards his mother. But maybe that's what she deserves for always doing everything differently, he thinks; eventually, people lose all respect for you! When his mother opens the door, however, the playmate has dropped his hands and acts as if nothing happened. He's well behaved and respectful. Perhaps his mother does have some authority after all.

There would be nothing wrong with the apartment where the boy and his mother live, if it weren't for the carpet. His mother doesn't talk about it, and for a long time he doesn't even notice it, but at some point, it can't be ignored any longer: the carpet is old, it's knackered. It has been there since the previous tenants. It's light grey. His mother always says that she likes the carpet because it feels inviting and it helps give the apartment the feeling of being flooded with light. She doesn't mention that it's threadbare, that it has long since detached itself from the skirting board almost everywhere and that you can see the screed underneath. The boy doesn't know anyone else who lives in an apartment with such a tattered carpet. Over the years, the screed spreads like the creeping desert. The distance between the edge of the carpet and skirting board grows. A carpet on the retreat. When Grandma comes to visit, she shakes her head. In her apartment in the Black Forest, she has an immaculate carpet throughout her entire apartment, except for the kitchen and bathroom, with neat edges right up to the skirting board. In the living room, there's even a second rug on top of the carpet, blue and dark red. If you run your hand against the grain, it straightens up and looks darker than the rest, where it's smoothly vacuumed down. You can draw shadowy patterns in the carpet that only disappear again when Grandma runs over them with the Vorwerk vacuum cleaner, sold to her personally by the Vorwerk reps who come to the door.

Strangely, Grandma is the only person who wrinkles her nose up at the state of their carpet. No one else seems to notice. On the contrary, his mother's improvised furnishing style, where book towers grow like stalagmites because the bookshelves are already full, is always praised as though it arises not from necessity but as an expression of his mother's idiosyncratic mode of living, her independence, her anti-materialism, which seems a source of delight to all their visitors. They always seem so jubilant when they sit down at the table, which his mother has lovingly set for her guests. And although the boy is ashamed of the carpet, to his surprise he has to admit he likes their light-flooded apartment with its large balcony. Sometimes he does wonder, though: shouldn't they have bought a new carpet instead of the expensive piano?

———

For a year, the boy goes to a kindergarten that the adults describe as anti-authoritarian. In summer, the kids run around naked, and because it's only a few minutes' walk to the River Neckar, they're forever going to the water to play. The river is lovely, but the constant nudity is unpleasant. The children can do whatever they want, nobody intervenes. At noon everyone sits down at long tables for lunch. Some dishes are popular with the children, others less so. The least popular is Thursday, when everyone's given a scoop of ravioli. No one likes canned ravioli, so the older children dump their leftovers on the younger ones' plates. There's nothing you can do to defend yourself; all you can do is leave it uneaten, even when you're still hungry.

In one room of the kindergarten, there's a wooden playhouse with lots of little rooms, dark and gloomy, with round porthole windows. There's a ladder to the upstairs. That's where they normally play Doctors and Nurses. The little ones lie naked on the mattress and the bigger kids give them a full-body examination. These role-playing games last until the doctor gets bored. It's only then the patient makes a full recovery and can escape.

Does he ever tell his mother about it? Not to his knowledge, although he has a stomach ache every morning when he has to go to the strange kindergarten that everyone else seems to love so much. After a year, his mother takes the boy out of that kindergarten, and he's astonished that somehow his mother knows that's exactly what he wanted all this time. He breathes a sigh of relief; the realisation that you don't have to endure bad things forever, that they can come to an end, is overwhelming.

There are two other kindergartens in Dossenheim: one Lutheran and one Catholic. When his mother, who is a Protestant herself, wants to register her son at the Protestant kindergarten, the pastor says he would love to have him, but he should be baptised first. The boy's mother is outraged. The boy has never heard her lay into someone with such fury and contempt. Then she goes to the Catholic priest. He simply says he would be delighted to have him. The Catholic kindergarten is just like kindergarten ought to be. You don't have to leap about naked, nobody makes you play Doctors, and the staff always keep an eye on the little ones and intervene before things get out of hand. And the children go home at noon and don't have to eat disgusting canned ravioli.

The boy has to take a deep breath before opening the picture book *Where the Wild Things Are*. How can anyone be as audacious as Max, the boy in the story, who, because of all the mischief he makes, gets sent to bed without his supper! Max scowls defiantly at his bedroom door. But his will can't be broken, not that easily. His bedroom turns into a forest, then the whole world. The boy steps into his boat, which bears his name: Max, captain of his own ship. He'll show Mama.

That's it, I've had enough, I'm sailing across the seas! You will never hear from me again! You'll cry when I'm gone, but it'll be too late!

He ends up on an island. The island where the Wild Things live. Here they come, emerging from the forest. They're ferocious, fearsome, with hairy bodies, eyes sparkling like lightning, talons for fingers; even their toes are claws. Max looks on from a distance, by no means sure of himself; the mood seems to shift a gear. But then he remembers his innate leadership and he looks the Wild Things in the eye, directly, without flinching. And thus, he subdues them; the Wild Things submit and crown him their king.

Now Max is in charge, his wish is their command. 'Let the wild rumpus start!' he commands. The Wild Things roar with all their might, dance and leap about, howl at the moon and shuffle like apes along the branches of the trees.

But good things always have to come to an end, and with tiredness comes sadness and loneliness. This jungle isn't really home, these palm trees aren't what he's used to. This is a foreign land. And the Wild Things are actually a bit scary. Even if he's their king, he'll never really be one of them. Unlike them, he's got a Mama.

Time to go home. Max steps into his boat. As he bids them farewell, the Wild Things break out into their deafening howls; they don't mean it badly, it's just their way of showing Max that they already miss him. Max sleeps as he sails, over calm seas, with a favourable wind. When he wakes up, he's back in his room. Moonlight streams in through the window. His supper's waiting for him, still warm. The stars are looking down on him; his mother would never let him down. He doesn't need to explain to anyone that he's from a distant land and that he's the king of the Wild Things.

The boy spends his holidays with his grandmother in the Black Forest. She lives in a village on a high plateau, 10 kilometres from Calw. The village is so small that he knows almost everyone who lives there. His mother has to work, so she puts him on the train in Heidelberg, in a so-called 'through coach'. Part of the train gets re-routed at Pforzheim. The rear carriages are re-attached to a train heading to Calw, while the front carriages set off for another destination. Both Mama and Grandma praise the principle of through coaches, which save you the stress and worry of having to change trains. The boy thinks it's actually quite fun to change trains, but it's even better when the carriage you're sitting in does the changing for you. You only notice when the train jolts. Shunting – that's his dream job. He would get to do what nobody else is allowed to do: get down on the track bed and crawl between the two wagons to uncouple them. If the boy doesn't become a bin man (not the driver up front, of course, but one of the two men who stand on the footplate on the back and jump down while the truck's still moving), then he wants to be a shunter on the Bundesbahn, the federal railway. Also because: wouldn't it be great to have a job with 'Federal' in the title? The Bundesbahn used to be called the Reichsbahn; he knows that because his grandfather, who died in the war, worked for the Reichsbahn in Breslau. His grandmother is still allowed to travel by train for free because she's the widow of a Reichsbahn official. Being able to travel by train for free is such an enormous privilege that the boy sometimes doesn't even know what to do with this joy, the idea that his grandmother of all people has it so good. No wonder she knows all about through coaches.

But not only about through coaches. She also knows where to sit on the train. Never up at the front, because in the event of a collision you're dealt a bad hand. From his own wooden train set (Brio, of course; as far as his mother is concerned, the Eichhorn train sets are morally questionable, because the wooden tracks aren't cut from one piece and the links are glued on – and although he loves Uhu because of the smell, he soon learns that glued-on things are something his mother looks down on), he knows that on tight bends the middle wagons are always in danger of derailing if the locomotive goes too fast. So he prefers to sit in the final carriage. Which works out perfectly, because the through coach is coupled on at the rear of the train.

In Calw, his uncle whose hearing was damaged in the war and Grandma are waiting on the platform. The station looks exactly like the one in the Faller catalogue. The model railway manufacturer Faller only has two proper city stations: Bonn and Calw. The fact that they chose Calw makes the place extra special. Grandma gives him a hug and says how proud she is that he's been so independent, coming on his own on the train. Well, he thinks, it was just a through couch, so you don't have to change, you just sit in your seat and eat the cheese sandwich and apple that Mama gave you.

At his uncle's, the boy can't tell whether he's happy or not about his visit. He doesn't speak much, and when he does, the boy doesn't understand him anyway because of his Swabian accent. His grandmother, who's from Silesia, always shakes her head, tutting about having to live surrounded by people who speak Swabian German. It's not the dialect she grew up with either. Her other grandson, his cousin Joachim (the boy fears

Grandma's fonder of Joachim, if only because they're in the same village and see each other every day) also has a strong Swabian way of speaking. The boy wouldn't say it out loud, but whenever Grandma pretends not to understand Joachim, to encourage him to try harder to speak High German, he thinks, 'Ha! You see.' (Later, when they're both in primary school, his cousin finds it hard going, academically. The boy does much better at school, but to his surprise, his undoubtedly superior performance doesn't seem to lead to a redistribution of Grandma's affections.)

The boy loves everything about Grandma's apartment. The L-shaped kitchen bench in the corner, with the seats that lift up, and the board games in the storage space below: *Barricade* and *Halma*. The cheerful music on the radio in the morning at breakfast. There's a place for everything and everything is in its place. Tatty carpets: unthinkable. If anything is broken or wobbly, it's repaired or replaced immediately. But above all, Grandma has a television and the boy can watch as much as he wants. She must think he has a lot to catch up on because he doesn't have a TV at home. He thinks it's great that Grandma has a TV, but is sometimes a little surprised that she isn't ashamed of it.

Once, before supper, he watches an episode of *The Invisible Man*. A man who can make himself invisible. It's unbelievably creepy. You really can't see him! When he comes into a room, the door opens as if by magic; when he drinks coffee, the cup suddenly floats through the air by itself. The boy can hardly bear it. Again and again he looks down at the floor instead of at the television. The idea that people can make themselves invisible is terrifying; it means they can lurk anywhere without you knowing they're there. He's haunted for ages by the Invisible Man. Worst of all on the loo. He imagines him rising up from the toilet bowl and grabbing his bum. Although that's pretty illogical, because the Invisible Man is invisible, not shrunk to the size of a goblin. Still, for a few weeks he is terrified of going to the bathroom and does everything he can to speed up the procedure.

Grandma's apartment is on the first floor. From the front door of the apartment there's an external staircase down into the open courtyard, which in turn leads onto a large garden. The garden and courtyard belong to the landlord. He's a figure of authority, but he's actually quite nice. He's fond of teasing the boy, saying things that he doesn't really mean. It always takes a little while before the boy realises from the landlord's grin that he was joking. Then the landlord laughs and ruffles his hair.

This is the summer that he learns to ride a bike. The landlord's son is a bit older than him. He puts the boy on a little bike and says, 'Easy-peasy! Just peddla, peddla! Don't stop, it ain't gonna keel over!' The fact that whatever puts you in danger in the first place should also protect you from danger doesn't sound as convincing as the boy-next-door claims, but because he's yelling 'Peddla, peddla!' at the top of his lungs the boy has no choice but to do precisely that. He's propelled onwards by cheering and all of a sudden he gets to the point where it all falls into place. The bike seems to glide along, he's doing one lap after the other in the courtyard, and the boy-next-door is screaming with delight, thrilled at his own talent, his ability to teach someone else to ride a bike, and the boy can hardly believe that something so amazing can actually be so easy. Much easier than tying shoelaces, for example. He has a lot more trouble learning to do that, although it is far less dangerous.

One morning that same summer, at the breakfast table, he hears voices coming from outside the kitchen. Grandma says it's slaughter day and people are going to slaughter the rabbits they've bred. After breakfast, he sneaks nervously into the courtyard where there are some large tubs and there's water and blood everywhere. Four or five men are hard at work. One is obviously in charge – he's giving the instructions – and the others are looking at him. The boy doesn't recognise him. A few gutted rabbits are already hanging from a long string, like socks on a clothesline. The boy is stunned. Breathless. He's never seen anything like it. He wishes he hadn't ever seen it, too. Even Helmut, the landlord, who always pats him on the head, looks completely different with this red-smeared apron; he seems distant and inaccessible, like he's in another realm. The boy is about to retreat quietly when the man in charge spots him. He sees the boy's frightened eyes and calls over to him. 'Shall we gut you too?' The boy turns ice cold. He turns and flees. Runs for his life. As he runs, he wonders if it was a joke – did the butcher mean it seriously, or did he say it with a laugh? But the risk of turning around and looking back at the butcher is too great; he's reached the steps, he just has to run upstairs, open the door and call for Grandma, then he'll be safe. The butcher won't chase him into the apartment, that just can't be, surely no one butchers children in their grandmother's living room? As he pulls the door open, he glances behind him for the first time, down the stairs; there's no one there.

As soon as the door has closed behind him, he sees the next problem ahead. Grandma hears him storming into the apartment in a panic. How's he going to explain it to her?

Now that he's safe, he realises that the butcher's threat must have been a joke. He fell for it. How embarrassing. Scaredy-cat! But before he has to explain what happened to Grandma, the landlord is already there in the apartment, hugging the boy, ruffling his hair. It was just a joke!

---

At home in Dossenheim, his road, the Bergstrasse, is lined with allotments, orchards and vineyards. In the summer months the boy strolls through the meadows with his friends. Now and then someone fires a shot to scare away the birds. The allotments are full of strawberries, cherries, raspberries and currants, but the currants are quite sour, he only likes them when his mother serves them with cream. Vegetables are boring, but stealing fruit is exciting. You have to scout out the area carefully and then get over the fence; sometimes your T-shirt gets snagged on a rusty nail. One keeps a lookout, his friend Christiane for example, while the other climbs the tree. If there's imminent danger, you have to dash back over the fence, your T-shirt dripping with cherry juice. If the garden owner shouts out to you, your heart starts pounding. Escaping danger: a marvellous feeling!

Christiane lives in the adjacent house, she's two years older and she has blonde curly hair. She's as strong as a boy and completely fearless. She always goes one step further than he would dare to on his own. When we play 'Ring-and-Run', she doesn't just ring one bell at the entrance to an apartment block, but all eight at the same time. But she never goes so far that it's scary or mental. 'Mental!' is the utterance of condemnation par excellence. The kids always say someone's mental when they don't like them. Then they say, he belongs in Wiesloch! Everyone knows what that means; the madhouse is in Wiesloch. It's only a small step between being cool and being mental. In the heat of the moment you're in danger of going too far, but at the last second you sense an inner restraint keeping you in check.

Christiane is the first girl he imagines kissing. Once she pulled up her T-shirt and showed him her breasts. They weren't fully developed proper breasts, but it was still cool. He imagines them both stalking through a field of tall corn and Christiane doing the T-shirt thing again. That would be the moment to kiss her. The thought is very exciting, and he wonders what would stop them from going back to the cornfield again and again. If he dared kiss her once, they could keep doing it. But he only has these thoughts in the evening, when he's in bed, just before he falls asleep, and he usually falls asleep very quickly. During the day, when he's playing with Christiane, there's too much going on, no time for fantasising. And when the mood gets cosy, for example at dusk, when they're sitting on the wall chatting and every minute feels precious, because they know the clock is ticking and either her parents or his mother is going to call them in any minute now, under no circumstances would he risk spoiling their time together by going in for a kiss.

---

One day he discovers something new. Christiane says that when they steal fruit it's actually just scrumping and it's not a criminal offence. The word fascinates him. When Christiane uses it, it sounds so precise, like an absolutely perfect circle drawn with a compass. And yet he doesn't quite believe it. It can't be true that stealing is allowed! It can't be right that you're allowed to climb over fences! The fact that they continue to be careful not to get caught during their raids is proof that neither of them really trusts this supposed licence to scrump.

When he's not roaming the vineyards, he often plays on the empty plot opposite their house. If anyone asks, he'll say it's his property. So far, no one has disputed this. Other children are welcome to play with him, but it's his. First come first served.

One day a digger approaches. It churns everything up, turning over the soil. The boy is horrified. Like a defeated general, he has to stand by and watch as his empire is flattened.

After a few days of powerless dejection, the construction work begins to fascinate the boy. Especially the concrete mixer, which rattles almost nonstop. Now his tenacious character pays off, his persistence, perseverance, concentration. For days on end, he stands at the edge of the building site, watching the builders until his single-mindedness impresses the foreman. He comes over and makes the boy an offer: if he wants, he can do some light work on site for thirty pfennigs an hour. Incredible! Real money for honest work.

As soon as he's back from school the next day, the boy starts shoveling sand, pushing the wheelbarrow if it's not too heavy and, above all, engaging in extensive discussions with the foreman. The other workers treat him with the greatest respect, because he's clearly under the personal protection of the boss. One day the foreman asks what his mother's profession is. A delicate subject. The boy knows her job title and he can say it fluently: child and adolescent psychotherapist. But it's a nail-biting horror of a mouthful. The worst thing isn't that there's no time to stop and breathe – that's OK. The hardest bit is you have to let it flow together so it sounds like one phrase, but where you can hear the distinct individual components. Pronouncing it is just part of the problem. What's even worse is that when the other person has heard the answer, they usually look like they've drifted off into a fog of confusion. The only way to remove that risk is to pronounce it as accurately as humanly possible. In fact, the boy sometimes worries that his mother doesn't in fact have a real job, and this phrase is just another of her weird eccentric notions that she dreams up just to be difficult. On the other hand, she's his Mama and it's a matter of honour as a son that he conceal the fact that deep down he shares the doubts of the person he's telling. He has to utter this mouthful of a tongue twister with just the right emphasis and just the right natural intonation that it sounds like child and adolescent psychotherapist is a completely normal, widely recognised profession. The other person might only be able to repeat it back with a stutter; that doesn't matter, as long as the boy manages to pronounce it swiftly, though not rushed, rattling along with a certain casualness. As tempting as it is to tear through it (like ripping a plaster off your knee: you have to do it faster than the pain can spread) so you get it all over with long before the other person can stare at you questioningly, unfortunately any such attempt is almost always doomed to failure. The other person never sees any shame in their own ignorance that they need to cover up, on the contrary, they embrace it as a welcome occasion to 'close a knowledge gap' and demonstrate their open-mindedness and their genuine interest in, even fascination for, his mother's profession. Again and again, the boy realises that something he would rather ignore as an embarrassing anomaly is precisely what other people find fascinating and brilliant. He's no stranger to hearing that he has an 'interesting' mother. There's nothing left for him to do then but nod.

So the boy bravely answers the foreman's question: his mother is a child and adolescent psychotherapist. The foreman squints a little, but with gentle eyes, pondering the reply briefly before going on to check that they're not talking at cross purposes: 'Ah, for kids who are a bit...' and at that point he waves his hand around by his head.

So now the boy is faced with a conflict of loyalties. It's not as if his mother isn't aware that her profession sometimes needs a little explanation. She taught him early on that there was no shame for a child in going to therapy, that her job had nothing to do with that accursed place that is regularly name-dropped at breaktime when kids say someone belongs in Wiesloch. When he's alone with his mother and her friends, he believes her. But here on the construction site it feels different. The rooster doesn't even get the chance to crow before he has betrayed his mother, nodding and confirming the foreman's definition. Mainly, of course, to get the matter over with quickly and avoid getting bogged down in any more explanations, but also because at that moment he thinks, 'Hmm, yes, the foreman knows what he's talking about.' His mother's words don't stand up to the reality test, they dissolve like mist in the morning sun. Grumpily, he goes back to shovelling sand into the wheelbarrow.

When the shell of the house is in place, the construction team disappears from one day to the next and new workers arrive. Tradesmen who know nothing about him and his preferential treatment. He's expelled from his paradise a second time. The house whose walls he helped to build is once more in the hands of others. The boy quietly swallows down his grief.

———

Worst of all is the boredom. It raises its ugly head on Sunday afternoons when there's nothing happening outside and the neighbourhood kids are out on family outings. No one comes to call for him, no book can tempt him, there's no television, his mother is busy, his toys lie lifeless on his bedroom floor. The boy has a constant tingling sensation in his legs and arms, as if his muscles were wasting away, dissolving like the foam in a bath. He could scream in desperation, 'Mama! I'm so bored!' But all she'll say is 'You need to be able to entertain yourself.' Or 'Go out and get some fresh air!'

But at times like this nothing is more boring than fresh air. Being inside is unbearable, and so is being outside. It makes no difference if you're here or there, it's all just as bleak and hopeless. You no longer want anything on offer, inside or outside. All you want is for the time to pass by quickly until something finally happens. Something has to happen again at some point. At some point there must finally be an end to this infinitely long Sunday afternoon, this infinitely long childhood!

How can the world be so dull?

Boredom isn't just physical agony, it also reminds you of your own loneliness. The sad, undeniable truth that there's no one to play with you.

And then, it's odd: the second it's over, it's forgotten. You can't see boredom coming, you can't dread it. There's no fear of it, and no memory of it, only the boredom itself. Whenever it hits there's no hope of escape, but then, when it's gone, it's completely and utterly forgotten. Suddenly you have a plan again, there's excitement again, you want something again, something is hilariously funny again.

---

At other times, the boy is constantly reminded that nothing ever happens. There's a red fire extinguisher in the basement of the house, for example, a wonderful thing. It's even got a seal so that nobody uses it illegally. The fire extinguisher can only be used in the event of a fire – but there's never a fire! It's unbearable. And then there's the emergency brake on the train, which he can never take his eyes off – no one ever pulls it! This 'emergency' is nothing but an empty promise! He would so dearly love to see someone pull the emergency brake – or even do it himself! There are always warning signs everywhere, but never ever an actual emergency. Disasters seem to be a thing of the past, something relegated to the good old days.

Because his mother shudders at the thought of the crammed Mediterranean resorts and loves a fresh, bracing wind, their summer holidays tend to be spent on long bike tours through northern Germany and Denmark, cycling from youth hostel to youth hostel. Sometimes the wind is so strong he's sure he'll be swept off his bike, and he could whoop for joy.

He also loves northern Germany, the sea, the ferries. He is eight when he first takes the train across the Hindenburg Dam to Sylt. He can hardly wait; it's a narrow causeway cutting through the foaming North Sea waves. But sadly, this is yet another disappointment: the North Sea is by no means crashing at his feet as he hoped, because the dam is wider than a motorway, and in places – comically, given the real danger and the real audacity – cattle are grazing on both sides of the railway track. The tide is out and there's no water in sight.

From Sylt they travel on to Hallig Langeness. A hallig is an island that's barely higher than sea level. It's pretty exciting on a hallig when there's a storm tide; once, in a book about lifeboats, he saw pictures of a hallig completely flooded by the North Sea during a spring tide (sometimes people say spring tide, sometimes storm tide – he still hasn't figured this one out). All you can see are the farmhouses standing up on their terps – man-made mounds of earth – like swimmers barely keeping their heads above water.

They're at Langeness for three days, staying at a farm. Since their arrival, everyone has spoken of nothing but the storm tide they're expecting. The sky is turning greyer, the clouds are moving faster, the wind is picking up. There's excitement on the day they're set to leave. In some parts of the hallig, the farmer tells them, the water has already come up over the banked shore. He's hoping to take them to the ferry, but he can't promise that they'll get through. They're in the car. Up ahead is the crucial point, the farmer says; if the water's higher than the car's axles, then he can't take them any further, because he wouldn't get back again with the water level rising. The boy hears these words but can hardly believe it.

Then they are there at the crucial point, and he can't believe his ears when the farmer says, 'No, no, it's no good, the water's too high.' He mustn't let it show, but inside he's whooping for joy.

The farmer turns the car round and drives back. Everyone's in full action mode now: driving the cattle up onto the terp, rounding everyone up, bringing humans and animals closer together. And then the sea is really there, coming closer and closer, and it's magical; the foaming. They're sitting in the rustic farmhouse, everyone's playing board games, and when you look out of the window, there at the edge of the terp, barely fifty metres away, rages the North Sea. '*Nordsee ist Mordsee*' as his mother always said. 'The North Sea is a murderous sea.' Finally, some truth to that phrase!

His mother has various rituals. Some of them – the ones that don't seem to feature in other families – make the boy suspect that his mother has invented them to make them seem like a real family with their own rules and traditions, not just a mother and son randomly deposited on Planet Earth. Their little single-parent family stands on shaky ground, he can feel it. He can sense weakness like a dog senses fear. And weakness provokes defiance. He has a disproportionately strong power of veto. There's no majority to vote him down. If he refuses to go along with something, his mother is a lonely woman in a losing position.

If she wants him to do anything it takes coercion. If he does join in eventually, it's usually not that bad after all. And then he feels guilty because he's aware of his destructive power, and he wonders whether they couldn't have got to this point without his defiance. Then his poor mother wouldn't look so exhausted. He doesn't want to see her sad, but he doesn't want to make it easy for her either.

He can't let anything go without a fight.

The hikes through the Odenwald are awful. At least at first. Once he's got into the rhythm and has got past sulking, he's quite happy walking. He actually quite likes the forest; he can run on and off the trail, returning to the path with long sticks, which are excellent for hacking at the undergrowth and the brambles. It's also fun to step on rotten wood and hear how it breaks apart with a crunch. When he's walked far enough, he comes to a clearing. The sun is shining and he and his mother find a fallen tree trunk and get out their cheese sandwiches. When sitting on a tree trunk like this in a clearing, he even likes the apples that go with the lunch. The first apple with the sandwich, the second with the chocolate. The only other time that cheese sandwiches taste this good is on train journeys.

His mother presumably invents her rituals in order to turn something she likes doing into something anchored in tradition: this is the way to silence his counter-arguments. And she thinks up names for everything. When they have to go for a walk in the Odenwald on 1 January, she calls it their New Year's Day walk, for example. It sounds like something everyone is doing and means he has to go along with it. But he has serious doubts that everyone else goes for a New

Year's Day walk. For his defiance he mobilises every ounce of energy in his small body. His mother has to pay for his company by enduring his bad mood; she can hardly ignore him. She needs his support if there's to be anything but frosty silence between the two of them.

When they finally set out after a seemingly endless struggle, there's always a point where his defiance turns into exhilaration. Funny that. But it doesn't make the next time any easier.

It starts to snow on one of their New Year's Day walks. Heavily. The boy drags his sleigh behind him. The forest becomes a soft snowy landscape. Snow is the most magical thing; a shame it's so rare. Now they're in the middle of the forest and their footsteps sink into the snow. That wonderful feeling when you pull your feet out of the deep imprints you've left behind! It's always satisfying to make noises and the crunch of snow is one of the most sublime sounds. Covered in snow, the world is like a fairy tale.

Then they head up the hill. Dusk is falling. There's almost something scary about being alone with his mother in the forest, yet there's something comforting about it at the same time. Before them stretches a long slope down into the next village; the boy and his mother sit on the sledge and glide down over the blanket of fresh snow. Here and there, it's so deep that you get stuck; his mother gets off to push, and as soon as they pick up speed she quickly jumps back on. They're alone the whole time, and the snow is theirs, until they see the warm yellow lights of the village. He has a slight sense of relief, because he wasn't entirely convinced that he and his mother would survive their twilight snowscape adventure unscathed.

When they reach the village, they pop in for a bite to eat at a pub. Mother and son both agree on one thing: a common love of popping in for a bite to eat. The phrase and the act itself. It conveys that whole feeling of safety and comfort. If you pop in somewhere at the end of a walk, everything's just fine.

The boy orders a Jägerschnitzel. The landlord smiles at him and pats him on the shoulder. He also seems to find it good that mother and son popped in to his pub.

Classical concerts are almost as bad as the interminable boredom of a Sunday without friends. It's only when it gets really loud, when the timpani and trumpets come into play, that the boy tunes in for a moment (sheer physical power is always impressive), otherwise a concert consists not so much of music as of an endless desert, its grains of sand trickling through the slender neck of an hourglass. (Death doesn't seem as scary if dying of boredom takes this long). At the beginning of a concert, it's absolutely inconceivable that he can ever survive to the end. The only way to divide the vast expanse of desert into manageable sections is to count the movements of the symphony. For some thoroughly arbitrary reason, symphonies always consist of four movements. But if it's Bach, sometimes there are only three. So the boy keeps track of the movements like a prisoner marking a tally on the prison wall for every day he gets through. You can tell it's the end of a movement when the musicians stop playing, but nobody claps. There's still the occasional bitter disappointment, though, because sometimes there's also a general pause within a movement. In the exhilaration of finally being able to clap, because, against all odds, he's still alive, he's survived the entire symphony, the boy is then horrified – like a hiker who thinks he's about to find the mountain cabin beyond this peak, only to discover that there's in fact yet another valley between him and his goal – to realise that he has miscounted. It's still only been three movements, after all. These embarrassing defeats have the paradoxical effect of training his musical ear. He listens much more closely, keen to avoid another demoralising mishap. Ticking off the movements (one, two, three, four) isn't necessarily what the adult world perceives as enjoying music, but at least it's something of a meaningful activity.

Most of the time, it's no problem to pretend there's nothing different about him. That he looks the same as everyone else and can't see some dubious, distant foreign land lurking in his facial features. As long as he doesn't raise the question of origins and Africa with himself, then it's not an issue. It doesn't just spring on you out of the blue. You can control it, keep it in check. Nobody forces you to state your identity; at most, people are only interested in his frizzy hair.

Not commenting on his hair seems beyond human strength. When you hear the way people talk about it, you might think that there's nothing in the world better than frizzy hair. Women are forever touching his hair and saying, 'Oh, how I'd love to have curls like yours!' How much effort they have to go through to artificially create something that nature has given the boy free of charge. The boy doesn't comment, he just rolls his eyes inwardly. Why would someone actively choose to have hair that makes you stand out from everyone else? The boy eyes these hair-crazed women with suspicion, sensing an insincerity that irritates him because he can't see what the point of it is, except perhaps to be nice to him. Maybe they really are just being nice. Or are they just trying to be nice because they think the boy has a hard enough time with this hair and that he deserves all the support he can get? This enthusiasm for frizzy hair doesn't seem to have any clear link to the rather more condescending way the continent where people with hair like this is viewed. Everyone would rather be German than African, everyone would rather send charity than receive it. Africa is the continent that people send money to, because people are starving there. For some time now, there have been posters on the walls of the school, the bank and the parsonage calling for donations for the Sahel region, with pictures of children with frizzy hair (and fat, bloated bellies. There are jokes about them, which the boy doesn't like to hear – not because he condemns them morally, but because he's worried that he might be associated with the butt of the jokes. He imagines someone telling a joke and then pointing at him while he's still laughing, challenging him, 'Why are you laughing about it?'). Perhaps some Germans do genuinely want to be Germans with frizzy hair, but he doesn't want to be their mascot.

He says nothing of any of this. He lets them stroke his hair because he knows that's all there is to it. For him, it's his hair, not his darker skin tone, that seems to flag up the questionable side of his existence, but people always stick to what's on the outside, they don't draw a link between his hair and the underlying shame, although it must be obvious enough. As long as he dutifully lets them ruffle his hair and doesn't contradict these women's ridiculous claim that they'd like hair like that for themselves, then he can just about navigate these treacherous waters. Then the topic is over and Africa is gone again, and he can go back to normal and can stop being fêted for an exoticism that delights everyone else more than it does himself.

Whenever his mother talks about Africa, he switches off and stops listening. But he doesn't make it too obvious, otherwise, if he's unlucky, he risks prompting an interrogation. 'Why are you being so defensive?' is a question his mother loves to ask. Whenever it can possibly come up. His mother is a psychotherapist, after all, so you have to be on your guard; everything you don't feel like talking about is seized on as an act of repression. The ground is strewn with these psychoanalytical traps and snares that you can step right into if you're not careful. Best to give them a wide berth. But the fact is that his mother avoids assuming that he's repressing something – a diagnosis she's usually quick to reach for – when it comes to Africa. When there's talk of Africa, she has a quiet, gentle persistence, but she doesn't bring out her usual psychoanalytical torture tools. As if she has mercy on the boy. She doesn't speak about Africa often, but regularly enough, and when the boy endures the conversation with a catatonic lack of response, she doesn't make a big deal out of it. While she usually embarrasses him with her requests for him to communicate, nudging him to talk about his feelings, when it's a conversation about Africa his mother at least spares him the need for any mortifying self-explanation.

But there are signs that no visitor can help but notice. Everyone stumbles upon the not-at-all-hidden secret. There's a crocodile on the windowsill in the living room, which the boy would rather not see in such a prominent place. It's carved from ebony. Like an envoy from that distant, dubious country. Like a heraldic beast of the equator. As if its duty were to remind everyone that this household has a special connection with Africa. There can be absolutely no doubt that the wooden sculpture plays the role of an ambassador who's keen to ensure that no one suppresses or forgets the existence of the continent that sent it. The natural habitat of the crocodile is the African continent; if you imagine a crocodile, you picture it against an African backdrop; the crocodile is a symbol of Africa. But that's not all. The crocodile is also made of ebony: not a local German wood, but one that's used to make objects and jewellery in Africa, and to top it all off it's black, as though the crocodile had taken on a dark skin colour in an act of solidarity with the people who share its habitat. Instead of a white marble bust, a black wooden sculpture. So blatant that not even a complete idiot can fail to notice it. You might as well just hang a huge sign around your neck.

When his school friends come by and see the crocodile on the windowsill, they ask what it is. It's a crocodile, he says with a poker face – and then he's always amazed how often the crocodile becomes part of their game without any more questions about its origin. Is he the only one who sees these connections? Don't the others notice? Is he worrying about nothing? Either way, he'd prefer the crocodile not to be sitting there on the windowsill. Just as he would prefer the coffee-table book with the African masks to be tidied away in the normal way on the bookshelf, tucked in with the other illustrated books instead of standing face out, its cover shouting out for attention. It's almost like his mother hanging a photo of his father on the wall. Well, not quite that bad, but almost.

Another book that carries out this theatrical attention-grabbing stunt is an exhibition catalogue entitled *Sumer, Assyria, Babylon*; on its cover is a bust, its face framed by strikingly even curls. Again and again the boy wonders about the catalogue, but no matter how hard he thinks about it, he can't find any way to allay his fears that *Sumer, Assyria, Babylon* might also embody Africa. Is his mother's interest in *Sumer, Assyria, Babylon* (what does that even mean?) somehow on the same level as her interest in Romanesque churches, or is it more part of that confessional zone where some connection with Africa is avowed by way of black crocodiles? Until he can rule out the latter with complete certainty, it's better not to give in to his curiosity about *Sumer, Assyria, Babylon* but rather to turn to the Greek legends instead. Otherwise it could be misinterpreted by his mother as an invitation to engage him in yet another conversation about Africa.

There's something else that always draws attention to itself, another deviation and anomaly. Why can he not just blend in? At primary school, whenever he has a long, hot shower after swimming (he's often late for the next lesson because he and his friend Marcus like nothing better than relaxing under the steamy jet of water; they're often still standing there feeling the spray on their faces when the hair dryers are already howling away in the changing room), it becomes obvious: he's circumcised. This is uncomfortable for two reasons; firstly, he has to explain it to others, and because he will have to explain it, his own mother has to give him at least some vague knowledge so that he's prepared for possible reactions. She keeps it short and simple, yes, but it's cringingly painful for him that something so personal is ever the subject of a conversation. Just the word 'foreskin' when spoken by his mother – who utters everything like it's the most natural thing in the world – doesn't feel natural at all. Quite the opposite. There's also something one-sided about the conversation; it goes without saying that the boy would rather die than broach the topic himself. It's fine, says his mother, he's been circumcised. Jews are also circumcised, but for religious reasons. He was circumcised for medical and hygienic reasons; she and his father decided together in favour of this progressive practice. There's less risk of infection, and there's nothing traumatic about it if it's performed soon after birth.

What she's trying to say is that being circumcised is something modern. The boy, on the other hand, likes modern things like the electric bread cutting machine his grandmother has, but his mother is not interested in modern devices like that and prefers to slice the bread with a bread knife.

If the reason for his circumcision is to do with hygiene, does that mean his uncircumcised classmates are unsanitary?

Some of the boys in his class are amazed when they see him naked for the first time. There are also those who know something about it and who shout out, their voices cracking: 'He's circumcised!' There's a frenzy of excitement. He doesn't exactly know why. Something that's perfectly sensible medically isn't a reason to get worked up. Or is there more to it? Perhaps it's not only Jews who are circumcised, but Africans too? Was he actually circumcised because he's African? Is that enough for him to be identified as African? But if only Jews are circumcised, then in a certain sense he must be Jewish. He could get used to that idea. If he has to be foreign, then better Jewish than African – they don't need the whole world to send them charity like the Sahel region; they're mainly known for being smart.

⸻

There's nothing the boy wishes for more than to have conventional parents, but unfortunately there's no mistaking one thing: his skin tone is an obvious clue about his father, even though almost nobody knows him. The boy was born in Salem Hospital, Heidelberg, on a spring-like 2 March, around midday. From this indisputable fact it's crystal clear that he's a Heidelberger through and through. In body and soul. He's seen the Heidelberg Tun on visits to the castle. The largest wine barrel in the world, no doubt about it. They say the Americans thought Heidelberg was so beautiful that they didn't bomb it. That speaks for itself. It's good to be a Heidelberger. Sometimes his mother sings to herself in a mix of German and English, '*Memories of Heidelberg sind memories of you*'. Heidelberg is so famous that it even appears in more or less English songs. That makes him proud. On the other hand, there's also something about that song that raises his suspicions. There's a lot of feeling in the melody, there's no denying it, and the boy has noticed elsewhere too that songs often focus on love, uncomfortably so. He would much prefer a world without love songs, it would be much less embarrassing, but adults – who seem to lose all sensitivity in the course of their lives – see it differently. But there's something more troubling about 'Memories of Heidelberg'; he can't rule out the niggling possibility that his mother sings it with such feeling because she's thinking of his father. What kind of 'memories of you' are they? There's something out of reach about his mother's memory wandering back to a time before his birth. He doesn't like it. If it was within his power, he would erase the past; nobody needs it. Even when she sings '*I've lost my heart in Heidelberg*', the boy sometimes suspects that it's not really Heidelberg she's singing about, but his father.

The boy understands full well that such things aren't for discussion. The way the world is, love is sublime, beyond any doubt. Even in church they say love is supreme. But for him personally, love songs have something unsettling about them, especially when sung by his mother. He is sceptical about love. It threatens the order of this otherwise so well-structured world. It is love alone that gives form to the absent father, love that lets him live on, unforgotten. If there were absolute silence about love, this absent father needn't have any role whatsoever. Unfortunately he can't forbid his mother from singing 'Memories of Heidelberg'. So he focuses instead on the song's other aspect. The fact that it's about Heidelberg. Heidelberg is so beautiful that it even features in an American song. Why would he want to be anything other than a Heidelberger?

His mother is always there for him. He has no fear of competition. There's just one time, in the summer holidays, on a tributary of the Elbe, when it seems things are hanging in the balance for a moment. Every night the boy throws his fishing line into the river and ties it to the jetty. When he runs across the dyke and down to the jetty in the morning to pull in the line, there's almost always a wriggling eel dangling from the hook. With the help of the hotel owner – who also takes him out sailing – he finishes the eels off and stuffs them in a transparent bag to freeze them. This is no easy task, because even when it's dead, the eel still squirms about on account of its muscle reflexes, and you have to be pretty deft and swift to tie the bag shut before the eel's tail pops out again.

After three weeks, the hotel owner lights the smoker on the lawn in front of the hotel to smoke the eels for the guests. There's also a large campfire. Everyone is drinking beer and enjoying the boy's catch. At the end of the evening, it's late and the campfire has burnt down with only the embers still glowing, and the boy sits on one of the benches with his mother and the hotel owner. He likes the hotel owner very much, but he doesn't like the fact that he has his arm around his mother, while the three of them sit there gazing at the embers of the fire. It makes him feel uneasy. What does it mean? What might become of it? Then his mother suddenly says in a resolute voice that it's late, time for the boy to go to bed, and she takes him by the hand and they head to their room.

When playing 'Cowboys and Indians' he can't understand why some boys choose to be an Indian. He always wants to be a cowboy. After all, why would you choose to be on the losing side? He doesn't get it. It's just as illogical as when he and his friend Volker play with Airfix soldiers in the garden and Volker always wants to be the Viet Cong. Although he doesn't know exactly what the Viet Cong is all about, he can only shake his head at his friend's choice. But at least that way there's no argument about who gets to be the American.

Volker's family lives on the ground floor. His father is an assistant professor of physics. Under no circumstances are you allowed to ring the Ackermanns' doorbell between 4pm and 5pm, even if you're desperate to ask if Volker is in, because that's when Mr Ackermann is taking his afternoon nap. When he's finished napping, he sits down at the piano. As soon as you hear the piano, you're allowed to ring the bell again.

Mr Ackermann is against nuclear power plants, and for birds. He hangs up triangular wooden birdhouses with a small round hole in the birch trees, for example, so that the swallows can nest in them. The swallows are the kings of the birds, they're very special, but sadly they're under threat, so Mr Ackermann helps to protect them. Before spring comes, he opens the birdhouses up and cleans them out, so they're nice inside for the swallows.

The boy learns from Mr Ackermann about the threat facing nature. Mr Ackermann influences his mother, too; she also starts subscribing to the magazine *Natur*. The boy likes the pictures in it; nature is really beautiful. Once the magazine even comes with some stickers and one of them has a bird looking at you sadly because its beak is tied with a thread. It can't chirp any more. Under the picture it says, 'Silenced by the noise.' The boy is shaken. This can't be happening! We have to do something! How can anyone ignore the fate of these poor creatures? He has tears in his eyes as he sticks the sticker on the door to their apartment, right under the peephole.

At some point the Ackermanns move to Marburg. His mother tells him reverently that Mr Ackermann has been given a professorship. Before they move, Mr Ackermann comes to their apartment and he looks solemnly at the boy; he's come to talk about the birdhouses. They should stay in the birch trees so that the swallows can continue to nest there, but someone has to take care of them, to take them down before the breeding season and give them a clean. Mr Ackermann immediately thinks of the boy for this important task. The boy is aware that this is supposed to make him feel honoured. Mr Ackermann has already prepared a document that the boy just needs to sign for the birdhouses to be granted into his care. With his signature he undertakes to maintain them. The boy has a serious expression as he signs. He never once cleans the birdhouses out and ends up feeling guilty about it for years.

———•———

The boy has a large collection of stamps, which hang up on a rotating holder like in officialdom. He has a date stamp which you can change; it won't cover every date forever, but it will last until a future date that's well beyond what he can imagine. There's another one for his name and address. Then there's the URGENT stamp and the PRINTED MATTER stamp. As a rule, the boy gives every document as many stamps as possible. The name and date stamp are a bit dull. The other two have more power. The URGENT stamp doesn't just convey information, it's an instruction that has a practical impact. Its power is particularly emphasised by the fact that it's a stamp. If he had handwritten URGENT on the document, the recipient might wonder what right the sender has to put him under such pressure, but because the request is made in the form of a stamp, it has an objective character, it's freed from his crooked handwritten scrawl and passes into the realm of official printed letters. The very existence of the stamp – which he didn't just come up with by himself, but bought in a stationery shop, meaning that it's a genuine stamp used in the real world of serious business correspondence – is a sign that the signatory is authorised from above to lend weight to his documents in this way.

But the stamp that's most satisfying is the PRINTED MATTER one. He always has the greatest respect for words he doesn't understand. PRINTED MATTER embodies the superior rank of impersonal communication. He's not interested in handwritten postcards where you get nothing but the puny voice of the individual; printed matter on the other hand has the power of the abstract. Behind the phrase 'printed matter' he senses the presence of an entire legal system, whose authority he can lend to his documents by virtue of the stamp. When he hears the words, he doesn't think of printing presses, but of correspondence from on high. Printed matter comes from officialdom and speaks in the name of the law – a shiver always runs through him when he reads these words. In films and books, state representatives gain entry into people's homes by knocking firmly on the door and shouting: 'Open up – in the name of the law!' Such is the power that his letters exude when he stamps them with PRINTED MATTER.

Anyone who has a stamp is actually practically a civil servant. That's a real job that you don't have to explain to a construction foreman while being seized with self-doubt. A civil servant is surrounded by a mysterious, impenetrable aura: no matter what, you dare not insult a civil servant. To do so would be to insult an officer of the law and that is a criminal offence. The boy can spend hours considering precisely how such an insult might come about. With what words. He's heard of a catalogue of penalties and fines depending on the swear word used against a police officer; you have to admire an administrative power that can put something like that into writing.

It's also a metaphysical process, because with the naked eye it's absolutely impossible to distinguish a plainclothes official from a non-official. The thought is maddening. The sheer possibility that someone could claim the rights and privileges of civil servant status when in truth he's not an official at all! It feels like a dangerous crack in the foundations of the order that he so admires. A breaking point that could bring the entire edifice tumbling down!

Fortunately, there's a remedy against such a danger and it's another word that is endowed with power by way of its mysteriousness: 'unauthorised assumption of authority'. Anyone who speaks on behalf of the state without being authorised to do so is guilty of 'unauthorised assumption of authority'. There's a catalogue of penalties for that too, guarding against the threat of someone coming along and having the audacity to stamp their documents with PRINTED MATTER.

His mother has a friend in America, Yvonne. He's heard so many stories about her, how they met while working for the church in a place called Cincinnati long before the boy was born. Yvonne is originally from Norfolk, Virginia, his mother says: a port city, home to one of the largest US naval bases. She has seven siblings and the family has always been disadvantaged because they are black. Although they grew up in difficult circumstances, everyone has made something of their lives. One is a lawyer, one's an engineer, one's a soldier, another's a teacher; his mother got to know the whole extended family. Yvonne grew up with her parents and siblings in a tiny house in a poor neighbourhood of Norfolk where only black people lived. They were all on top of each other in that tiny house, but that only made them closer as a family. Besides, the Delks – Yvonne's family – had a real fighting spirit. Back then, African Americans came together in their churches, which are nothing like the churches in Germany (there's a completely different *spirit*, his mother says), their courage and fighting spirit dedicated to their struggle. His mother always says *struggle* when she talks about the fight for black people's rights in America. As a child, Yvonne had to sit at the back of the bus because only white people were allowed to sit up front. There were universities for whites and universities for blacks, and even the water coolers came in twos (the boy always wonders, what's a water cooler?). It was unbearable and they couldn't take it any longer; they took to the streets, often risking their lives. African Americans fought for their rights in the Civil Rights Movement and Yvonne was up there leading the way.

His mother always mentions Martin Luther King Jr in this context. 'I have a dream' she quotes, emotion in her voice. It was his dream that all people should be treated equally, regardless of their skin tone. He also preached non-violence. He was then murdered, but his spirit carried on. Yvonne was also a great fighter, and she drew her courage and her faith from Martin Luther King Jr.

The boy is outraged whenever he hears stories of racial discrimination in the United States, but he can't pinpoint whether it's theoretical outrage or one that stems from the fact that it concerns him too. He senses that it's hard to tell the difference. He feels empathy and admiration for everyone who marched to Washington with Martin Luther King Jr, but doesn't want it to be his problem – and heavens, it's really not his story either, Dossenheim near Heidelberg isn't Norfolk, Virginia! When his mother speaks of Yvonne and Martin Luther King Jr, and the black struggle and question of skin colour, she never makes it sound like it concerns him personally. She makes no comparisons between Yvonne's skin colour and his. But perhaps – the boy can't help wondering – perhaps the parallel is so obvious that it doesn't even have to be pointed out?

Yvonne comes to visit every few years. It sounds so funny when she says 'Dossenheim' in her American drawl. She always says it with great enthusiasm and gusto as though Dossenheim was her favourite place after Norfolk, Virginia. Her visit is always a major event. Her commanding presence fills the apartment and she leaves her mark on everything and everyone.

As long as they don't leave the apartment, the boy enjoys the charisma of his mother's best friend. But then his mother wants him to take Yvonne to the post office to post some letters. He wonders how he can get out of it, but he can't come up with a convincing excuse. He is full of respect for Yvonne and her wit and acumen. Can she see through him and his cowardly shame? His shame towards Yvonne is now twofold: he's ashamed of his shame. But if he walks with her in public to the post office, something becomes irrefutable: next to Yvonne's ebony skin, no one will be able to ignore his own skin colour and pretend it was nothing remarkable. His brown was too light to stand out ordinarily, but in Yvonne's company it would be unmissable, everyone would scratch their heads and wonder how they failed to notice this obvious truth all this time. Of course, they would say; how could we have been wrong about him for so long? So that's his background! Maybe people would even think that Yvonne is his real mother and Mama is just an adoptive mother? It would be difficult to prove otherwise.

The man at the post office counter is the father of a classmate who has always been very nice to him. (Although his mother is so different from other Dossenheimers, everyone's always very nice to him. To his mother too, which surprises him a little. Why do people think so well of his mother, even though – with no husband, television or car – she doesn't conform to even the most basic standards?). Now the boy has to be strong, he mustn't let his stomach ache, nerves or panic show; he has to stand by Yvonne, no matter what. He just has to pretend everything's normal. As he so often does. He's a pro at it. Perhaps his ability to adapt is so great that it rubs off on his surroundings, and he turns Yvonne into a Dossenheimer while he's at it?

The postal clerk doesn't speak English (neither does the boy, of course), but he is kind and attentive towards Yvonne. His behaviour towards the boy is no different to normal, either.

The boy watches the scene with bated breath (it's implausible that he'll survive this hopeless venture without lasting damage), and meanwhile the transaction is completed, the envelopes are franked, the airmail stamps stuck on, the post office clerk and father of his classmate cheerfully stamps on the postmark (a wonderful, huge wooden stamp in the shape of a hammer!) and wishes them a good day, and the boy and Yvonne leave the post office. Nothing bad happened! Buoyant with relief, the boy bounces along beside Yvonne on the way home. He can hardly believe his luck. He got away with it yet again, and, exhilarated, he realises that something that you think will be unimaginably difficult can sometimes be quite easy once you tackle it head on.

But Yvonne has also made a deep impression on the post office clerk. She comes across as self-assured, charming and regal. It doesn't cross her mind to hide or be timid. Stylish and confident, she oozes genuine authority. The boy is impressed by the fact that his mother has such a sophisticated woman as a best friend, and it makes him see Mama in a new light; maybe he underestimated her. Perhaps she has more standing in the world than he imagined.

What annoys him about his mother, however, is her eternal 'Talk to me, talk to me!'. You always have to tell her something, even when there's nothing to tell. 'Darling, you have to communicate': a much-heard phrase. A phrase he can't stand. Sometimes his mother acts like she's deeply offended, muttering in an exasperated voice that they won't get anywhere without communication. She then comes across as very lonely. She uses the word *communication* as a form of blackmail, it exudes moral pressure and coercion, as though it were an article of faith to profess and live by. The truth is much more banal: his mother likes talking to the boy more than the boy likes talking to his mother. So what? There's no reason to make a big deal out of it and act like your son has problems communicating.

Perhaps the truth is even worse, and that makes him all the more stubborn: she wants him to talk more because there are only two of them. If they were a normal family, it wouldn't be so obvious who was communicating and who wasn't. So now he has to to pay for his mother having no husband!

When his mother has guests, she asks everyone to tell stories, often in the form of a game where there's a ritual for deciding whose turn it is next. The boy finds it unbearable even just watching, but the guests seem to enjoy it – by God, it's weird, but he can't deny it. Everyone who leaves their apartment seems to feel like their soul is lighter. 'You always get such interesting conversations with Ms Mangold,' they say.

This is just something he is going to have to get used to.

———————

There are mayoral elections coming up in Dossenheim. On all the lampposts are election posters with either the CDU or the SPD candidate. You're either a supporter of one or the other. The boy supports the man from the SPD, although he has a beard, which he doesn't like, it always looks so fierce. His mother and all of her friends are going to vote for the SPD man. It is no wonder really, because you have to be an odd fellow to vote for the CDU. Actually, the boy can't even imagine what kind of people CDU voters must be. In any case, the good people vote for the SPD.

The SPD candidate's first name is Peter. In the neighbouring town of Schriesheim, there's a CDU mayor whose first name is also Peter. People always talk about the 'red Peter' and the 'black Peter', but his mother confuses matters by saying she thinks that the Peters from both parties would get along splendidly. That's utterly absurd, thinks the boy; why would they get along when one is CDU and the other is SPD? His mother thinks that this says a lot about them, the red and the black Peter. The boy gets her point, but he's not convinced. Surely you have to decide which side you're on?

Then something strange happens. His best friend Marcus's parents are SPD. On Saturdays, you can see them handing out SPD balloons at the market square. Marcus has always been an uncompromising supporter of the SPD, but then one afternoon suddenly everything changes. Marcus tells him that the CDU candidate is their neighbour; he points to the house. For real? Yes. The boy has to take a deep breath. So the man on the posters lives in the house next to theirs? Exactly, and he's very, very nice. Marcus knows him by sight, and since realising that he is the CDU candidate, he's kept his fingers crossed that he'll win the election. He hasn't said anything to his parents. Of course not.

This changes everything. A whole new reality is opening up. So the CDU candidate isn't a nasty piece of work at all, on the contrary, he's very nice? In view of these new facts, the boy wholeheartedly joins his friend's party. On the way to school, he stops at every lamp post that has a poster of Marcus's neighbour hanging on it and looks fervently, almost a little besotted, into the eyes of the CDU candidate, while swearing unconditional allegiance to him. The Hitler moustache, daubed on the man's face on many of the posters, had thus far met with his approval, but now it stirs outrage in him.

Election Sunday is approaching. Marcus and the boy don't tell anyone about their change of sides. Like spies, they defected secretly to the enemy camp. At times they marvel at their own audacity. But the sense of isolation is a bit oppressive. Was it perhaps a mistake after all?

On the evening of the election, they're there on the town hall square. Then the election result: the red Peter has won with a clear majority. The adults cheer and clink glasses, the mood is jubilant. Nobody talks about the CDU candidate anymore; the boy has almost forgotten him too. It's so nice to be part of the winning team. He furtively glances over at Marcus, who's hopping about and clapping with joy. His father ruffles his hair. The weeks of their secret apostasy are erased in an instant. The boy is now clapping too and is really so relieved that the good guys have won. He can no longer explain how he could have ever supported anyone else.

The thing he fears most – but of course only when he thinks about it, and he doesn't think about it very often – is nuclear war. An atomic bomb explosion is so powerful that you can't even imagine the consequences. But he can't understand how it was that the American pilot who dropped the atomic bomb on Hiroshima wasn't himself ripped to pieces by the explosion in the air. Was he flying that high? Or did the bomb have a time fuse? That would be neat. That was probably it: it must have had a time fuse.

Once, there was a copy of the magazine *Stern* lying around at home. The cover featured an article about the rise of the far right. The boy doesn't actually read newspapers or magazines yet, but he knows this is a truth he mustn't shy away from. When his mother leaves the apartment, he flicks through to the article. He reads it like he's duty bound. Outside it's a beautiful summer day. But his thoughts darken. He's aware that this article is about him too. It's a description of a threat that has him in its sights. The neo-Nazis in the article hate foreigners. And as he reads, he wonders whether it's possible to interpret the neo-Nazis' hatred of foreigners in such a way that it doesn't include himself. But although the article mainly talks about Turks, he has to realise that there's no reassuring way of reading it that takes him out of the line of fire. As far as the neo-Nazis are concerned, he's a foreigner. He needs to be on his guard.

He's very worried for the next few days. Up until now, he's only been afraid of Christian Klar, the infamous terrorist who is in prison in nearby Bruchsal. The boy is haunted by the idea that Christian Klar might escape from jail, hide in the forest and ambush the boy when he's playing in the woods. But this new fear is on another level of reality, that much is clear. It's a lot more tangible. More abstract and simultaneously more real. Something has changed, and with its warning tone the article leaves no doubt about it. The right-wing movement is growing stronger, which means that up to now everything was fine, but now everything is bad. He's going to have to adjust to tougher times.

The places mentioned in the article are far from Heidelberg. That's reassuring, at least, it's something to cling to. He doesn't tell his mother about his worries. He wonders whether the neighbours will think about him when they read an article like this and if they might ask him about it. That would also be awful.

But nothing happens. People don't speak to him about the article, nor do any neo-Nazis cross his path; his world and the world of worrying news don't overlap. When the magazine disappears into the paper recycling bin under the stove pipe he breathes a sigh of relief.

———— • ————

Sometimes the boy is genuinely astonished by who he has for his mother. As if, like Moses in the reeds, he had been found by a woman who is nothing like him. Do they have anything in common? Although they're like chalk and cheese, it doesn't make him feel any less loved by her. But what does that even mean? To be loved is a given. Mothers always love their children. Naturally, he would never say this to her – he cares about her, of course, and doesn't want her to be sad – but a mother's love, surely that's just something to take for granted, it's not something to be grateful for. It's more the other way around: she should be grateful to him that he's there to be the object of her love. That's why there's no need to be too lavish with his affection: he only lets her hug him when there's really no getting out of it.

His mother's love is like a force of nature; you can rely on it like the ebb and flow of the seas, like the return of the seasons, like the lunch that's still warm on the hob when he comes home from school, like the supper waiting for Max when he gets back from his adventure with the Wild Things, like the tinkle of the little bronze bell that his mother rings when she pushes back the curtain to reveal the nativity scene and the mound of presents under the Christmas tree (there it is: the German Crocodile, series 194, in green, a locomotive so powerful that it can even pull long freight trains up over the Geislinger Steige; OK, the Swiss Crocodile is even longer and stronger, but it's also more expensive, which is why he only put the German Crocodile on his wish list), like the bathtub his mother has already filled with hot water when the boy comes in shivering after sledging – but the water's too hot for his frozen feet, so he learns the knack of sinking his upper body into the water first, while keeping his feet out of the water until they've slowly thawed. All of this is beyond any reasonable doubt, and yet their two-person household sometimes strikes him as somehow questionable. Fragile, vulnerable. He senses when his mother's worried about whether she can manage it all, or about her account being blocked again. Is it perhaps not her eccentric obstinacy that the boy so objects to, but her inability to find a firm footing? Is her entire gospel of communicating just a kind of smokescreen to detract from the mundane poverty that means there's often not enough to tide them over?

It's not until after puberty that he abandons his reservations about his mother, when he realises that she's something of a celebrity among his school friends. He's amazed when a friend tells him how easy she finds talking to his mother. She takes you seriously. She doesn't have rigid prejudices like most adults, this friend says; she really listens to you; she understands what young people need. Well, he wouldn't have said so himself. He decides not to be ashamed of his mother anymore. The constant worry about causing offence or attracting puzzled looks is a thing of the past. Where he once looked on, annoyed, at his mother's overdrawn savings account, now this delicate, vulnerable mother-son team is one of the higher earners, morally speaking. Even if he is still often annoyed by her (and enjoys winning the affection of his friends' fathers), it's now no longer his weakness, his Achilles' heel, but the source of a special admiration.

# Silesia

My mother was born in Silesia in 1939, in a village called Pilgramsdorf near Breslau, now Wrocław in Poland. Very little has survived from that time. There's one photo of a two-storey house surrounded by a small garden. There are hollyhocks in the borders up against the house. You get the impression of a modest, but respectable and well-kempt household. Spick-and-span, as they might have said back then. Written on the long side of the house was 'Paul Witteck's Bakery – Bread, baked goods, confectionary; Flour, cereals, grains, animal feed'. It sounded like animals and people came to feed from the same trough.

Paul Witteck was my great-grandfather: my grandmother's father. The entire family is gathered in the photo, with the proud stance of an Antwerp craftsmen's guild in a Flemish genre painting, in front of the garden fence separating the house from the street: Paul Witteck, his wife Anna and their children Helene (my grandmother) and Erhard (whom I only know from the stories told by my mother and her sisters; he was always 'Uncle Erhard'). Plus the dog, a Spitz. If I've guessed my grandmother's age correctly – she was born in 1906 – then the picture must have been taken around 1924.

Mama loved talking about Grandpa Paul's bakery. The warmth of the oven, the impressive machinery, the smell of freshly baked bread, the rusk biscuits topped with icing. The hustle and bustle of esteemed craftsmanship. Even when she scurried about between Grandpa Paul's legs, she was never in his way.

There was a lot of singing at the Wittecks and indeed good singing – which was important to them. It was taken for granted that you should be able to hold your own in a polyphonic harmony. Grandma, a sparkling soprano, learned the piano, Erhard the violin. This love of music was something the Wittecks had in common with the Mangolds, who were originally Berliners; my great-grandfather Alexander Mangold was born into a prosperous tailoring business. He fell out with his parents when he married beneath his station against their will. Disinherited, he moved to Silesia with his wife, where my grandfather Willi was born in 1904.

In 1929, at the age of 23, my grandmother married Willi Mangold. He was a 'twelver,' meaning he had served for twelve years in the Reichswehr and had earned the right to a high-ranking position in the civil service. He left the military with the rank of Stabsfeldwebel and began his civilian life with the Reichsbahn, the German state railway. In their wedding photo, Grandma is wearing a white wedding dress and has a cheerful, quizzical expression on her face; her husband stands beside her in his Reichswehr uniform, a little stiff, but by no means shy (it wouldn't necessarily occur to later descendants that he was a sensitive player of the zither). Twins arrived just a year later: Willy, who bears his father's name, except that the *i* became a *y*, and Gerda. Inge followed in 1935, my mother Ulla in 1939 and finally, the baby of the family, Heidi in 1943.

The seat of the larger family remained the Witteck bakery in Pilgramsdorf, but Helene and Willi moved about a lot with their young family because of Grandpa's successful career as a civil servant. The Reichsbahn transferred him to several new posts around Silesia. The highest rank he reached in 1944 was senior civil servant, but the papers documenting his promotion were lost when the family were displaced and forced to leave as refugees.

In the late summer of the same year – and this was often talked about in my family; it was, so to speak, the point at which things turned sour – my grandfather suddenly enlisted for the front. Of his own volition. To his wife's consternation. After all, there was absolutely no reason for it; he was working in the Breslau railway administration, a reserved occupation. Whatever his job consisted of, he was needed where he was for strategic reasons, so why did he sign up to go and fight? War fever? Patriotic fervour? He was a member of the Nazi party, and he was the right age to benefit from the new opportunities this offered, but does someone really leave behind their wife and children to throw themselves into a war that's already lost? This would have required an almost martyr-like fanaticism – and he was never described as a particularly ardent National Socialist.

The period between 1944 and 1949 was a regular topic of conversation in the family. As a child, the end of the war and my grandmother and her children were more vivid for me than any other event in my mother's life before I was born. We were a refugee family. That they had 'lost everything' was something that Grandma wanted her grandchildren to understand. Life would have been different if they hadn't 'lost everything'. Becoming a burden to others had always been a source of shame, a dreaded nightmare. But that was precisely what happened.

There was no end of speculation in our family about why my grandfather might have enlisted voluntarily. Whenever the conversation took this direction, Grandma backed it up, adding details or chronological facts to my mother's reflections, but not insisting on her own interpretation. It could have been that, her expression said, but ultimately it remains a mystery. There's so much it's hard to know for sure, even about your own husband.

My mother also spoke about it with a number of reservations. It was conceivable, she'd say, that Grandpa was directly involved in the deportation of the Jews through his work for the Reichsbahn; there probably wouldn't have been much normal passenger traffic at that time, and Breslau was an important transport hub. Grandpa might have witnessed, perhaps even been an accomplice, in the extermination of the Jews, and perhaps he just couldn't stand being part of that apparatus. Better to die at the front. Was his decision perhaps a way of escaping what was unbearable?

As a child, I had a lot of distrust for this story. Not because of the whitewashing of my grandfather (the sensitive zither player), but because it just seemed highly unlikely to me that the fate of our insignificant family should be so directly linked to the course of world history. Somehow that seemed rather grandiose. He was just a railway employee! It's only now, when I think about it again, that something completely different occurs to me. Maybe that really was the case, and maybe Grandma knew full well, but she chose to adopt this tone of speculation because it helped subdue the scandal at the heart of grandfather's life – being a cog in the machine of the deportations – and make it more bearable. This is also mere speculation, but it also threatens any presumption of innocence. Anyway, the fact is that my grandfather went back to being a soldier. And was sent to the Eastern Front. Grandma received his last letter by field post in December 1944. After that there were no more signs of life, but no death certificate either. From now on she was alone with her five children. All that remained of him was the Silesian expression for father, Vatl. Besides that, very little Silesian survived in the diaspora – just this one word.

'Vatl played the zither so beautifully!'

Before Breslau was declared a military stronghold, Grandma and the children moved to Pilgramsdorf to live with her parents. There was room for them there. But with others, not on their own. The first refugees from East Prussia arrived in January 1945 and had to be found somewhere to live. One of the refugee children had diphtheria and infected Heidi. At the end of January, three months before her second birthday, Heidi died.

Meanwhile, the Russian front was approaching. The air raids were focused on Breslau, but Pilgramsdorf was also bombed, and throughout the night they could hear the injured cattle bellowing in agony. Two weeks after Heidi's death, the family decided to flee. My great-grandfather and Vatl's sister Käthe, who had married a farmer, hitched a covered wagon to some oxen and set off. Oxen, not horses: the wisdom of this decision has always been lauded, as oxen are more resilient. As a child I imagined how I would have skipped along beside the wagon (oxen are really slow), thrashing the nettles on the verges with a stick and giving the animals' glossy fur an occasional stroke.

On 20 January, the regional Nazi leadership, led by Gauleiter Karl Hanke, declared that anyone in Breslau unfit for military service was to be evacuated from the city. The Mangolds, heading west from nearby Pilgramsdorf, must have been caught up in the huge stream of refugees making their way through the snowy landscape. Fortunately, Käthe had brought cured pork with her from the farm, so the extended family was given accommodation in a barn here and there along the way in exchange for food.

They arrived in the Sudetengau region. Their hope of encountering the Americans there was not realised. Instead, it was the Russians! The family's Promised Land had been Bavaria, but at that point they decided, 'We're going back; at least we've got our houses there.'

In April 1945, the situation in Pilgramsdorf changed completely. The Soviet Army conquered Silesia; only the fortified city of Breslau held out until 6 May, in a self-destructive mania recalling the Twilight of the Gods. The first Poles, themselves victims of a gigantic resettlement drive, reached the western territories and took possession of whatever they could find. The machinery was ripped out of the bakery, and Käthe's farmstead was torched by jubilant Russians. There was still no replacement administration to put things in order. 'It was no man's land and we were fair game,' my aunts say, their eyes to this day wide with fear and at the same time with a look of resignation, as if they had long since given up hope that anyone might understand the monstrosity of what they went through. There was no routine, no school. The expulsions began. But while more and more Germans were being forced out of their houses, the Mangolds and Wittecks were allowed to stay for the time being, because there was still no Polish baker who could have replaced Grandpa Paul. So they were among the last Germans to remain.

In April 1946, the Polish militia were suddenly at the door. It was a Friday evening. No explanations, they just came and took Grandma away. She was locked in a cellar for a day and two nights, the water up to her knees. She had a tough time of it. They let her go on the Sunday morning – the day of Willy and Gerda's confirmation, apparently a prompt for compassion in the Polish militiamen, pious Catholics that they were. She looked awful, her thighs covered in bruises. It was clear they had no future in their homeland. But what a decision – to have to leave everything behind!

Their relatives had already left. In August, Grandma set off with the children. This time by train, heading north-west. When the train stopped, they were in Brandenburg.

I was young when my mother first read me a poem that warmed my heart, Theodor Fontane's *Herr von Ribbeck at Ribbeck in Havelland*. I liked everything about it: the tender glow of the autumn evening, the old man's kindness, his German dialect when he says 'Lad, fancy a pear?' I loved pears, and a pear tree seemed to me to be a far better grave decoration than flowers. I loved the name Havelland, the dreamy sound of it. And I loved the old man's sage foresight in anticipating and preempting his son's stinginess. The old Herr von Ribbeck, who always handed a pear to the village children as they passed his castle, suspected that his stingy son wouldn't continue this philanthropic tradition. So he decreed in his will that a pear should be placed in his grave. Just a few years after his death, a beautiful pear tree grew on that spot, and when a boy or girl passed by, the leaves would rustle, 'Come here, I'll give you a pear.'

The only thing I didn't understand about the Ribbeck at Ribbeck poem was the funny repetition of names, but you got strange names in fairytales and stories, too. Convinced that the son would blush with shame every time he visited his father's grave, I was filled with the thought that this tale represented justice for children and a demonstrative punishment of greed. The more he saw the pears on the tree, the less the young Ribbeck could ignore his own shameful behaviour.

Most of all, I loved the pears. The trees glowed in the golden autumn light, and the poem's pears were so juicy and sweet that every time I sank my teeth into an earthly pear I lamented my misfortune when it turned out to be only half-ripe. The fabled Ribbeck pear was the gold standard.

So you can probably imagine that as a child it seemed completely absurd when my mother told me that our insignificant family had stayed in Bagow am Beetzsee, in Brandenburg, in a castle that had for centuries belonged to the Ribbeck family. Yes, Mama insisted, the same Ribbecks, whose ancestor was the old man from the Fontane poem. However, it wasn't the main castle with the famous pear tree, but another one that the family owned. Mama must have loved it. It was as if she had found a place of childlike exuberance there for the first time after the chaos of their escape.

It was a difficult time for Grandma, the 'famine years,' as she liked to call them, but for my mother it was a completely different experience: the dungeons in the castle's basement! The dark corridors! At night she could have sworn she could hear chains rattling. While the nine-year-old Gerda had to help with the harvest in the fields so that the family had something to eat, she was romping around in the castle grounds, which stretched as far as the River Havel. She learned to swim in the Havel and could jump straight in from the castle grounds.

I didn't believe a word she said but, considerate son that I was, I kept my doubts to myself. There were famous poems and there was our insignificant family; that both should coincide at a certain point in cosmic space-time seemed to me to have emerged from the same desire to overemphasise our family's significance as my grandfather's alleged involvement in the deportation of Jews. No wonder; after all, they lost everything back then, so perhaps there was the temptation to conjure up this or that detail to comfort the injured soul and relocate oneself into a fairytale castle. If you can have phantom pain, then why not phantom happiness?

The family lived in the castle by the Beetzsee lake for almost two years. Not alone, of course; the house was full to the brim with refugees who, like them, had moved to Brandenburg from the eastern provinces of the Reich. The Ribbecks themselves had long since been dispossessed (in fact, the Gestapo had dragged Cavalry Captain Hans von Ribbeck off to Sachsenhausen concentration camp in 1944, where he died). Grandma was given a small room on the first floor, where they lived, slept, cooked and ate. On the first floor there was a kind of hall that was used as a schoolroom. Mama had her first schooling there at the age of eight; she still had to learn to read and write. Sometimes a classmate whose parents owned a grocery store would give her a snack – she would just slip it into Mama's pocket without saying a word.

At one point, Inge had appendicitis; the only people in the town who owned a car were the parents of the popular singer Rudi Schuricke; they got her to the hospital in Brandenburg just in time. From then on, whenever Aunt Inge hears the song 'Capri Fischer', she always remembers the singer's helpful parents.

As a refugee from the East, you had nothing but the clothes on your back. If the father of the family had survived the war, it was easier, but my grandmother was alone with the children. She didn't get her widow's pension in the Soviet occupation zone. She received some produce from the farm by helping with the harvest. At some point, the carpenter from the neighbourhood, who looked out for her, suggested they move on. 'Go over to the West, where your relatives are. Here you're completely on your own, you can't manage like this.' In fact, her sister-in-law Käthe and her family were already in Westphalia, near the town of Steinheim, and so was Grandma's father Paul.

It's the end of 1948 when they set off for the West. Moving on is no big deal; the two years were too short to put down roots. The refugee helpers lead them to the border zone at night. They wait for dusk in a grove behind a hill. When the first dawn lights up the sky, the small troop marches across the green border to the West. Nobody sees them, it all goes well.

My mother finished secondary school in Steinheim. Grandma received a widow's pension, albeit not as much as she was entitled to with her husband's final salary grade. The dream of a senior rank, although indeed a reality, had evaporated like fog.

Those were challenging years, hardly a kind word is spoken of that time. Grandma kept one hope alive, that her husband would walk down the street one day, one of the last to return from captivity. She often stood at the window of the apartment, looking out at the street, sizing up the passers-by, but the man she was waiting for was never among them. Instead, she also lost her son Willy, who couldn't cope with life there, having racked up impossible debts during the economic boom, and could only see one way out of his malaise: he crossed over to the East, going against the tide. Even with the best will in the world, no one could see it as an act motivated by political conviction. Willy had just done a runner in a big way. He seems to have brought a lot of children into the world, but there was never any contact. Once we heard from the grapevine that he was in prison, but even that seemed like baseless rumour and certainly not enough to transform him into some heroic dissident idealist. Grandma never heard from him again, the lasting torment of her life. A year before her own death in 1993, the news reached her from the then new German states that he had died.

In the early 1960s, my mother trained as a parish assistant at Burckhardthaus in Gelnhausen, an institution of the Protestant church. Burckhardthaus, under the directorship of the renowned theologian Jörg Zink, was a place where believers grappled for a progressive, politically conscious Christianity; no sign here of a spiritually desiccated faith. The word they used, *ringen* – 'grappling' – seems to me characteristic of the milieu: these weren't people who were happy to follow the path of least resistance. Nazi sympathisers in the Third Reich had taken the easy path; now it was time for a new, grown-up Germany, one that wasn't afraid to put up a fight. The focus was on 'Bible study', and I remember that, when reminiscing about Burckhardthaus, my mother always positioned 'Bible study' with a certain creaky Prussian grit, probably to distance herself from the happy-clappy guitar piety that became prevalent later. Sometimes she defined it with the adjective 'rigorous'. For her, 'rigorous Bible study' meant that philological analysis had far greater standing in her value system than mere effusive enthusiasm. She wasn't about to let her son think they sat around chatting aimlessly back then; my mother maintained a deep, life-long mistrust of facile, effortless morality.

The words that Austrian playwright Franz Grillparzer puts into the mouth of the spokesman of the Bohemian estates in his play *Family Strife in Habsburg*, 'We're building on a solid foundation, on the written word', could also apply to my mother. She also saw the written word – scripture – as the foundation to build on. By no means just the Bible, but books in general, the letters that she wrote and received in large numbers, a written tradition to refer to and learn from. Scripture, for her, was the tradition that opens up our lives to everything that has ever been, strengthening and broadening our inner world. I imagine Burckhardthaus, with its 'rigorous Bible study,' meant access to the study of scripture even for those who hadn't finished high school; a back-door route to literary studies and at the same time a place dedicated to the world and to its improvement.

She spent the summer months in so-called development camps, where young Christians from all over the world volunteered on work projects to renovate useful public facilities, a hospital in Greece, for example; borders were crossed, new communities emerged, and their physical work was lent a spiritual dimension through shared Bible study. When I go through her correspondence from this decade, letters addressed to her which she kept, life's questions are constantly linked to the readings of St Paul. One particularly eager correspondent is a young Greek man whom she must have met in the summer of 1960 in a development camp in Vienna. Basilius. His letters gushed with passion. Some of them read as though he were speaking in tongues. On the one hand. On the other hand, he addresses my twenty-one-year-old mother with the formal form of the word 'you.' She can't stand him addressing her as 'unforgettable Ulla' – it sounds fictitious. How, he replies, can she accuse him of writing fiction?

Basilius is full of doubts: should he pursue a career as a priest or apply for a scholarship to study medicine in Switzerland? He has already studied Orthodox theology in Greece, but he's no longer sure about continuing that path. Theology and medicine, he ponders, aren't polar opposites, are they? Luke the Evangelist was also a doctor. Basilius constantly asks my mother for advice. Her advice means a lot to him, he writes, her letters speak to a good blend of idealism and realism, and after each letter from her he sees things more clearly. He also thanks her for writing so 'clearly'. For him, someone whose German is ambitious but shaky, her cursive script can't have been easy to read.

This choice between the priesthood and a secular profession is complicated by a further aspect that isn't stated explicitly: one obvious advantage of studying medicine in Switzerland is that he would be closer to the person whose advice he so values. That God is love (*deus caritas est*) is a sentence repeated a little too often for him not to lose some of his angelic innocence. It quickly turns into a slippery slope. But no sooner has Basilius drifted from *caritas* to *eros*, than he's apologising for his emotional exuberance. Incidentally, it's not just my mother's words that are pure, so too is her heart. He includes a photo of himself in one letter: he's sitting on a terrace, in a dark suit, white shirt, narrow tie, his legs crossed, a book in his left hand. He doesn't look unpleasant, but you also get the spontaneous desire to tell him to relax a little, stop being so uptight; his eternal one step forward, two steps back isn't a great strategy for making an amorous conquest.

Basilius decides eventually to study medicine, and the St Paul quotations are replaced by Sappho quotations, but it's no good, he has to send his last letter (the last one she receives, anyway) to the USA, because in the meantime my mother has set off for Cincinnati. After an intense four years the correspondence ends.

A flight would have been pricey, so in 1967 my mother booked herself onto a cargo ship from Bremerhaven to New York. That suited her perfectly: even later on she thought that we have to take charge of, or 'construct', our experiences in life, and in the process, it takes time before the outer world becomes our inner reality. (How it used to annoy me as a child when she explained why she didn't take any photos on our bike tours: 'I'm capturing the memories in my mind.') Six days of crossing, then, and as the silhouette of New York emerged on the horizon, even though she knew that she would return after two years, she felt a little like the countless emigrants who had left Germany for the USA before her, looking for a better life, hoping to breathe the air of freedom.

After completing her training at Burckhardthaus, my mother had worked for four years doing youth work in a parish in Münster, and now she had been sent by the Protestant Church to Cincinnati, Ohio. The church there, located in downtown Cincinnati, was originally a German one, and you could still read biblical passages in German in the church windows. But Cincinnati was seeing demographic change. The German speakers were moving out to the suburbs and the black community was moving in; this was having an impact on the parish, where for the time being the two church communities met under one roof. The new parishioners could no longer decipher the old church windows. And yet baptisms, weddings and funerals were still recorded in the church register in German.

To help this transition go more smoothly, two young women were hired, one German, the other African American: my mother and Yvonne. From such different worlds. Up to this point, Yvonne had had almost no contact with whites, her friends were all black, she only met whites on a professional level, and otherwise very cautiously. Their formative experiences of humiliation and debasement were something they had in common only with other people of colour, and there was an openness only with others who had this shared lived experience. And now this young white woman had rocked up at the now black First Reformed Church of Cincinnati, and on top of that from Germany, where six million Jews had been killed because of racism just a little over twenty years ago. Yvonne had an older brother in his late fifties who had been stationed in West Germany for years; what he had to say about his time there wasn't conducive to painting a rosy picture of the country. The Germans, he said, used to say black people had tails like monkeys. So how was this young German church worker going to prove herself in Cincinnati?

My mother had very rudimentary English when she arrived. Maybe that's why it took a while before they both got to know one another. Early on, Yvonne observed from an interested but respectable distance how the last remaining older parishioners beamed as they spoke German with Mama. Then my mother started organising children's activities in the community; Yvonne insists that it was in Cincinnati that the foundation stone was laid for Mama's future career as a child and adolescent psychotherapist. Mama's interactions with the children must have triggered something within Yvonne. The dam broke, there was no stopping it. Now they spent almost all of their time together. Yvonne wanted to know what it was like to have grown up in the war, to flee your home, to lose your father at the front. Mama, in turn, listened to Yvonne's life stories, which essentially revolved around the experience of growing up in a society where she was perceived by the law as inferior. 'So you had to wait in the supermarket until the last white person in the queue had been served?' Some time later, when Yvonne took my mother to meet her family in Norfolk, they already felt like sisters. Both born in 1939, both Christian, both deeply rooted in their families. Mama went with Yvonne to their home church, the Macedonia United Church of Christ in Norfolk, and on their return she baked apple strudel for all the Delks.

My mother learned in the USA the true meaning of political engagement. Not by interpreting Marx in communist 'K groups', but by singing the Gospel with street workers. When she returned to Germany in 1968, the student movement struck her as theatrical, poserish and academic – indulgent, even. Although she was driven by some of the same motives, she never felt part of the world of these sons and daughters of the bourgeoisie, and that these eloquent students kept talking about the working class just seemed ridiculous to her. The struggle of the African Americans, on the other hand, as she had encountered through Yvonne, had nothing ambiguous about it, the suffering and injustice they rose up against was real, their fight was therefore concrete and tangible. She mistrusted abstract programmes for world happiness, and you would never hear a grand dogmatic pronouncement pass her lips. She believed only in tangible relationships that could be established between individual people.

Working for the church, where spiritual community and political engagement were intertwined, had shaped her life and had become a source of happiness and deep friendships. Where her relationship to the kingdom of God came from I don't know. It took me a long time to even realise how much her faith meant to her. You could go a long time without being aware of it. Was she a genuine believer? Or a happy agnostic who had simply chosen the more appealing of the two possibilities – that God probably exists? Or was she nothing but a Protestant by culture, who had learned the scriptures and kept up the traditions? She would have been as reluctant to relinquish the Christian holidays and her baptismal statement as to miss their customary hike through the Odenwald at Pentecost. She was uncompromising on these points, she was deeply attached to them, but you never had the feeling in her presence that a little less faith would be more pleasant for everyone.

The adjective 'concrete' was undoubtedly one of my mother's favourite words. The concrete was inherently superior to the abstract; only the concrete was tangible and observable. Morals that were not concrete were just empty talk. After many of the psalms she noted triumphantly in pencil: 'Concrete application in the world!' For her, the church work to which she had devoted so much enthusiasm in her twenties had been a manifestation of concrete action, and she valued the liturgy for the same reason: as the concrete performance of something beyond our senses, which almost made redundant the question of certainty of faith.

When my mother returned from the United States, her work for the Church ended. She wanted a new direction, so she moved to Heidelberg, where there was an institute that taught psychotherapy for children and adolescents – at that time, a vocational rather than an academic profession. This was a great opportunity for my mother, who didn't have the high school diploma that she would need to go to university. I don't know if that was part of her motivation, at least subconsciously – that she could pursue a professional activity which had a certain amount of academic prestige without needing a Bachelor's degree. In any case, she would come to love her job, because it was, as she put it, 'concrete work with people'.

One day she went to a meeting of young Nigerians and German church officials. A civil war was raging in Nigeria, and they wanted to discuss a shared strategy on how to push German politicians to take a more decisive stance. My mother and father found themselves sitting next to each other.

Nigeria, granted independence in 1960, was at risk of being torn apart by ethnic conflict. In January 1966, Igbo officers from the national army had seized power in a military coup, because they felt marginalised by the Hausa Muslim majority in the north of the country. The Hausa general rallied troops and staged a countercoup in July of the same year. There were pogroms in the north and a huge stream of refugees, hundreds of thousands, returned to the south, to the predominantly Igbo region. The country was being split in two. On 31 May 1967, the military government of the Southeast, the territory where the oil wells are located, proclaimed the independent Republic of Biafra.

The civil war didn't end until 1970 with the defeat of the Igbo and the end of the secessionist state. A million people were killed in the war and famine took the lives of millions more. The besieged Biafra tried early on to draw the world's attention to what was going on in Nigeria, and the Igbo diaspora around the world formed support committees to influence the governments of the countries where they lived. In Switzerland and the USA, professional PR agencies were even hired to campaign on behalf of the Biafrans. Would the world stand by and watch as the Igbo population was subjected, as many believed, to genocide? In August 1968, *Der Spiegel* ran the headline 'Biafra – death sentence for a people'. And *Stern* had 'Damning photos: the starving children of Biafra.' The public was finally forced to wake up.

Letters had been going back and forth between my mother and father since August 1968. Unfortunately, I only have his. He was a medical student in Heidelberg at the time. The political fate of his homeland plays an ever-present role in his letters; my father reports who's just been elected president of the committee, that there's still no agreement on whether to recommend a total boycott of Nigeria to the German government. He passes on to my mother any news he hears from his family in Nigeria. But above all, his letters are about everyday matters: exams, having too much work at the hospital, how expensive his rent is, and who says hello to whom. He buys a second-hand car (an Opel), the engine fails not long after, and in another letter he describes how easy it is to hitchhike in Germany, even over long distances. The first letters are signed Lewis, but he soon switches to Ozurumba – not without recalling in his decisive baptismal letter how long she, Ulla, had nagged him to tell her his Igbo name, and how cross she had been that he had even introduced himself with his English name, which had so little to do with him and his past. He, Ozurumba, couldn't deny how happy he was that she called him Ozurumba.

Shortly after this, he got a job in Saarbrücken. The hospital was badly understaffed, but the team worked extremely well together, he wrote, so he was learning a lot. There was a telephone in the corridor of his apartment block. He had Saturdays off, so he planned to visit her in Heidelberg. Or would she be visiting her mother in Steinheim next weekend? If so, he asked my mother to send her his best regards.

Once he asked my mother about a conference she had attended in Stuttgart. 'It's interesting that an anti-authoritarian girl takes part in a discussion about anti-authority. Did you get your point across?' Despite his slightly patronising tone, he doesn't seem to have any doubts about her assertiveness.

It isn't easy to tell from the letters at which point the friendship turned into a love affair. It certainly happened at some point, and my mother became pregnant not long after.

# PART II

# Tenno

The scenes we remember, the ones most vivid in our mind's eye, those that are always there to be called upon, ready to be narrated to ourselves or others at will, these well-archived memories that belong to the core repertoire of ourselves, are by no means unadulterated. The better we remember something, the more often we have summoned it to the forefront of our minds, the softer and suppler it has become from our repeated manipulation, moulded to fit our requirements. As with a game of 'Broken Telephone,' we mutter the anecdotes of our past self into the ears of our later self in an infinite chain, with the difference being that the stories, because all our selves are so familiar with one another, don't become more absurd, preposterous and meaningless from one telling to the next, but rather they become ever more compact, more rounded and more palatable. This is how it comes to be that our most reliable memories are also the least authentic. As the sea wears away the rock, so do we hone our memories as we subject them to the rules of storytelling. We refine them like we refine petroleum. We trust them now because they've accompanied us all our lives, we trust them perhaps more than the fleeting memories that flash by unexpectedly, a surprise and a challenge, because we haven't yet formed an opinion of them. We know full well that the memories that are especially familiar to us are not a direct connection to our previous life, but rather memories of memories. We remember them as we remembered them the last time, and that too, as we are also well aware, was only the memory of an act of remembering even longer ago.

Much of what I tell here is an established part of my autobiographical folklore. Other stories, on the other hand, were long forgotten and only speak up now that I'm looking for them, decades after they happened. There's a particular episode that's one such straggler. I can't remember how old I was when it happened, or more precisely, when it happened for the first time, because I think it's something my mother told me about more than once. It was with a kind of intensity that I couldn't escape: when she spoke like that, it was a matter of listening and accepting. African Americans, she said, are doing well for themselves in America, but mostly in show business and sports. And as nice as these successes are, we need to be careful not to restrict black people to the entertainment industry and the role of the clown, we also need black lawyers, doctors and politicians. It's important that as a people, they are taken seriously, too.

These memories are still raw and untreated. They're from a distant place in the dark unlit recesses of my mind. I turn the frequency dial hoping to reduce the white noise and hear the rest of what she said, but all I get is Mama's reminder that it shouldn't be just sport and entertainment. Was it some kind of educated, bourgeois scepticism about popular culture? An exhortation to moral austerity? Was my mother trying to talk to me about something related to my future career aspirations? Did her words place an obligation on me, or was it just an attempt to dismantle a cliché and to open my eyes to the vast horizons before me?

I also can't remember much of my reaction to what Mama said, I just remember that this time I didn't tune out. Did I associate what she said with my own passion for sport? Back then I was an athlete, a middle-distance runner, and I was training at least five days a week. When sport was later replaced by drama club, did I have the feeling that I was too accurately carrying out her prophecy in spite of her warnings?

All I can say is that I didn't block out what my mother said like I so often did. For once she talked about black people and I listened. I was somehow intrigued by her observation. Perhaps not so much by what she said as by the realisation that there was anything to observe at all; that a certain group of people took on certain professions. This observation was my first, as yet completely unconscious encounter with the realities of society.

Thinking of what Mama said, I couldn't help picturing Harry Belafonte. His was the only pop LP in my mother's record collection; sometimes I would put it on, irritated by the catchy music that made me cringe a little, the voice that seemed to show no restraint in its attempt to get everyone dancing. I looked at the singer on the record sleeve and asked myself if I had anything in common with him. He looked so slender and lithe, so flexible, so elastic, but he also seemed somehow exaggerated in his physicality, his sexuality, like a comic figure. Was that what Mama meant?

In any case, a completely different moral austerity emanated from other record covers – for example, the stately golden horn on a red background that was on the cover of a Mozart horn concerto. In general, these LPs had something intimidating about them: the classical music industry at that time clung to a solemn, histrionic style. With eyes that flashed the madness of genius, a stare that crushed all mediocrity, Beethoven stared down from the cover of his 9th Symphony. But my mother's record collection also contained the ethereal, meditative transfiguration that radiated from a bearded man who had recorded Bach's Violin Concerto in A minor. And there was the man whose facial features had been the subject of much talk in those days, features that one associated with the personality cult of totalitarian dictatorships and Roman divine emperors, that man with the eagle's beak of a nose, the silver-grey hair, chiselled features, whose gaze always looked up, into the depths of the cosmos. Ideally he would be standing before a steel-grey shimmering cliff face, its sublime grandeur lending a craggy monumentalism to his countenance. This was a look that left an austere impression on the beholder. An expression so imperious, so relentless, so absolutely humourless, that unsurprisingly there was barely a record to be found without the portrait of this semi-divine disciplinarian of music, whose name was so baffling with its preposition in the middle that it seemed to be not of this world: Herbert von Karajan. You could hardly have two faces less alike than Harry Belafonte's and Herbert von Karajan's, even if they were staring each other in the eye in my mother's record collection. Who would blink first? Such an anatomical necessity as blinking was presumably beneath someone of von Karajan's stature, whereas Harry Belafonte would spin three times on his own axis within the blink of an eye, with moves as fluid as mercury, too swift to freeze, outwitting gravity, no need to strive for majesty.

Was I somehow associated with Harry Belafonte because we had the same skin colour? I couldn't see it. Others might, of course, have come to a different conclusion, because naturally they couldn't see inside me, they could only judge by external appearances, and this might indeed suggest that we had something in common and came from a similar place. My mother exercised a tender reticence about such questions, and only now and then was she overcome by an educational mission – or would it have been a moment of rapt memory of my father? Then she would come across like an ambassador for the distant continent, reminding me that Africa was a part, and indeed a very dignified part, of my identity.

My mother was happy to mention that my first name was an Igbo name. The word Igbo meant something special. When my mother used it, her voice took on a hint of jubilation. In the Biafra War, the Igbo were militarily inferior, but the moral victors. The Hausa might have held the reins of power in Nigeria, but the Igbo had the education and the IQ. Emotionally, just the term Africa would have been enough for me to pinpoint my paternal line, and although I had no idea of borders within Africa, I was ready to talk about Nigeria, if only to show my goodwill. But being specific about the Igbo connection? That was going too far for me. It seemed to me like a mathematical pedant trying to learn the number pi by heart up to nine decimal places, even though you're almost certainly never going to find yourself in the quandary of needing to calculate something using it. So what was the point in this excessive precision? Why zoom in on that distant continent so closely that suddenly a word like Igbo was given life and detail and depth of field? It seemed absurd to me. If it was an unspoken invitation to associate something of myself with this word, let alone some form of noble ancestral narcissism, then I rejected it out of hand.

So, I blocked all conversations about Africa. When Mama talked about Africa, I listened passively, with a vacant stare; I didn't object, but I didn't ask any questions. Mama never kept it up for long, and then it was over. She probably suspected that there was no point in pushing me, so for once she didn't drag out the moral bludgeon to remind me I needed to *communicate*.

I started high school in 1981. It was my wish to go to the more academically-focused grammar school, the Kurfürst Friedrich Gymnasium, an old school which overlooks the River Neckar, because my best friend, the one with whom I once bet on the wrong horse in the mayoral elections, was also going there. His father was a Latin teacher and had once taught at KFG himself. Mama was initially sceptical about my choice of this high school of all places, given that it had rather an elitist reputation, and she warned me that she wouldn't be able to help me with Latin. But for some reason I couldn't articulate, I now had my heart set on KFG, although I had no idea what this school stood for, with its over 400-year history.

'Fine,' said my mother, when she saw how determined I was, 'but then we'll sign you up for Greek, too.' This was a resigned 'May as well go the whole hog, then', as if she wanted to test how serious I was. But would I get a place? The principal – to whom my mother and I had to introduce ourselves, and who was concerned that the numbers taking Greek were dwindling, until eventually there would no longer be enough pupils for a proper Greek course and the core identity of the school would be threatened – accepted our choice with an affectionate smile. He congratulated me on my decision, one which opened up a huge, meaningful world, and I thought, amazed, that – for once – this was a smart move Mama had made.

When I started in the autumn, I found out my year group was known as 'sextains.' Before the summer holidays, we had been 'fourth graders', now we were sextains; this was more than just a chronological leap, it was a completely new mode of existence. So there we were, in our very first lesson, sitting at our rows of desks in the unfamiliar, awe-inspiring classroom, the Latin teacher, who was also our class teacher, asked each of us to say our names. When it was my turn and

I had said mine, he fell briefly into deep thought; something had clearly thrown him out of step, and he was mulling over the best way to bring the situation back under control. Then his face lit up, and he solemnly declared that although the surprising -a ending, which we encounter in my first name, usually indicates a feminine, Latin also has exceptions such as *agricola*, 'farmer,' a masculine noun despite its ending. And straight away, the anomaly was dispelled and my name was successfully assimilated by the blessing of Latin. I accepted my Latin teacher's analogy with relief. After all, I wasn't a girl.

Everything was unfamiliar at this new school. It wasn't just that the card deck was shuffled afresh, you didn't even know for sure what values the cards had that you held in your hand. What rank or status would you have in the class? Were you destined to be one of the leaders or would you find yourself at the bottom of the pecking order, where unfortunate souls eked out a pitiful existence, those who get left behind in PE when the team captains took it in turns to select players, dismissing the stragglers with – 'You can have the rest…' – only to be taken to task by the PE teacher for such arrogance, but still, it was worth it.

The first months were a time of shifting constellations, power structures forming and crumbling. Someone rose to the top, only for their preeminence to turn out to be based on deception, a misunderstanding; they were in fact one of the weaklings, the unsporty, the uncool. It may have looked at first like they had some natural claim to authority, but now they found themselves unceremoniously dethroned. These were mere teething problems at the start of the school year. But soon enough a hierarchical system emerged as a fixed alignment, where there was seldom a fall from grace or a promotion in rank. The ruling form of government in the class was the oligarchy (apart from the democratic election of the class representative, a post that didn't come with any actual power). As in every classroom. A small number of grandees at the top were the ones who set the tone. I still didn't quite trust the peace that had been negotiated, but apparently, to my surprise, I found myself in the inner circle within our class, and then eventually – by now we were 'quintains' – I was part of the so-called 'Group of Six'.

The Group of Six, which eventually became simply 'the Six,' were three boys and three girls. They didn't call themselves that from the start. They just spent a lot of time together, being careful not to waste time talking to anyone else. Once, all six of them had a sleepover hosted by one of the girls, at her apartment – or more precisely, in a small wooden hut on the large roof terrace. Before they went to sleep, her father told them stories from Brazil, where he grew up; they were good stories. Then he took some pictures of them lying side by side in their sleeping bags like sardines in a can. When the photos were developed, they looked at them at breaktime at school, sitting on the desks in the classroom. The others peeked over their shoulders, eager to be let into the secret.

Gradually they started to sense the magic that emanated from the name. When they started calling themselves the Six, everyone else looked on with envy. They didn't hold back from asking if they could join the Six. But the Six was a conservative structure, they didn't accept new members. How could they, anyway? It wouldn't be a group of six if it had more than six members, would it? Some people just didn't get it. The more often people talked about the Six, the more the rest of the class sank into insignificance. The best thing was that the Six didn't have to do much to maintain the air of mystery; a bit of whispering to each other at breaktime was enough for their eminence to grow.

The Six went to the cinema to see *The Last Days of Pompeii*. The one possible hitch: it had a 12+ certificate, but they were only eleven. All morning they had planned what they would say at the box office. 'Six tickets for *The Last Days of Pompeii*, please.' Would they be let in or would they be laughed at? Would they get in trouble? If they did get in, their fame would skyrocket.

They were nervous as they queued up for the afternoon showing. Was it really such a good idea to try and get into a 12? But in fact they had no problems at the counter; they paid and were given their tickets. They were high as kites. The film was pretty intense, with gladiator fights, a volcanic eruption, blistering lava everywhere and a city being ripped apart, but that wasn't the most exciting thing. Sitting in their cinema seats with bated breath, they were already imagining how they would play it tomorrow at breaktime. The best thing would be to just look conspiratorial and if necessary drop an enigmatic codeword in passing. It was crucial that they didn't blurt out the sensational news themselves, that there be a build up, the rest of the class longing to know what they'd been up to. Let them beg. That was the only way to reveal their secret, after a show of reluctance.

And the amazing thing was that it worked. There was always someone who was desperate to know what the Six had been up to. You could tell from their faces that sneaking into a film that was a 12 was actually pretty bold.

They just had the knack. No question about it.

The ultimate showstopper was when they featured as an agenda item to be discussed at the teacher and parents meeting. This meant they had pretty much achieved diplomatic recognition as a sovereign state, a powerful entity that could no longer be ignored. This wasn't immediately apparent to the rest of the class. When word went around that the Group of Six had trouble coming their way, some started celebrating, but they didn't realise they were signing their own death warrant – this controversy only propelled the Six even more into the limelight.

It wasn't easy for the parents to channel their concern into an effective counter-strategy or to knock together a credible indictment. The standard route would be to charge them with some grave misdemeanour, with evidence to back it up and a consequential ban on criminal association. But they had nothing to pin on them! The Group of Six couldn't be stopped that easily. They slipped through the fingers of their detractors. In fact, as soon as anyone talked about the Six, they vanished like a phantom; and even if no one was talking about them, they still dominated the room. The fact that one of the most irreproachable girls in the class, known for her faultless, responsible behaviour, was part of the Six, didn't make it easier to catch them red-handed. They hadn't done anything wrong. You couldn't even prove that they called themselves the Six. They just liked to do things together, that was allowed, wasn't it? In the end, the parents asked, almost begging, why they didn't want to play with the others. The Six replied with drooping heads and a mixture of disinterest, weariness and contempt. Of course, they *could* play with the others. A disdainful pause before the word 'others' made it clear that there was an infinite distance between them.

Nobody at school seemed to particularly notice that I looked exotic. There were of course foreigners in the Federal Republic of Germany at the time, but I wasn't one of them. When we discussed xenophobia at school (and it came up a lot), it never occurred to anyone to ask about my experiences. My unfamiliar aura was not only not mentioned, it wasn't even registered. I can't say why that was, because I didn't notice it myself for a long time. Probably because of both my ability to adapt and Heidelberg's relaxed, cosmopolitan atmosphere that was favourable in so many ways. And of course there was something else: a foreigner was – and is! – someone who causes problems. Foreigners have to belong to a problem group, otherwise they're not foreigners, they're just someone with an interesting life story, a background you might ask about by starting, 'So, tell us about yourself!' But you wouldn't ask a foreigner about their life, because you already know the narrative arc: school dropout, parallel universes, honour killings.

The only ones who weren't deceived were the genuine foreigners. First it was the Yugoslav and Greek greengrocers, then the Turkish ones. They all served me with an emotional warmth and exuberance that for a long time I presumed was a regional temperament, until at some point it dawned on me why I was such a hit with them: it was solidarity among foreigners! We were brothers in arms because we knew what it was like to live among Germans. And maybe there was also a glimmer of admiration that I got on so well with these tricky Germans, because they knew only too well that it wasn't easy.

It was Yugoslavs, Greeks and Turks who were like this with me, but not Italians. They had already left the ghetto behind them in the 1980s and they no longer saw themselves as foreigners. And they weren't seen as foreigners either. You were a foreigner in the Federal Republic for as long as people griped about the smell of your corresponding guest worker group. I can still remember that in the 1970s, Italians were thought to reek of garlic. I swear I heard people on the street say that they had nothing against Italians, but it was a shame they stank like that. Basically, until well into the 1980s,

Germans considered themselves the only genuinely clean people in the world. Even with Austrians, people had doubts about hygiene in their hotels.

When Italian cuisine established itself as the prevailing culinary standard in the 1980s, it was suddenly just the Yugoslavs and the Greeks who stank of garlic. Since Germans considered themselves to be immaculate, the smell of garlic was taken as a form of uncleanliness. Some people – you would hear this time and time again – wouldn't go to the Greek restaurant because it was dirty. This didn't ever have to be proven.

I also had a keen ear for such undertones because I always saw myself as being at risk of guilt by association. And it was a real danger, even if it never actually came to anything. As a result, I was hypersensitive to what I overheard. I started doing a lot of athletics in sixth grade; in my age group, I held the Baden record for the 1000, 2000 and 3000 metre races. Once my trainer, who had a heart of gold, raved about me to someone else: 'He's got lungs like a horse!' I winced. Days later I was still picking his words apart, worried that 'like a horse' might have been an allusion to my African roots, because people liked to ascribe Africans a certain animalism. In general, I was uncomfortable about the fact that so many famous runners were African; was I only confirming a common African characteristic with my athletic ability? (Just as people would often say to me, 'You must be a good dancer!' I wasn't, although it would have been nice.)

The word 'negative' triggered a similar horror, and strangely enough, this state of alert has persisted to this day. Because it's only when the speaker reaches the third syllable that I know I'm safe and they're not about to say the word *neger*. It has almost never happened, but I've always been on high alert. Like a soldier guarding a nuclear weapons facility: nothing ever happens, but he can't drop his guard for a second.

Every time I went to the barber, before he started cutting, he made an obviously redundant statement: 'Same as always?' As though there were plenty of alternatives for me, but because I was so incredibly happy with my hairstyle I stuck with it time after time. The sad truth was there was no alternative. Before going to the barber, my hair was a little longer, afterwards a little shorter. That was it. There were only gradual differences, but there was no question of a new hairstyle. That's why it was ridiculous when the barber held a hand mirror behind my head when he was finished, so I could check I was satisfied with the way he had shaved the back of my neck.

It had been the same for years. Then Udo Lindenberg came into my life. When 'Sonderzug nach Pankow' came out in 1983, I bought the LP *Odyssey* and every song was good. Especially the lyrics. The things he could say with his songs! The sorts of things that if you dared say them yourself, everyone around you would be speechless. I particularly loved the song 'Beim Bund' which had one completely insane line, full of unknown words I savoured on my tongue. Such a dense concentration of expletives and foreign words that I had to examine each individually to surmise the meaning. Absolutely genius, I thought, that the foul-mouthed *Spieß* had a complex, because it suddenly shifted the balance of power. It wasn't the recruit who was the poor sod, but the high-ranking *Spieß* (whatever a *Spieß* was? A sergeant? Sounded like *Spießer* – a bore? Hmm, that could kind of make sense).

It wasn't just the idea of talking like Udo Lindenberg, I also longed to look like him. I did actually manage to locate a kind of floppy Fedora like the one he wore. However, on my head, it really didn't look anything like how it did on Udo Lindenberg; the Udo look came down to the combination of hat and long hair, so I needed long hair too.

The next time I went to the barber, I was extremely nervous. Because this was the day that I was going to answer the question 'Same as always?' with a defiant 'no!' Provided I could pluck up the courage. It was so hard to do something different for the first time. There were still two customers ahead of me. Most of all I just wanted to leave. Then suddenly it was my turn. The barber asked, 'Same as always?,' and I answered hesitantly, because I had no idea how you were supposed to put it. 'Well, I'd like it longer at the back.' The barber stared at me. I winced. I realised he was stumped. He asked what I meant by 'longer at the back'? There was only the hairline anyway; my hair wasn't *long* in that sense. I was close to despair. How could I tell him that I wanted hair like Udo Lindenberg? Shakily, I added, 'Don't cut off so much at the back.' He nodded slowly and seriously. 'I won't shave the back of your neck, then.'

When I get home, I checked my new hairstyle very carefully in the bathroom mirror. It looked exactly the same as before.

There was a lot that was new and exciting, but it wasn't always easy to know how to make sense of it all. Certain words were particularly tricky. There were important and mysterious words that you were supposed to know, but didn't really understand what they meant. For example, the English phrase 'double feature' had been cropping up a lot recently. It sounded cool, and my classmate Mirko had used it before, and everyone was in awe of this phrase. But of course I couldn't ask Mirko what a 'double feature' was, I had to find out myself. But how? I couldn't rule out the possibility that it was one of those extremely mysterious words that had a suggestive secondary meaning. That was the danger with any new phrase, that it might have a sexual connotation, and if you weren't careful, you could end up being mortified. It didn't sound like it with 'double feature', but I couldn't rule it out for sure. Didn't 'double' mean 'two'? And two, well, that was the basic configuration for something sexual, and, oh God, were their 'features' somehow, er, penetrated?

Then there were words that had nothing suggestive in terms of their meaning, but if you isolated their components, they had quite a different meaning. You couldn't read the word *fiktiv* ('fictional') without thinking of it as *fick tief* ('fuck deep'). Even if someone mentioned a 'graphic artist,' everyone would snigger. And what about Boris Becker, a Heidelberger like us, whom the tabloid *Bild* had renamed 'Bum-Bum-Becker'? Was it supposed to make you think of *bumsen* (shagging)? Some kind of commentary on the thrusting action of Becker's serve?

Speaking of *Bild*, older women liked to call it the '*Bums Blatt*' (shag rag) which was hilarious – didn't they know what they were saying?

And what was 'petting' exactly? Where was the line between 'petting' and 'banging'? In *Bravo* magazine, a girl who had slept with her boyfriend for the first time wrote: 'And then we saw the stars.' Would you also see the stars when 'petting' or only while 'banging'? And where did these stars suddenly come from?

Burning questions, but I had no idea who to discuss them with. We had outgrown the Group of Six, we had lost that basic trust and no longer had much to say to each other. Life wasn't so easy any more. I was horrified to see some fluff forming on my upper lip.

But certain books were suddenly fascinating. In one history lesson, I gave a presentation about Friedrich Engels' essay about the peasant uprisings. Engels, if I understood correctly, was a Marxist, and what's more, he was a friend of Karl Marx. Even though he came from a wealthy family, he fought for the proletariat. The word 'proletariat' was just as intriguing as the word 'double feature', albeit in a different way. Maybe I was also a Marxist myself? It wasn't such a bad feeling, I realised. And it clearly made an impression on everyone that I talked about Friedrich Engels. I stood on the side of the oppressed peasants, while Luther – it couldn't be said often enough – had opportunistically taken the side of the princes and betrayed the peasants.

My history teacher was happy with my presentation. But then the bomb went off.

At school, there was a teacher of Religious Studies and Hebrew, Mr Vaupel, a man of the old school, a real Cold War type, who liked to proclaim himself (thereby suggesting that we should also be) a *Gesinnungspreuße* – a Prussian in spirit. Coming from Heidelberg, he could hardly be a genuine Prussian. Hence, Prussian *in spirit*. Now we had to reconsider what we had been taught all this time. At our school they liked to tell us we were privileged because we were born within the borders of the Roman Empire. We'd walked along the Limes on the school trip to Taunus, after all. But according to Vauper, that was just an ancient cultural backdrop! Anyone who couldn't count themselves among those lucky Romans might at least have been born within the borders of the Carolingian Empire; beyond that dwelled the barbarians. And now all of a sudden, being *Prussian in spirit* was where it was at. Of course, as students, we didn't take identifying with either the Romans or the Prussians very seriously; both were ridiculous, reactionary and anachronistic, but what was remarkable was the shift in the cultural and topographical axis with which Mr Vaupel professed his loyalty to Prussia.

He wore a badge on his lapel declaring his membership of the CDU, the Christian Democratic Union. He once threw a girl out of class for wearing the purple scarf of the Evangelical Church Assembly; it turned out the girl's father was a big shot in the local church, and the matter ended with Mr Vaupel being reprimanded by the School Board. He had always boasted of his special connections to the School Board, too, and now they'd left him out in the cold! The old loyalties clearly hadn't stood the test of time. All the same, he seemed to revel in his isolation.

Since I, an unbaptised heathen, didn't take Religious Studies, Mr Vaupel wasn't my teacher. Nevertheless, he got wind of my presentation. At breaktime, I was standing in the corridor when he rushed towards me. Red-faced and fuming at the ears, he shook his head, waved his arms, gasped and trembled all over with rage. 'You've backed the wrong horse, young man. Very, very wrong!'

Everyone overheard his tantrum. It was incredible. I had literally just become a Marxist, and the class enemy had already lost it.

Another time, when we were doing a school project on the power of advertising, we had to interview people on the street to see whether they thought they were influenced by advertising or not. The idea was that people would insist they weren't, but – ha! – we knew better. We'd see how deluded people are, and that's always a good feeling.

I was standing with a classmate in the pedestrian zone, asking passers-by for a quick interview, when a short man with wild, anarchic curls, and a round belly that gave him a content, even smug look, came up to us. His shirt was only half buttoned and hung over his trousers, he was wearing wire-rimmed glasses, and he handed us his business card. He was from the radio broadcaster Süddeutscher Rundfunk. He said what we were doing was really interesting, he'd wanted to do a feature about the manipulative effect of advertising for a long time, it was a really relevant topic we were working on. The problem was, he explained, that if he asked people, one adult talking to another, they wouldn't answer honestly, whereas we boys had the advantage that we would get more authentic answers. Would we be happy to do the same for him, but with recording equipment? His address was on the card. If you pressed the buzzer with his name at the same time as the one on the top left, the door would open by itself. 'Ha ha,' he sniggered, like he was sticking two fingers up to the busybodies with their faint-hearted need for security. Why didn't we just drop by his tomorrow after school? We could have lunch together, then he would lend us his tape recorder and we could make a start. And by the way, he said, everyone called him Tenno.

This was the start of the Tenno era.

Tenno's unusual, cave-like apartment with its small inner courtyard (overgrown with wild vines) in Heidelberg's old town would see regular visits from scores of teenagers and young men. The Tenno youths, who hung out in Tenno's grotto after school. I found it a bit strange that Tenno's adolescent following was recruited exclusively from the Kurfürst Friedrich Gymnasium, while at the same time he never missed an opportunity to ridicule the school, which saw itself as the elite institution that churned out the next generation of Heidelberg's upper class. He seemed to see in his young followers a secret task force that could attack the venerable institution from within. Tenno's key message for the boys was that each and every one of them was vastly superior to their insipid teachers. His perspective found fertile ground.

Tenno, who had studied music and composition, particularly had it in for one of our music teachers. When the school orchestra had performed a concert in the town hall under his direction, Tenno wrote a customary review in the *Rhein Neckar News* where he praised the students for their animated performance, but accused the music teacher and conductor of making a hash of an opening in Brahms' Fourth Symphony. At another concert he was outraged that the music teacher in question had silenced the audience with a brusque gesture from the conductor's lectern, when a few students had accidentally started to clap between movements; there was no need to stifle the exuberance of the students with such pedantry! Too many teachers believed they were misunderstood geniuses, when in truth they were mediocre. As Tenno put it, ludicrous little runts.

When I met Tenno, I was 14 years old and at loggerheads with most of my teachers, so I was in my element – or as we said at the time, it was 'an inner Nuremberg rally' – being able to conduct a psychological argument against them where I was undefeatable. They were just sad, pitiful figures who couldn't cope with not being geniuses like some of their students whom they resented – and not without good reason!

Tenno was always delighted to tell the tale of how he got his nickname. In the Scouts they were lounging around a campfire one time and, while stretched out on the floor as if on a chaise longue, he asked another scout to bring him something to drink. The kid replied, 'Get it yourself, you're not the Tenno!' And since then he has liked to make it abundantly clear – he is the Tenno. Unfortunately, I didn't know who the Tenno was. Oh, the Japanese emperor. I laughed quietly, the way you do when you're not absolutely sure that you got the joke.

Wasn't it a bit odd that someone who in other ways argued for socialism and equality, and liked to kick authority in the shins, adorned himself with the title of emperor? Yes, but maybe that was precisely the ingenuity here: he would take on board anything anyone else said, turn it around in surprising ways, and always make an exception for himself.

Indeed, rebelling against the authorities and celebrating oneself were, as I learned from Tenno, two sides of the same coin. You could almost get the impression that the battle against the former was only worth waging in order to gain more space for the latter. Narcissism was only a character flaw if you were timid about it; if you confessed to your narcissism unreservedly, it was considered an expression of nonconformity. As Tenno liked to say, 'Vain? Undoubtedly so!' And he would break into a big beaming smile.

One of Tenno's go-to quotes was a line from Goethe, which to my surprise, I had already heard uttered by Mr Vaupel: 'Only a nobody is modest.' These were all new opportunities for Tenno's young acolytes to become more assertive, more self-confident. If someone accused you of being cocky, you would counter with the Goethe quote and an ironic grin.

'Stick it to the lot of them!' was Tenno's oft-repeated war cry. Most of all, it was aimed at my 8th grade German teacher. Clearly someone who was highly unlikely to see himself as a genius, he was fragile and lonely, a bit prone to self-pity. He felt constantly misunderstood and wrongly unloved by the students whose happiness and success were all he desired. When he was at the end of his tether with me, he summoned my mother to a meeting to complain about me. Afterwards my usually so compassionate mother reported back, revealing in her intonation her irrepressible contempt for the display of unmanliness with which he had exclaimed, 'Your son, Ms

Mangold, wants to be treated with kid gloves, but he doesn't treat me with kid gloves, far from it!'

As I said, he didn't consider himself a genius, but he tended to get emotional about the fact that he could speak Alsatian German, and in this regard he was completely self-absorbed – something he simply couldn't hide. In spite of our well-known hard-heartedness, he seemed to hope that his knowledge of Alsatian German would enthrall us as it did him, and consequently he was deeply disappointed when it turned out that our souls were not, so to speak, in harmony with his. We dreaded his oral demonstrations; his pronunciation tended to be rather moist, and someone in the front row even opened an umbrella, with the bold comment that it had started to rain.

We also sensed that this Alsatian German had something suspicious about it, something that went far beyond the status of a dialect. Alsace no longer belonged to Germany, let alone to the Federal Republic. It belonged to France. Anyone who spoke Alsatian German was presumably a revisionist, rather like a Western-facing mirror-image of a displaced Silesian.

This teacher loved Johann Peter Hebel. Not me. Back then, anyway. I found him stuffy. What was all that about the Alemannic dialects? When you think about it, it was almost as questionable as Alsatian!

I was once given extra homework as punishment for inappropriate behaviour: I had to retell a story by Johann Peter Hebel, in the form of a precis, i.e. written in the present tense and without subjective evaluation. I was still fuming when I got to Tenno's after school and I ranted to him about this outrageous injustice. He agreed with me; my teacher had a nerve and he shouldn't be allowed to get away with it. 'Give it to me,' said Tenno, and I handed him the photocopied pages with the Hebel story. He read it quickly, chuckling to himself mischievously. Then he sat down at his electric typewriter and with a roguish enthusiasm he set off. After 45 minutes he handed me his finished version of Hebel's story. I read it and couldn't believe my eyes. It was pure genius! It was so *incredibly genius*, I didn't even know that such a *genius* gambit was even possible with mere words! Tenno had retold the short story in such a way that even the dimmest reader would realise what a miserably regressive story it was, and that it could have only been thought up by the most sinister authoritarian. And at one point, and this was truly the icing on the cake, Tenno described one of the protagonists in brackets as a 'misunderstood genius with an inferiority complex', so that my German teacher, unless he was utterly imperceptive, would know straight away that this referred to none other than himself! My cheeks were burning. To come out with an insult like that aimed straight at the teacher, but at the same time to arrange the whole thing so skilfully that for him to feel offended would mean admitting that he thought he was a misunderstood genius – that was *incredible*! I'd have my teacher cornered. And on top of that, it was all written so incredibly well that it was absolutely clear that it couldn't have come from an eighth grader. How would my teacher react to such a blatant insult?

I handed in my extra assignment. I couldn't wait to get it back. Basically, there were only two options: I'd get a 1 because of its sheer brilliance or a 6 because of the blatant disrespect (to Hebel and the teacher).

But no, my teacher acted like it was nothing at all out of the ordinary. When he handed it back to me, all he said was that it was supposed to be written in the present tense. Mine was written in the past tense, so he'd given me a 2-.

It couldn't have been a more miserable outcome. There were now no bounds to my contempt.

Tenno loved to cook, and whenever we pressed the two buzzers together after school finished in the afternoon and – *open sesame!* – the door flung open, he would already be in the kitchen preparing a delicious lunch with lots of garlic. By this time, it was very fashionable to show off that you cooked with a lot of garlic. Anyone who cooked with a lot of garlic was cosmopolitan. The demonstrative consumption of garlic was second only to an unconditional commitment to Riesling, which was to be drunk in large quantities, preferably in the legendary bar Weinloch, with its 1968 lefty vibe, whose unadorned, cellar-like sparseness in no way detracted from the main purpose of meeting there. Its famous name Weinloch – 'watering hole' – suited it well. Time and time again, Tenno repeated the Bismarck quote which says that any Riesling that isn't drunk has failed in its mission. Except that Bismarck, that drunkard of the East Elbe, had champagne in mind.

For a while, I was going to Tenno's every other day. There were always five or six boys hanging out there, all older than me – 11th, 12th and 13th graders – so I looked up to them, marvelling at their witty repartees. They seemed so confident and poised. Tenno loved talking about their success with the girls. They went weak at the knees whenever they saw Clemens or Tobias, he would boast.

Throughout the course of the afternoon and evening, all sorts of people tumbled in, all without exception exuding an air of culture and refinement. On arrival they were served a glass of Riesling, even the choirmaster and organist at the Church of the Holy Spirit, who took the art of misanthropy to truly Olympian heights. I remembered his scowl once during the applause after a performance of the Passion of St. Matthew, which left no doubt about the scorn he felt for his tone-deaf audience, even as the sycophantic Heidelberg bourgeoisie kissed the ground he walked on. Masochism is an essential part of the bourgeois appreciation of culture. In Tenno's grotto, on the other hand, the choirmaster was very affable, though he cursed the ignoramuses in the Heidelberg cultural administration. 'You wouldn't believe it. Idiots – the lot of them!'

Or the artist Klaus Staeck (whose famous postcard 'Workers! The SPD wants to take away your villas in Ticino!' I had framed on my bedroom wall) would show up with an expression of the most austere Protestant conscientiousness, a 'regrettably very busy' diary under his arm. Staeck lived in the same block and Tenno treated him with unusual respect.

Another regular was Lothar, from the building next door. He actually lived in Berlin but had a second apartment in Heidelberg. Lothar cultivated the aura of a noble misanthrope à la Schopenhauer, an attitude that was completely unknown to me up to that point, but which I found fascinating. He only had a thin grey ring of hair, hollow cheeks, always moist lips, and not an ounce of fat on his body – clearly not the result of physical activity. He radiated something deeply unhealthy, which in turn gave him a somewhat ethereal look. He told me again and again about his wonderful adoptive son, a 'mulatto' like me, who, to Lothar's delight, had followed a path that was in complete contrast to his own. He was studying sports or business administration, or perhaps both.

Tenno and Lothar were bound together in a deep-seated mutual hostility. When Tenno was once more cooking up plans to hold up the mirror to the SWR director, his boss, and make the glass crack with the scandal he would unleash (I gasped; wasn't that going a bit too far?), Lothar's only response to such sensationalism was the sort of cynical smile you'd give a minor who's not old enough to be taken seriously. His cynicism extended to everyone, including himself – and that gave him a touch of the gallant hero. The only thing, he said, that distinguished him from a useless good-for-nothing was his love and self-sacrifice for his adopted son. If Lothar let out a misanthropic sigh without good reason, he was probably contemplating the fragile context of the world and his struggle to find a place in it.

Tenno didn't so much see Lothar as a bore than as something almost more dangerous: a historical pessimist. Lothar had a painting in his apartment of Frederick the Great; Tenno thought this was really a bit much. He couldn't walk past the painting without doing a gesture to suggest he had a screw loose. If that wasn't enough to let off steam, he would make fun of the nerdy little flute concerti the Prussian king had composed. Lothar ignored him; perhaps he was musing about the Katte Tragedy.

Every now and then, Tenno invited the parents of his young acolytes to a party in his cosy courtyard. They were mostly affluent and at ease with the lively, brash atmosphere at Tenno's. They were quickly persuaded that their sons' acquaintance with him represented a harmless, even Socratic broadening of their horizons. My mother also had the honour of an invitation and fell firmly under Tenno's spell.

At Tenno's we enjoyed every conceivable freedom, and if it ever got a bit late in the evening, he would call our parents for us and allay any concerns. There was only one aspect where he maintained a strict and unrelenting regime that no one dared to violate: the only music we were permitted to play was classical. Tenno could not abide pop music. His god was Bach, his religion was monotheistic, and only motets, chorales, organ toccatas and concerti grossi would sing from the loudspeakers of his impressive sound system. Even the talkative parrot Rico, a rather arrogant character who perched on Tenno's shoulder and snapped at everyone, knew the rules; when Bach was playing he kept his beak shut.

In Tenno's grotto there were books piled up in every free corner and shelves on every wall up to the ceiling, many of them so-called review copies, which publishers actually sent him for free. The lucky devil!

That's when I started reading in earnest. Tenno encouraged it, even if he unfortunately never found the time (or the interest?) to talk to me about my newly acquired aesthetic insights and literary experiences. I would have loved to find out from him who in the maddening arguments in Thomas Mann's *The Magic Mountain* ('the aristocratic question!') was right, in his opinion: Naphta or Settembrini? But although he always made a big fuss about his books, I sometimes had the slightest suspicion – but surely it couldn't be? – that he hadn't read them at all. Of Thomas Mann – this stiff, self-loving man, 'one of the greats,' as Tenno referred to him contemptuously – all he could think to say was an alleged quote from Brecht: 'A talented writer of superfluous novels.' A sentence that moved me, unsettled me in fact, because I had just finished reading *The Magic Mountain* and had loved it; it was a true revelation. So if Tenno (and Brecht) rejected Thomas Mann, then I wanted to discuss why. To my astonishment, however, he wasn't interested at all. I found that a bit strange. He was supposed to be an intellectual, after all!

With music, too, I was an eager student. I had stopped listening to pop music in an act of aesthetic thrust reversal and was now obsessed with classical music. Not necessarily Bach, but Beethoven and as much opera as possible. Shivers ran down my spine when Alfredo and Viola confess their love in

Verdi's *La Traviata* or when Rigoletto realises it's not the duke's body he's carrying in the sack over his shoulder but that of his beloved daughter (with an emotional farewell duet between father and daughter squeezed in for good measure). I packed up my German new wave LPs, Udo Lindenberg collection and even the Frank Zappa album I had only just bought, and dragged my treasure, which had once meant so much to me but was now completely worthless, to a second-hand record store. I didn't get much for them, but I skipped away with a light heart and, in another record store, I bought myself a comprehensive anthology of recordings of contemporary composers from Hans Werner Henze to Wolfgang Rihm for 60 Deutschmarks.

And then I discovered Richard Wagner. The temptation was great, because unless you were a complete idiot, if you were a pubescent boy in the mid-eighties, you couldn't fail to notice that the only things that still had the magical allure of taboo were things that had been discredited by the Nazis. When I shuddered during the final chorus of *The Master-Singers of Nuremberg* ('The Holy Roman Empire may have melted away / But Holy German art is here to stay'), the ecstasy would have been far more restrained, my passion extinguished, if the music wasn't also tinged with the aroma of all that is forbidden, dangerous, aesthetically licentious. The ambivalence was particularly alluring: while Thomas Mann had denounced Hitler's Germany, he had never renounced his love for Wagner, and continued to find increased aesthetic appreciation in its ambiguity.

I read, read, read, I listened, listened, listened. With regard to Wagner, too, I hoped for insightful explanations and critique from Tenno, but again – nothing. He didn't think much of Wagner, and when I once put on *Das Rheingold*, he could only stand it for the duration of the prelude, then he switched to Gustav Mahler's *Lied von der Erde*.

Mind you, he did take me to the 4-hour-long film *Parsifal* by Hans-Jürge Syberberg. Tenno said that you had to see it, even though Syberberg was of course a Nazi.

Speaking of Nazis, I was surprised every time Tenno put in a good word for the Boy Scouts, because I always thought that with their uniforms, their discipline and their hierarchy, they were to be seen as mini Nazis. In truth, Tenno explained, he hadn't been a boy scout either, but had been part of the Bündische Jugend, a less authoritarian alternative. This was all a bit too complicated for me.

Since I had become a member of the Tenno Order, I hadn't had much to do with my classmates. Besides, I had felt lonely and misunderstood by everyone since I started throwing myself into reading. I had no one to share my immense discoveries in the realm of the mind. At Tenno's apartment, on the other hand, you could take a book off the shelf and read it, precisely in keeping with the environment. And so whenever I was at Tenno's, I read while he typed away on his electric typewriter, we'd drink tea from a clay teapot, and then as it became late afternoon, his first friends started to arrive with a bottle of wine. Once, before the first visitor arrived and the chatter started, I tried to quickly get one question in.

'Tenno, what do you think of Wolfgang Leonhard's *Die Revolution entlässt ihre Kinder*?'

'Hmm,' he murmured, briefly looking up from the typewriter. 'It's pretty good.'

I was actually hoping for an answer that would explain to me how a leftist was supposed to reconcile the fact that the Soviet Union had unfortunately turned out not to be a paradise for humanity after all, but this conflict didn't seem to bother him in the same way as me. 'Fucking fat cats,' he added, making it clear that he felt no responsibility for the squares beyond the Iron Curtain.

Of course, my classmates quickly realised I was no longer interested in coming with them after school to buy an ice lolly or a bottle of Coke from the kiosk, and preferred to head off on my pilgrimage to Tenno in the Old Town. Besides, since I'd started dropping foreign words into my parlance, they all thought I was full of myself. It did hurt, but I was powerless against the flow of vocabulary that gushed out of me. I couldn't forsake these new-found riches; I firmly believed that through them a higher truth was revealed to me. As a witness to the truth, you had to accept a certain amount of isolation.

And my classmates couldn't deny that a breeze of freedom blew in from Tenno's direction, though they tried not to come across as envious. Still, I had to tone it down a little sometimes, otherwise I might start thinking I was better just because I knew Tenno. Once, at break, Mirko – who I had been very close to when we had the Group of Six – said, 'So you're seeing Tenno now too. That gay sod.'

Well, yes – there was little doubt that Tenno was gay, but as Udo Lindenberg put it on one of the LPs I'd just flogged, 'So what?'

Basically, everyone knew that the main thing Tenno enjoyed about his lads' company wasn't that they let him participate in their epiphanies about the works of Thomas Mann. There was give and take on various levels, but you didn't have to talk about it; it was obvious and you didn't need to make an issue out of it. When I stayed at Tenno's occasionally because it was too late to cycle home, and he had had a bit to drink, he would sometimes drape an arm around my neck and pull my head in to his chest, but then you just had to squirm out of the loop akin to a dog shaking himself out of its leash and that was the end of the matter. What was more annoying was when Tenno slurred a little phrase like, 'So, my little *negerle*.' But he was drunk that time and he wouldn't have said that in front of the others. It was probably supposed to be taken as some kind of indirect vote of confidence. When I sent him this chapter to read, Tenno said he was horrified and ashamed of 'the (one!!) blundering little "*negerle*".' He added very confidently and generously, 'If that's how you remember the Tenno episode, then I think that's how you should write it.'

When the Odenwald School in nearby Heppenheim was celebrating its 75th anniversary, I went to the gala event with Tenno. Tenno didn't have a car, but there was always someone who would give him a lift when he wanted to go somewhere outside of Heidelberg, which wasn't often. The writer Klaus Mann went to the Odenwald School, Tenno told me, and I was very impressed. I had just read his autobiography *The Turning Point*, where the phrase 'death wish' came up a lot in the final pages of the diary entries. Again and again, there were the words 'death wish' until the diary entries broke off and the announcement was made that he had killed himself. Since I often felt lonely and desperate, and moved by reading *The Turning Point*, I once wrote 'death wish' in my own diary. Unfortunately it looked completely ridiculous, but it didn't make much sense to cross things out of your own diary when you're its only reader.

In fact, Tenno continued, one of the President's sons, a true *enfant terrible*, was a pupil at the Odenwald School, and I would probably meet him at the event. This was really something. I was thrilled at the possibility of meeting the son of the President of the Federal Republic of Germany. This was beyond my wildest hopes. Even shaking hands with the artistic director of the Heidelberg City Theatre, again in Tenno's company, took my breath away, but the son of the Federal President – and what a Federal President he was!

At that time, we were stuck with the anti-intellectual mediocrity of a Federal Chancellor, who was from the nearby Palatinate. What was worse? His small-town cronyism or his attempt to draw a line under the past? Perhaps the two converged: he obviously had no problem with presenting the local speciality *Pfälzer Saumagen* to the French President in Deidesheim. Sow stomach sausage? What a faux pas! Offering a French bon vivant who was used to a degree of savoir-vivre a rough and ready German dish like that! Surely that was exactly the shameful Germanness we had all learned to repress with our summer holidays in Provence. If we had known at the time that Mitterrand had read Ernst Jünger, it would have turned the world upside down. Ernst Jünger and Pfälzer Saumagen were, to a certain extent, ideologically, on the same page: manifestations of the Germanness that we had to learn to overcome.

People liked to bathe themselves in the gleam of the Federal President's silver hair. The man knew how to talk, you could see yourself travelling abroad with him, he was a man with class. Sure, his father was a Nazi, but State Secretary in the Foreign Office wasn't as bad as it could be.

The grounds of the Odenwald School were large with a touch of Romantic wilderness. It looked like the setting for an adventure film. The students, scattered in groups across the grounds, looked incredibly relaxed. So, I thought, this is how the children of the rich and powerful live. I wasn't jealous; we tend only to be envious of what is within close reach and essentially attainable, whereas this world, where the children of presidents lived in a film set, was too far removed to be within range of envy.

And then all of a sudden we were sitting in a room with four students, and one of them was indeed the son of the Federal President. It was *so cool* to see how the conversation bounced between the four of them, as they lounged back in their chairs and on the sofa, as though they were nodding off from weary ennui, only to score a stunningly good punchline the very next moment. And this amazing banter – nobody seemed offended if a joke was at their expense, because the carousel was always turning. The President's son kept winking at me encouragingly, as if to say that I shouldn't be afraid to join in, but if I preferred to sit and listen – given my age – that was fine, too. I was genuinely happy not to say a word, but on the car journey back to Heidelberg with Tenno, I daydreamed for a moment about what it would be like to share a dorm with guys like that.

These were formative years, intense and enriching, and bringing the Tenno era to an end after over two years wasn't easy. It was the first self-initiated feat of my life, a conscious decision, where I deliberately switched tracks – I had no idea until that point that life was so malleable, that you could change things by way of a conscious decision, just like when my mother took me out of the anti-authoritarian kindergarten and handed me over to the Catholics, only this time the responsibility rested on my shoulders alone. What would Tenno say? How would I explain it to my mother? Would anyone expect me to justify myself? Would I be seen as ungrateful? Would I suddenly be isolated and lonely? What would my days and evenings look like in the future? I had no answer to any of these questions.

I only knew one thing; that I didn't feel like Tenno took me seriously, that he had begun to take my presence for granted, that he didn't have to make any effort with me. I felt my pride was wounded, and it became ever clearer to me that we needed to go our separate ways.

However, Tenno had no idea that I had long been growing more distant, so he must have been surprised when I suddenly stopped coming by. But my decision was irrevocable. He was sure to deny it, but the truth was he wasn't interested in me, at least not in what I saw as my best side, my thoughts, which he had played such a big part in influencing. He was always making grand speeches, but whenever I tried to tell him something that needed a bit more time, a bit of quiet and concentration, perhaps to talk about something I had observed when reading Döblin's *Alexanderplatz*, that was when I realised that in fact he wasn't there for me, although he put on the act of being a great litterateur. Suddenly I could see through his cultural affectations.

I was also jealous. Because Tenno now had a new boy under his wing. Lars, who was younger than me – by now I was in 10th grade – and who he obviously preferred. Lars could do and say whatever he liked, Tenno would always bang the table and howl with laughter in approval. I didn't understand Tenno; couldn't he see the nerdy school boy in this baby-faced Lars? He couldn't be serious, surely? What did he see in him? It was humiliating to be forced to watch this flirting. For Tenno's other disciples, who were already taking their final school exams and preparing for university, Lars was no competition because of the age difference, but for me the competition was real: we were in the same league, and it was truly grotesque to hear Tenno fawning over Lars's viola playing, which was supposedly out of this world. Lars could go and shove his viola up his arse! I couldn't bear to watch any longer, I didn't need this. And in the meantime I had, to my surprise, made some new friends my age and they weren't stupid, unlike some people! Some of them even knew Thomas Mann better than he did. At the end of the day, Tenno had taught us to disobey, so why shouldn't I turn that virtue against him now? All his ranting about 'those damn fools' was hollow, the way he styled himself as Socrates, who wouldn't let the *polis* get away with untruthfulness, was completely ridiculous, little more than pubescent posturing. His affected style was over the top, and the irony that his constant self-celebration was based on really wasn't all that sophisticated. In addition, although he mocked others for showing off and parading their knowledge, this was in fact precisely what he did, and I could no longer ignore the fact that all he had to say about literature was boastful empty catchphrases. What was this ritualistic community I had fallen prey to? Hadn't I always been against peer pressure?

I renamed "Tenno Hollow" in my diary as "Tenno Hell." When Mama asked with a concerned frown why I no longer went to see Tenno, I didn't say anything.

# Drama Club

Turning my back on the Tenno fraternity was made easier by the fact that I had found myself a new tribe: the theatre. In 9th grade, I gave up athletics and joined the school drama club. It was clear that as a novice I wasn't going to get anything better than a minor role in Shakespeare's *The Winter's Tale*, but that was fine with me. Anything more than that would be terrifying. People would presumably assume that a Shakespearean noble couldn't be played by someone who didn't exactly look European? There might as well be a hundred Bohemias by the sea. A few years earlier, as a 'quintain,' I had been chosen by my Latin teacher to play Hercules. I had sat pondering the decision: should I give in to the temptations of vice or choose the steep path of virtue? Too young to appreciate the refined pleasures of vice, I opted for virtue; I grabbed a club and slew the Nemean lion. But Hercules was a mythological figure, so the colour of his skin wasn't so important. It seemed different with Shakespeare. It was a relief when I landed the role of Lord Antigonus, who abandons the queen's baby on the Bohemian shore before being mauled to death by a bear (but I also had a decent monologue before that bit).

The following year I got the lead role in the Edward Albee play *Everything in the Garden*, which takes place in an American middle-class setting where black people's agency was limited at best to cleaning the pool, which nobody seemed to object to. For me, however, the role as the lead in Albee's play meant more than just theatrical success, it was proof that I was free to do what I wanted. No one would ever say: 'But that role doesn't suit you!'

Once someone from a casting agency called me and said they needed another GI for a film; could I send in some photos? I asked Christian to help me with the pictures. We sat in his room, our eyes twinkling. This was really something: he was being called on as a photographer, I as an actor. Life, this glorious life, was actually taking us seriously for once! Just one problem. 'You don't look anything like a GI.' Christian did his best to rough me up, styling me in a denim jacket, unbuttoned to glimpse a little chest hair and summon the illusion of swagger, but it was no use; there was no making a GI out of me. I didn't get the role.

All the same, we were surprised that someone had wanted to cast me in a black role. My blackness only really came up when it came to demonstrating familiarity, cultivating a cult of friendship. Someone might make a joke about Africa, not because they thought it was good, but because it emphasised what close friends we were, which meant they could get away with it. Take, for example, the endless debate at school about whether or not the chocolate brand names Mohrenkopf and Negerkuss were racist. I had the resounding authority to dismiss it all as ludicrous, which made it difficult for the other side not to look bitter, and this left my friends feeling proud, not because they cared about these terms, not at all, but because, compared with the moral gain that was to be won by calling these terms out as discriminatory, it was far more ethical and progressive to be close to someone who could be offended and this was morally superior to getting bogged down in verbal correctness. (Incidentally, these days I would take a more critical view, discerning a trace of the Roberto Blanco effect here: 'Ah yes, he was our *favourite Negro*.')

On the other hand, as we got older, people got more interested in hearing stories about the racism I had experienced. Sadly, there weren't very many stories to tell. Once I was sitting with a friend on someone's front garden wall when the owner came out and shouted, 'Get lost! Go back to where you come from! Back to Greece!' But that was more of a case of someone being, as they say in Heidelberg, 'too dumb to piss a hole in the snow'.

It was only in the last year of school – but now I'm having to reach far ahead – that I had a really good anecdote to share. Everyone wanted to hear it again and again; they couldn't get enough of it.

I was travelling from Heidelberg to Munich for an interview for my civilian national service. With me in the compartment were five grannies. From the moment I sat down, they had beaming faces, incessant smiles. I could tell it was only a matter of time before they dragged me into their conversation. At a certain point they couldn't hold it in any longer. The first lady spoke to me while her friends smiled as if they were about to be served coffee. *Where was I from?* Well, I said, from Heidelberg, which is where I just got on. *How lovely, Heidelberg! A beautiful city.* But what she actually meant was, where was I from, as in where I was born? They all nodded encouragingly, eager to learn something about the world!

Of course, I was no stranger to this interrogation game; I knew how to hold back and not satisfy the questioner's curiosity straight away. That would be too easy. With consummate innocence I replied, 'In Heidelberg.' Now the ladies shook their heads and tutted, as if they had never encountered anyone so obtuse. This fully justified their ratcheting up the cross-examination technique.

'But where are your parents from?'

I replied, 'My mother's from Silesia.'

Finally, they had what they were after! There was a sigh of satisfaction all round; nothing was more gratifying than being confirmed in your own assumptions. The ladies shouted, as if in chorus, 'Tunisia! Yes, you can see that right away!'

I had to concede to their victory. For the rest of the train journey, questions of ethnicity were no longer an issue and we talked about this and that and everything in between.

Were there feelings of being an outsider, of being excluded? Yes, but they had nothing to do with the colour of my skin, and more to do with my inclination towards literature and classical music. When you read Thomas Mann at 16, it's not just that you understand Thomas Mann, but above all that you feel understood *by* Thomas Mann, and better than by your contemporaries, namely your schoolmates. And so my love for Thomas Mann and Richard Wagner seemed to be the real stigma of my life: it made me the weirdo who didn't belong and wouldn't get to enjoy a sense of belonging. Fortunately, this very problem had been addressed by none other than Thomas Mann himself. Like Tonio Kröger, portrayed by Mann as the Romantic hero, I longed to go over and join the ordinary people, the Ingeborgs, the Hansens, the blonde, blue-eyed majority, but it wasn't about ethnic backgrounds and appearance, it was about artistic isolation, about a certain aesthetic *Weltschmerz*, an ennui or weariness with the world, that keeps you off the paths trodden by everyone else around you; my self-pity was limitless. And it really was true. If you listened to Schubert and Bruckner, people looked at you like you weren't just from another continent, but from another planet. It had been different in the Tenno-sphere, but now my taste in music was something that separated me from my peers. So I kept it quiet as much as possible and lived in the constant fear that someone might ask about my favourite band. As the German new wave band Spliff put it, jazz and punk were where it was at; Wagner made you queasy and Mozart made you puke. Neat lyrics, but the sentiment didn't match reality. Trying to posture as subversive, I liked to pretend that Wagner and Mozart were normal, and jazz and punk were the savage deviation; the tables were turned long ago.

Noticing our contrasting track records when it came to snogging at parties, my classmate Mirko (not known for profound thought, and who in later life, at least as long as I was around, never experienced an even vaguely comparable moment of diagnostic enlightenment, but whose lucky phase of somnambulant self-assuredness meant he went with the flow and encountered no resistance from the girls) cut straight to the chase when he remarked, with true compassion and the harsh brutality of the truth: 'You know, ten years ago, you would have been unstoppable with the ladies – they were all into intellectuals back then, you know, the '68ers. Today, it's all about looks and muscle; you've got to be Arnold Schwarzenegger to get a look in. Books won't get you anywhere nowadays.' Basically, he was just articulating what I already knew.

The fact that I had adopted as my patron saint the most German of all German writers, Thomas Mann, seemed to me proof that it wasn't 'German-ness' or German society that I felt excluded from. What set me apart was my arrogance combined with an enthusiasm for art: a classic accelerant.

Reading led to isolation – that much was clear. For a long time I didn't see that it also earned me respect, a certain distinction. 'No need to be so pompous,' they used to say, and since then I was careful to keep my fervour for language to myself. So reading was a lonely thing. The only person I could talk about books with was a neighbour who was a trained bookseller and later a sales rep for a publisher.

Oh, the fearlessness, oh, the lack of constraints of that pubescent era! It was at that heroic age that I scaled the steepest towering walls of my reading life, conquering the territory that would become my comfort zone. At 16, I read Joyce's *Ulysses* to the last page, even though for at least two thirds of the text I understood more or less nothing. But that didn't put me off. This was by no means mere arrogance – it was precisely the incomprehensible that struck with the most force; the more accolades a book had, the more revelations it contained, surely. And what satisfaction was to be reaped when I stumbled on a passage in *Ulysses* where I could orient myself again. It was like reaching the first cabin on a hike in the Alps.

I also discovered a good remedy for the incomprehensible: learning by heart. I played my vinyl recording of Gründgens' production of *Faust* until I could join in with all the important scenes. And the opening words of Ulysses, which I read in the German translation by Hans Wollschläger: '*Stately, plump Buck Mulligan came from the stairhead, bearing a bowl of lather on which a mirror and a razor lay crossed.*' If you knew a text by heart, you didn't have to understand it, the music of the words was gratification in itself. And I could sense the cool blending of blasphemy and tradition in Joyce, without being able to articulate its components. I'm sure I would have loved to call out, like Buck Mulligan on his 'stairhead': '*Come up, Kinch! Come up, you fearful Jesuit!*'

One day Mama gave me a book that – though it's only now that I realise it – encapsulated in one tome almost everything that I was interested in. It was the volume on Thomas Mann from the *Text and Criticism* series. I scanned the table of contents: fourteen essays on the life and work of Thomas Mann. Amazing – this was like lights switching on in my head. Now I could really get into what I had previously been intrigued by in the dark. But how great was my dismay when I discovered that most of the essays amounted to little more than ugly point scoring at the expense of my favourite writer. They refused to condone his *Reflections of a Nonpolitical Man*. They considered him an opportunist who had adapted to the Weimar Republic, but remained a reactionary at heart. Even his emigration was, so to speak, twisted; it wasn't a demonstrative act of resistance, but an expression of indecision, complacency even. When Hitler seized power in 1933, the 'great writer' was on a lecture tour in the Netherlands ('The Sorrows and Greatness of Richard Wagner'), biding his time, as it were, and realising the strong position he was in, he simply didn't return to Germany. Walter Boehlich reduced Thomas Mann's relationship to politics to an unflinching, short and snappy formula: 'Too little, too late.' Was that all there was to it? I was beset with doubts; ought I to distance myself from Thomas Mann?

There was an essay by a certain Yaak Karsunke with the title 'On the absurd desire to be special: a re-reading of Thomas Mann's *Death in Venice*'. This text was so caustic and disdainful that it spelled its own demise. Perhaps this Karsunke was simply wrong, but in that case I didn't understand why his words were even printed.

I fared much worse with the collection's opening essay by Martin Walser. It was at least as polemical as Karsunke's, but was much better, which in this case meant written with much more panache. He also mocked Thomas Mann, as a representative and beneficiary of the bourgeoisie, but at the same time he wrote an irrefutable exposé of the poetological method of *The Magic Mountain*, which to him consisted of nothing but the insipid juxtaposition of contrasting terms: enlightenment versus absolute despotism, development of the ego versus discipline and sacrifice, a series of terms and concepts that were put into the mouths of the adversaries, Settembrini and Naphta. I had simply lapped up these quarrels between Settembrini, defender of progress and humanity, and Naphta, the Jesuit, whose sharp tongue allowed him to articulate his medieval views with stunning rhetoric. Like God and the Devil in *Faust*, with their endless squabbles, the two seemed to be wrestling for the soul of Hans Castorp, 'life's loyal problem child'. But who was right? To my surprise, Hans Castorp decided the matter for himself in such a way that Naphta was mostly right, but Settembrini came across more sympathetically. That seemed to me to turn everything on its head; I would have said, of course Settembrini was right, but Naphta was the more compelling character. Settembrini's views were self-evident (in favour of life and against death, in favour of what is desirable and against terror, for equality and against the aristocracy, for classical moderation and against the Gothic glorification of pain, for Apollo and against Christ with his crucifixion wounds), whereas from Naphta's positions emerged something daring, forbidden, dangerous. Something siren-like and at the same time a somehow deeper understanding of existence.

Did I have to choose one of the two sides? If I didn't, the whole thing would be just a game. Thomas Mann himself, it seemed to me, as I delved further into the subject, had to decide, namely opting for Naphta's side until 1918, only then, as an advocate of the Weimar Republic and opponent of Hitler, to switch sides and campaign for Settembrini's ideals of humanity. Of course, I was more sympathetic to Hitler's opponent, but the more outrageous certain passages of *Reflections of a Nonpolitical Man* seemed, the stronger a hold they had on me. German culture versus French civilisation – did these formulae of pathos correspond to any reality? It was precisely the ambiguous, ambivalent and problematic that I found so attractive.

That also applied to Wagner. Certainly, I loved the composer and his music, but this Wagner cult was also the possibility of rebellion against one's guardians in general. I had learned that from Tenno: that we shouldn't let our parents' generation get away with anything, that we should constantly challenge their intellectual complacency. Rebellion, however, against a generation that stood firmly on the side of nonconformity, wasn't so easy. If you could expect to encounter a taboo anywhere, then it was with Wagner, since immunisation against pathos was at the heart of the Federal Republic's educational programme. It was right to be suspicious of all forms of pomp, which was taken as being tantamount to contempt for humanity. Nothing ought to stand on a pedestal anymore, nothing should appear larger than life. That was the key lesson that a young person was taught in the '80s, everywhere – at home, at school, on television. One of the pretentious foreign words that you learned early on in West German grammar schools was aestheticism. You had to be on guard against it. The first film director, after Alfred Hitchcock, that any high school student knew by name, was Leni Riefenstahl – the teachers warned you against her work like a priest warned against masturbating, awakening a craving that hadn't been there until that point. Just mentioning a title like *Triumph of the Will* sent a creepy shiver down your spine, like a forbidden fetish for those with a predilection for the anti-authoritarian.

With this in mind, our German teacher showed us the propaganda film *Hitlerjunge Quex*, Hitler Youth Quex. The poison had to be injected under supervision so that we could develop the appropriate antibodies.

Richard Wagner and his work were the ultimate cipher for the demonic aesthetic of the Third Reich; the expansion of the Wagner Orchestra in a way preempted Heidelberg minister for architecture and armaments Albert Speer's visions for Germania. Of course, I found Wagner's anti-Semitism primitive and repulsive, but I also didn't want to come across as someone intellectually and morally incapable of appreciating both the greatness and the ridiculousness of Wagner's work at the same time. Curated thoughts and emotions were something to be wary of.

I was 15 when my mother gave me a ticket for a performance of *The Master-Singers of Nuremberg* at the Mannheim National Theatre. It genuinely was just one ticket, because it wasn't cheap. Our theatre in Heidelberg – which hosted concerts, drama and dance – was perfectly respectable, but its orchestra pit was too small for Wagner. At best they could stage *The Flying Dutchman*. So anyone who wanted to see Wagner had to go to Mannheim. This was my first Wagner performance. I was so determined (triumph of the will) to experience a life-changing initiation that evening that I ended up being so tense that my synapses shut off and the music remained bafflingly external the entire time (failure of the will). Nevertheless, after the six-hour performance I took the tram back to Heidelberg with the feeling that I could now rightly call myself a Wagnerian.

I couldn't ignore the fact that the opera was all about being German. In the final chorus, Hans Sachs sang:

*What is German and what is true*
*No one would know*
*Were it not for the German Masters!*

That sounded like something strictly forbidden. On the other hand, the *Master-Singers* were against the petite bourgeoisie. The opera told the story of an outsider who was eventually successfully integrated into mainstream society. At least that's how I understood it at the time.

Walther von Stolzing, a knight from beyond the realm, a genuine invader, comes to Nuremberg, where he meets Eva. They fall in love, but Eva's father, the rich goldsmith Veit Pogner, has already promised his daughter's hand in marriage to whomever wins the singing competition on Midsummer's Day. So Stolzing tries to get accepted into the Master Singers Guild and shows up to sing. Beckmesser, of all people, who also hopes to woo Eva, holds the post of the judge of the singers' performance. Now Stolzing has a natural talent, and something of the Sturm und Drang about him, but he's not familiar with the venerable rules of the Nuremberg art of singing. No matter. What are rules for a genius like him? But during Stolzing's performance, every one of his violations of the traditional rules is scratched in chalk on a slate by Beckmesser, who would prefer to disqualify his rival in the preliminary stages. The turmoil in the Master Singers Guild! It's like when the Impressionists were first exhibited in the Salon in Paris. Only Hans Sachs, moved by the young knight's emotional temperament, defends him against 'the old masters.'

I was a little unsettled by the punch-up at the end of the second act (conveyed musically as a large choral fugue). It's Johannisnacht in Nuremberg, the eve of Midsummer's Day, and the testosterone is running high among the fired-up revellers. The mood is tense, not least because of this outsider who threatens to rip apart the fabric of their society. Everyone piles into the fight that breaks out; the charming locals quickly descend into a raging mob. The next day, Hans Sachs philosophises in a somewhat misanthropic tone, 'Madness, madness. Everywhere, madness!'

Wagner of all people, who had such a seductive influence on Hitler, himself the seducer of the masses, had demonstrated onstage how ready and willing people were to resort to violence. That struck me as something worth bearing in mind. I already knew to be wary of crowds. In the plural, humans are transformed into an archaic horde. Only a wise authority figure like Hans Sachs can get the better of them. As an outsider, there was no getting around it: I was going to need to keep close to the Hans Sachses of life.

But while the locals were still at it hammer and tongs in the punch-up scene, the jubilant horns can already be heard, heralding the start of the festivities. A moment ago, the people were still a wild mob, now they are transformed into revellers at the Midsummer feast. Violence is just the flip side of elegant manners and customs. Stolzing has adapted to these customs by now, but he's also made his mark on them. Everything flows. The outsider Walther von Stolzing protects the community from becoming sterile: he bows to the rules of master singing and at the same time develops them further. The people who had briefly locked horns now cheer happily when Walther von Stolzing marries Eva Pogner.

Meanwhile, school was all about exclusion and belonging, but more in the sense of hierarchy and social recognition. The pyramid of ranks at the Kurfürst Friedrich Gymnasium was almost as finely stratified and — at least at first glance — as inexorable as a caste system. This was a regime based on social criteria in the broadest sense, rather than an ethnic paradigm, and the ranking system was complex and sophisticated. It was also more open to surprises and changes, more open to promotion and demotion through the ranks than you might imagine, when you're sitting there on your step of the despotic pyramid, seemingly anchored there for all eternity, conscious that while communications downward were an act of clemency, any attempt to communicate upwards through more than two steps up to the rarified levels where the air is thin was a foolhardy venture that could be punished at any time with humiliation. When, in the smokers' corner of the school yard, I once got a little too close to one of the top dogs, a dealer who held sway over our school, he said with relish, while everyone in earshot grinned uneasily (they knew that next time it could well be them), that annihilating rhetorical question, 'Who on earth are you?'

It was by no means money that determined your rank, although it did play a role. Everything was connected under the surface, like communicating vessels, and money was just one aspect. Nonchalance and a bold, outgoing nature were winning qualities; your background could help, but only in conjunction with other characteristics. Attractiveness meant absolute power, but even here there was some give and take. There could be an act of immense exaltation if the top dog suddenly recognised the allure of a girl who until then had been overlooked as a wallflower; it was only once the prince had kissed her that the veil was lifted and everyone could see what beauty had always been hidden in her shy face. Self-destructive alcohol and drug use could earn you points, but only if you kept up appearances – you still had to somehow look good even when off your head, you had to keep up with the witty banter. Interestingly, very, very good grades could be a deal breaker, but also a source of social capital if you managed to pull off the act as a cool brainbox and not a nerdy swot.

And at some point, for some reason, the school Drama Club also became a factor of social recognition. I could hardly believe it, but there was no denying it: Drama Club was like an elevator that took me ten floors up within the course of a few weeks. I left the middle level of the pyramid far below and now stepped out on a point where I was within easy reach of the apex. Now I was seen as someone who might plausibly go on to drama school. There was actually no longer any reason for Tonio Kröger-style self-pity.

But it was at this time, aware of my new status, that I first began to be ashamed of the fact that we didn't have a villa on Philosophenweg, that we only had a three-room apartment in Dossenheim. I shook my head defensively when my mother said one day, 'You're always being invited to these birthday parties. It's fine with me if you want to have a party here for your next birthday.' No way! I would rather have died. These birthday parties were always on the grandest scale, in prime locations in Heidelberg, with lavish buffets, fridges full of sparkling wine and a castle view from the terrace. Of course, I couldn't tell my mother that our modest apartment was simply not an adequate backdrop for a party of spoiled seventeen-year-olds. Even the thought of the unglamorous way that we would be crammed into our living room made me hyperventilate. I took careful note of people's reactions when a school friend naively dared to invite us to his parents' much larger apartment. For fear of damage, they had hung plastic sheeting over the bookshelves in the living room. Nobody danced that evening. Weeks later, people were still laughing behind his back about the plastic sheeting.

In the 11th grade I became friends with Florian, who was also in Drama Club (we were rehearsing for Sartre's *Nekrassov*). He was a year older than me and had just got back from a year in the US. He liked to say, 'Another anecdote from Phoenix, Arizona!' We were all impressed by the fact that you could simply announce an anecdote like this and then launch into a narrative where you yourself play the leading role. The fact that he put the name of the state after the city name 'Phoenix' seemed to me like a bit of an affectation, but I saw that Florian could get away with it.

He could get away with a lot, if not almost everything. Maybe it was because he was gay and being an outsider had made him more astute and independent. It was as if this distinction gave him authority over the whole year. His bon mots were sharp as nails, and whomever they targeted was done for.

Florian had the power to reverse established value systems, and suddenly a new code of conduct came into force. Until then, when you were out in the car with someone who already had a driver's license, there had always been a petty squabble about who was allowed to sit in the front; sitting in the back was like being strapped into a child seat. Until one day when Florian said in a calm voice, quietly, but resolutely, 'I'd rather sit in the back.' A staggering about-turn, it seemed to us, brought about by the willfulness of one individual. After that, we didn't exactly fight for the honour to sit in the back – we weren't complete imbeciles – but there was an ongoing contest to see who could most lucidly articulate his indifference with regard to the seating arrangement.

Florian wasn't particularly good looking, at least not in the usual sense. He had delicate features, but his face was full of character. He didn't adhere to any of the usual school fashions: he wore ankle boots and jeans with a jacket or waistcoat, and yet was always unshaven, as though making a point of casual distraction, in contrast with his more consciously planned dress sense.

He often complained about his acne. He complained so frankly that the acne soon lost the character of a problem that was a source of shame; rather, he became the acne specialist, as well as the sovereign philosopher who could speak frankly about any matter that afflicted mere mortals. Florian was a trailblazer at our school in the use of sincerity as a gesture of superiority.

This also brought a new atmosphere to Drama Club. He played his roles with an urgency that paid no heed to whether it made him look attractive or not. He created his own mode of expression, a repertoire of gestures and intonations that were not drawn from his normal life, but were distinctly hammed up. When I saw Florian on stage, my own acting felt flat. In Sartre's *Nekrassov*, I played an impostor, and I felt like one when I saw the abandon with which Florian threw himself into his role.

We were both ardent supporters of Botho Strauss, a playwright who had strong grounds for a place in the canon that was then dominated by Brecht. We took a particular liking to his *Trilogy of Reunion*; our German teacher had got us a VHS recording of the stage production by Peter Stein, which was much talked about. We watched that video over and over. We had long ago looted Strauss's script as an anthology of quotations for our own use, but the highlight was when Florian taught me to talk like Libgart Schwarz in the Stein production. Libgart Schwarz was a revelation. Her acting style went far beyond plain old realism. How she stretched her words, emphasised certain phrases to absurdity, and rolled her 'r's, sounding at times like she had an Eastern European accent! At first we could hardly believe that someone dared to enunciate in a way that was so exalted, so artificial, so completely gaga. But then we realised, this was art! And for

Florian there was the further realisation that we should treat life like art, so why not ham it up as much as possible?

Florian lived in the Weststadt, an elegant district of Heidelberg. His mother's medical practice was on the ground floor of the Gründerzeit era town house; the family lived on the first and second floors. At Florian's, you were always treated like an adult. Florian described his father as a house husband. That was unusual, but somehow it fitted Florian's unconventionality. However, if you phoned between 1pm and 3pm, you'd find yourself speaking to a grumpy father, who wanted to know who had dared to wake him up. Otherwise, he was a lone wolf and as long as you didn't disturb his siesta, you didn't see or hear much of him. Years later Florian would say, 'Lone wolf? Hmm, you could call it that. He was just an alcoholic.' But we didn't see that back then.

My mother also loved Florian, she immediately recognised his formidable individuality. Florian was always very charming towards her, and this mutual tenderness helped me to view my mother with more respect. Maybe she and Florian shared a genus? It dawned on me that it might have been petit bourgeois anxiety that had made me underestimate Mama.

I was proud to be friends with Florian, but I wasn't entirely confident about our friendship. Florian was so imperious on insisting on his freedom that you were never sure you could count on him. There were no routines, he tended to forget about commitments when they no longer interested him, and that was what I feared most: his indifference to things he had lost interest in. One day he could be feverishly obsessed with something that a week later he said was only for bores. It was important to be ahead of a trend and to discard it as soon as too many joined the bandwagon. He had a heightened sensitivity to that tipping point when a few became too many. 'We few, we happy few, we band of brothers...'

But why should I belong to the 'happy few'? I didn't really get it. Why did Florian, who had access to our school's inner circles, consider me worthy of his friendship? What did I have to contribute besides my erudition? Well, reading didn't get you very far; *Tonio Kröger* had taught me that much. On the contrary, it led to isolation and loneliness. I couldn't formulate barbed witticisms like Florian, and I certainly couldn't keep up with his penetrating psychological gaze. Whenever I said something in his presence, I was always worried I might bore him senseless.

This was a general problem I was still grappling with later in life, though. I thought you had to be razor-sharp all the time, always armed with a witty response, or people would get bored with you. Pauses in conversation were to be avoided at all costs! I couldn't imagine that someone could be likeable without having to say or do anything. I thought you had to keep proving yourself, keep talking like your life depended on it.

Florian had an older sister, Nora, a fashion designer in Paris. Up until that moment, I had thought it impossible that a fashion designer from Paris could be directly related to someone I knew. After all, one thing was reality, the other was the stuff dreams are made of. But that's how it was. Well, she only had a small studio; you could have also called her a tailor or a seamstress, but that would only enhance her bohemian appeal. In all questions of style, Florian referred to his sister; for us, her word had the infallibility of a papal declaration on the doctrine of the faith. 'This is what they're doing now in Paris' – Florian was the only one who could get away with saying that. That line impressed me almost as much as when Florian said of the musical *Cabaret* that it was 'simply a declaration of love for life.' Like you needed a vast Parisian backdrop to talk about life like that.Yeah, of course. The anecdotes from Phoenix, Arizona had been supplanted by examples of French *savoir vivre*. At some point Florian started coming to school without a school bag, he simply carried his books and notebooks under his arm. Extremely impractical but so casual. That was what the students did in France, he told me later. With his books under his arm, he seemed as free as a bird, while the rest of us remained chained to our heavy school bags. (15 years later, when Florian was assistant to opera director Gerard Mortier, he complained to me, 'Gerard always thinks he knows how to do things properly. He recently told me, "Florian, when you're in a hotel, whether it's in Tokyo, Sydney or Oslo, always head to the carvery. Never mind the other restaurants, always the carvery!"')

Nora had a very similar skin tone to me. She was Florian's older half-sister, and she too had an African father. Although there was this unusual parallel between us, it was never a topic for Florian and me. Florian didn't say, 'You have to meet my sister, you're so alike.' When Nora was visiting her family in Heidelberg, I was captivated by her, because she was so glamorous (Paris!), not because we had something in common. It just wasn't of interest.

Nora made some highly unusual pieces of clothing for her little brother, which Florian then wore as if he were just dropping by our classroom from the Marais to hand in his homework on his way back to the bistro for another café au lait (yes, archaeologists of social mores, there was indeed a time when the watchword of the hyper trendy wasn't latte macchiato or galão, but, believe or not, café au lait). When you wore clothes like he did, you no longer had to go on and on about having just been to see your sister in Paris; everyone could see. So you also got points for understatement, this was high class. Florian had given me a kind of waistcoat made of red velvet with gold buttons, and I wore it with genuine zeal. It was not in the slightest bit subtle, but I didn't care if people looked, I didn't feel insecure because I trusted implicitly that something from Nora's hands was beyond any doubt.

Nora's boyfriend, who was also about six or seven years older than us, seemed larger than life, majestic. When I saw him (Florian had taken me to Paris), I thought to myself: this is how you need to look to score a woman like Nora!

Of course, I couldn't fail to notice that my friendship with Florian had enormously enhanced my social standing. Drama Club had catapulted me up out of the hordes, and Florian dragged me the last few metres to just below the summit of Mount Olympus. And there, in the cloudy heights, dwell the gods.

Our school's lofty nobility consisted of a group of perhaps ten or twelve students. If – as seldom happened – there was a newcomer to this elite, the astonished masses stood with bated breath observing this historical event. But even this most distinguished upper echelon was itself stratified into ranks. The legitimate bearer of the crown was Rebecca.

Tall, slim, but not lanky, intelligent and of immaculate beauty that had nothing cheap about it, she was a moral overachiever in a way that didn't necessarily make her more likeable, but gave her a certain unassailability. Her greatest weakness was blushing when she made the slightest error, which only happened once in a blue moon, be it missing the irony of a remark, or catching herself resorting to petty meanness. In fact, it was a miracle that someone who displayed such tight self-control could be so sexy at the same time. She was like a stern governess, who ruthlessly pilloried others' misconduct, and yet she didn't come across as stiff; she had sprezzatura and could be downright funny – so much so that there was a mischievous pleasure in imagining who the poor victim of her next joke might be. It must have been her own ideal of perfection to blame for the fact she even occasionally made an ironic joke at her own expense.

Rebecca's eyes were never still; nothing passed her by. She was quick to pick up on even minor tremors and shifts in the social tectonics. Shrewd and perceptive, when she needed to she could pull off a nimble about-turn to stay in the realm of the moral upper hand.

Of course, the Student Council didn't command the slightest respect. Its members were students you had never seen before and, above all, people you had no intention of being seen with. Who would seriously believe that the result of a fair, general election, where everyone had only one vote, said anything about the real balance of power at the school? Hierarchies didn't come about through elections organised by the school office. The Student Council was for timid mousy nerds, and the dominion over which they had a say didn't include anything that actually mattered.

Until one day Rebecca and her boyfriend Marius waded in. Now the word on the street was, you simply had to get involved. Something Rebecca and Marius did couldn't possibly be uncool. You could have a legitimate dread of Marius's lethal intelligence and arrogance, but no one could take him for a nerd. Now they were cooking up quite a storm on the Student Council. Their every move was closely followed and scrutinised in the school yard; for a while the topic on everyone's lips was the upcoming Student Council social trip – after all, two nights away! The school's drug baron was even going to bring his sound system and be the DJ!

Suddenly anyone who was anyone was trying to get onto the Student Council. Rebecca was elected, the uncrowned queen of the school legitimised by a plebiscite.

One day, during the longer morning break, Florian and I were standing by the drinks machine. Florian was restless, all flustered, like when you have a breakthrough, a sudden realisation. That was when he asked: 'Have you noticed how the best-looking girls here are all from rich families?' He went on to define what he meant by 'best-looking', this winning quality, but I was already thunderstruck. Where did he come up with that? Wasn't that sick? And yet this observation had something to it. There were also families with money that had inconspicuous daughters, but the five or six girls who were – by a long distance – at the top of the field, who sat at the apex of the social pyramid, unchallenged in their status, because their beauty and self-confidence formed an impregnable fortress, these girls (who incidentally also had pen pals in Cuba and raved about Castro's healthcare system) all came from wealthy families, with party-friendly villas on Schloss-Wolfsbrunnenweg and holiday homes in the Balearics. These girls weren't showy or bitchy; they looked down on anything tacky. Their wealth wasn't anything to boast about; it was accepted more like a slightly embarrassing whimsy of fate. In the meantime (involvement in the Student Council had something to do with it), they made a point of avoiding arrogance and of interacting with the representatives of lower-ranking castes without condescension, with a certain willingness to help, even warmth. But stopping short, of course, of being friends with them.

And these girls were all mad about Florian. It was invigorating, thrilling, to see how they admired and feared him at the same time. Consequently, it was primarily thanks to Florian's enviable position that we both found ourselves invited to Mallorca in the summer holidays, to Rebecca's parents' holiday house, and then to her friend Jette's on Formentera. It was astonishing, I could hardly believe it, although it was perhaps not entirely accurate to say that Rebecca and Jette had invited us – Florian had invited us in a spontaneous surprise coup after they had told us about their summer plans. I felt a bit uneasy about it, but Florian insisted there was no reason to be embarrassed.

First Mallorca with Rebecca, then. Her parents, who were unable to suppress the delight at their own bohemian spirit, clearly found Florian a bit too cocky and insufficiently contrite when he broke a piece of Mallorcan pottery on the first evening. No matter how many joints they smoked, they couldn't forgive Florian, who, for his part, when we were alone in our room that evening, was unmoved and actually said, quite without remorse: 'They make like they're cool '68 hippies, but then kick up a fuss about that ugly vase! Totally fake.' This was breathtaking self-confidence. Not only was he entirely unapologetic, but he was also accusing the injured party of being posers and of having bad taste.

I, however, was warmly welcomed by Rebecca's parents. Once again, I found that my classmates' parents found me pleasant and well brought up, which was always a surprise; I never imagined that my mother, who had no driver's license, no television, and no husband, could have possibly brought me up well. I should clarify at this point that my view of my mother had changed in the meantime – I came to see that her obstinacy was something I could also get carried away with – but that didn't change the fact that we weren't a middle-class household, that we lived in a three-room apartment on the outskirts of Dossenheim, where the carpet was still threadbare (unbelievable, I know, and Grandma was genuinely ashamed when she visited us now). Somehow – you pick these things up gradually – I associated being well brought up with having a villa on Philosophenweg and therefore I found it hard to believe that it could apply to me.

I couldn't easily switch off my deep-seated shame at our constrained circumstances ('There's no shame in being poor,' they said, but I had heard this phrase a little too often to fall for it), but gradually I realised that, at my school at least, education was more important than money (after all, the university rector enjoyed the most prestige) and that from this point of view, Mama and I radiated something downright heroic, coming down fervently as we did on the side of education, even if money was sometimes a bit tight. On Christmas Eve we always sat in the front row of the Heidelberg theatre – my mother thought it important that I could see the orchestra – and we would still be talking about *Fidelio* long after the performance, although my mother, for whom any kind of arrogance was completely alien, wasn't impressed when her son dismissed the director as provincial. There was only one time – we must have been only just keeping our heads above water – that Mama had to suspend her theatre subscription for a year. That was a real blow, and she was almost bitter about it; she saw it as something she had a right to. Piano lessons were never suspended, though, not even in times of greatest need.

When Florian and I were setting off for Formentera to stay with Jette – Nathalie, the third best friend, would also be there – Rebecca gave us a letter for the two of them; she would be arriving later. It annoyed Florian no end, not knowing what the letter was about. He had an inkling that something might have been up with Rebecca's boyfriend, and he was desperate to know what it was. We had a stopover in Ibiza, and Florian couldn't bear it any longer. 'We're opening this damned letter now!' I, in my legalistic righteousness, which I'll probably never shake off, urged him not to, despite his burning curiosity, but discovering something about the love life of these goddesses was a temptation impossible to resist. My heart was still pounding in a mixture of remorse and lust for gossip, when Florian plunged the letter into the waters of the Mediterranean. 'We'll just say that unfortunately the letter fell into the sea and it came unstuck.' It was ridiculous. Outrageous. It didn't fulfil any of the criteria of a decent excuse; it was sheer audacity. But Florian was convinced he could get away with it.

The content of the letter exceeded our wildest expectations. Yes, Rebecca was breaking up with Marius because she was actually already together with the boyfriend of her other best friend... How was she going to break it to her? Wow, that wasn't an easy one.

Florian would have certainly had some advice to share, but we had to feign complete ignorance. When we got to Formentera, he handed over the storm-buffeted letter, the ink smudged. 'Shit, sorry. It fell in the sea.'

Jette snorted. 'What a load of crap!' she said, shaking her head.

Things were a bit frosty for about twenty minutes, but then that was it.

Really, the world worked in mysterious ways.

Going back to what Florian said about the best-looking girls at the school, the moment I heard him say that I, in a sense, lost my innocence. For all that I had thought about the world so far, the fact that sociological laws were so visibly accessible still came out of the blue. Florian's observation couldn't be denied, however uncomfortable it might feel. His cool, detached perspective was fascinating, but what did it mean for me and the modest circumstances in which I lived with my mother?

Florian's observation had consequences for me that he couldn't have imagined. In my view of the world at that time, equality was not just a goal to strive for, it was a given; people *were* the same, even if they looked different at first glance, because we had to think of them as the same. That the goods of the world were unevenly distributed was a socially conditioned abomination, but it didn't cast doubt on the essential, underlying equality. The fact that intellectual gifts were also distributed unevenly was due to social conditions and upbringing, a circumstance which, for reasons of tact, was best not discussed. We should support the class struggle, yes, but class-specific observations were frowned upon. At the end of the day, the question of whether our school goddesses really were that gorgeous (yes, they were!) and whether the daughter of the man who ran the Italian ice-cream parlour wasn't also pretty gorgeous (yes, she was, but she was a bit of a nobody at our school) was secondary. The exciting thing for me, what was new here, was that you could actually utter this obvious truth. That you could say out loud that the wealth of the parental household had an impact on the success of the children, thereby articulating what was happening in the world so much more incisively than through our amorous obsession with the Cuban health system.

After the summer holidays in Mallorca and Formentera, I thought for a long time about what this vacation meant for me. It was undisputed that I had spent my holidays in the homes of the two most powerful girls in our school. Not just one, but both. I had to laugh; it still seemed so implausible. I knew it wasn't thanks to any achievement of my own, it was entirely Florian's doing. However, when I thought about the opened letter, I realised something else: the embarrassing thing about it wasn't the breach of confidentiality, but the humiliating fact that we had dined like mice on gossip crumbs dropped from the master's table, or in this case, the ladies'. We were voyeurs here, spectators – not actors. Like flicking through the tabloids for tidbits about the life of the princesses of Monaco, we had scraped in the gutter for gossip on Rebecca's love life. The broader truth left an even worse taste in my mouth: on closer inspection, this humiliating black mark only applied to me and not Florian, because he was gay, so for him this was a voyeurism free of sexual interest.

In this context, I expanded on Florian's diagnosis with a few empirical observations of my own: not only were the most beautiful girls from wealthy families, their friends had also grown up in the villas in the same neighbourhood, so they had all known each other since kindergarten. I didn't want to downplay my inferiority complex, but I felt that this fact should be noted at least once.

Jette had a Danish mother and was blonde like the girl with the pigtails from the Rama butter commercial. She was incredibly good-looking and had an unbroken relationship with outward appearances. Her friends Nathalie and Rebecca, with their Protestant ethos, sometimes rolled their eyes when Jette surrendered to all that is beautiful and rich in life without any critical reflection, but somehow there was also an impressive power in her abandon, her blithe ease with herself. Blonde jokes rolled off her like water off a duck's back, precisely because they seemed to be made for her. It was Florian who was ahead of us again in this regard when he explained that it doesn't always have to be about what is true, beautiful and good, that sometimes beauty was to be worshipped for its own sake. For Florian, Jette embodied this form of pure beauty to a tee. And suddenly, Jette was no longer a superficial blonde, but was *l'art pour l'art*. I could hardly comprehend that such beauty could walk on this earth... Jette was so unattainable, she lived in such a completely different sphere that I couldn't even fall unhappily in love with her. And yet I found myself on good terms with one of her boyfriends. Of course, they were always older than us, that goes without saying. Andreas, whom she was dating at the time, was even in his early twenties, but above all he was a yuppie. He traded stocks. The fact that something that we only knew from the movie *Wall Street* had suddenly materialised in Heidelberg was a major event, and that this 'something' also involved Jette was just too exciting. Maybe I could ask him how to pronounce the 'u' in yuppie correctly? He ought to know, after all. In fact, we hated yuppies – as far as it was possible to hate someone purely theoretically. How would Rebecca and Nathalie, with their solidarity with Cuba, react to the fact that their best friend was now with a yuppie of all people?

When Jette brought Andreas to a party for the first time, it wasn't easy for him, you could tell he felt uncomfortable. As if money were bashful in the presence of education. There was something clumsily heartfelt about his boyish face. So, I asked, he was a stockbroker? He'd have to explain it to me. Which he was delighted to do. He gave a short historico-philosophical lecture about how the '70s were over and things were different now. That all sounded familiar; Mirko had said something similar before. The fact that the times were changing – which for me was so devastating – played perfectly into Andreas's hands. Great, I said, so then, however you're supposed to pronounce it, you're a real yuppie! At which point I was amazed to see how you can take the edge off a term that was meant to be derogatory, insulting even, by applying it to yourself, because Andreas exclaimed, yes, exactly, a yuppie! It's fun making money!

It has to be said that he wasn't a poser, he didn't brag, and he didn't consider his success to be a personal achievement, but rather he considered it to be something like fate looking kindly on him. He'd been born under a lucky star, or had drawn the right lot in the tombola – wow, gosh, suddenly there's a Porsche outside! And he spoke with far too strong a Heidelberg dialect to come across as cosmopolitan or intimidating; you could tell he hadn't been a student at KFG. The fact that I didn't react hostilely to him was obviously a relief, because he had a touching awkwardness. He lacked the polish and poise of the educated middle-class, and the Porsche didn't make up for that. For a moment I thought, maybe Andreas had an even bigger inferiority complex than me? But that didn't stop him from putting his arm around Jette at that point to assert to the world his claim to her.

A few years later, I was sitting in a Heidelberg bistro when he came over to my table. He was wearing a waiter's apron. With a warm laugh and a genuine smile, he told me, 'I lost it all! Everything I'd earned – gone!' There wasn't a trace of bitterness in his still boyish face.

At the end of 12th grade, Florian declared that it was time to leave Drama Club; everyone was joining now, it was getting ridiculous. It was true, acting had by now become a sport for the masses and students were signing up who we had never seen before; Florian noted with spite that he didn't know half of them were even at our school. We were outraged when these newcomers voted against the play we old grandees wanted to put on; a disdainful majority voted for the cringeworthy, rookie play *The School of Dictators* by Erich Kästner.

But we were the aristocracy of the art form!

I, too, was seething with rage. It was obvious why the majority had opted for the wretched Kästner play. There were no explicit main roles; all the roles had more or less the same weight. The most vulgar egalitarianism had won out, thoroughly dismissing our ancestral rights.

I was deeply wounded. But Florian saw immediately how the defeat could be turned into a victory. Let them try and stage it without us. We would found our own theatre group, and it would have nothing to do with KFG, it would be far more grown up. Florian already had a play in mind: *Picnic on the Battlefield* by Fernando Arrabal. It was so-called theatre of the absurd, very mannered – right up our street. Besides, there were only seven roles, so that was perfect. Florian would direct, I would play the lead, and Florian didn't have to think twice about the three female roles: Rebecca, Nathalie and Jette (in this particular case, we didn't view the fact that Jette couldn't act as an obstacle). The real coup was that if Rebecca, Nathalie and Jette were to leave Drama Club along with us, its social prestige would be in tatters.

Florian was always very good at convincing others of his ideas, so it didn't take him long to get the school's three queens on board. Separation, secession, forming a new rival group; this was in our blood as KFG students. We would approach Fernando Arrabal in the purest Libgart Schwarz style; aesthetically, we would set sail for new shores. The final performance was quite an event, at least socially, because it wasn't open to every Tom, Dick and Harry. 'By invitation only!'

# Prussian in Spirit

The only person who talked about my unusual looks during my school days was Mr Kaufmann, the father of Christian, my photographer friend, who had once tried to make a GI out of me. It was obviously impossible for him to not comment on my different appearance. His children were always hideously embarrassed and told him off, but I saw it as an expression of our special relationship. We got on well. For someone who – due to my lack of experience – had a weakness for eccentric patriarchal figures, Mr Kaufmann was the perfect casting, while he appreciated my visits as a chance to discuss his newly acquired history books, especially about the Third Reich.

When he was sixteen he was drafted as an anti-aircraft gunner. He was a conservative old chap and his children groaned every time he offered his views on the world. He was haunted by his war experiences, and he told them again and again, but in a way that was bereft of any moral stance; he neither glorified nor condemned the war. He had been hit in the eye by shrapnel, and a plucky field surgeon had cut out his shredded eyeball without anesthesia. He had had a glass eye since then which he liked to take out and toss in the air of an evening, after a couple of bottles of wine. He had a child's love of scaring people, whether with his glass eye or his political views.

Fundamental to conservative thinking at the time was the conviction that the younger generation had it far too easy. Mr Kaufmann was able to formulate the sentence 'You've got it too easy' in endless variations. It was hardly fair, because even if the younger generation did have it easy, it wasn't their fault, in fact it was thanks to the likes of Mr Kaufmann who had worked and worked until he could bequeath a house in Heidelberg to each of his children. With a few complete sets of bed linen thrown in, because he was fond of keeping up the tradition of the trousseau.

Mr Kaufmann was an orthodontist, and because he had a Prussian concept of duty and correctness, he had brought several lawsuits against the health insurance companies, all of which he had won – in ten cases, as he put it, he had been 'the victor'. The health insurers were so impressed that they had hired him as an expert. Whenever he had an intellectual quandary he needed to unpick, Mr Kaufmann explained from time to time, he would simply translate the facts into Latin and the structure of the problem would emerge.

His practice, however, was not in Heidelberg, but in Ludwigshafen, over on the other side of the Rhine, where the chimneys of the BASF chemical plants puffed away. The industrial city – 'Lumbehave' in the local Kurpfälzisch dialect – was a world far removed from Heidelberg. A BASF board member who lived in Heidelberg might report back on life on the Rhine plain and that was about the extent of the connection. Well, Mr Kaufmann knew this rougher side to life, driving through it every day. We – who, as he loved to remind us, had it too easy in our cosy Heidelberg cocoon – had no idea what was out there in the real world! He thought this was especially true of me with my sunny disposition. I had it far too easy, albeit in a different way to his children and heirs. 'Come to Ludwigshafen with me; that'll wipe that smile off your face.' The fact that my foreign-seeming phenotype hadn't posed any obstacles in my life was only thanks to the mild, but entirely artificial protective climate of Heidelberg; in Ludwigshafen, on the other hand, an arena of genuine hardship, I'd soon get used to fending off abuse. And that might well have been the case, but the annoying thing was that Mr Kaufmann never revealed which state he himself considered the more desirable: the meek Heidelberg artificiality or the harsh Ludwigshafen authenticity. The motto of all conservatives, 'See things for what they are,' was always geared towards a certain anthropological pessimism: man was a wolf to fellow man. If I wanted more insight on the matter, I was always welcome to drop by his Ludwigshafen practice.

I gleaned from Mr Kaufmann's remarks that race and class were inseparable, linked under the surface like communicating vessels. The higher you were in the class hierarchy, the less significant the question of race was. There were no foreigners in the upper classes, only Argentinian cousins.

The Kurfürst Friedrich Gymnasium was considered an elite school. Most teachers used the term ironically, if at all; we students, on the other hand, despised the description and mocked anyone who used it, we would die for the political struggle against the elites – however, in the midst all the bluster, the suspicion suddenly crept in that we might just have been getting high on a moral win-win situation. We boasted of incorruptibility, rejecting titles we could actually claim for ourselves, but the louder we condemned all talk of elites, the more we just confirmed our entitlement. After all, why reject the term if you're not under the slightest suspicion of belonging to an elite yourself?

The only one who cultivated an uninhibited relationship, to put it reticently, with the concept of the elite was Mr Vaupel, the Religious Education teacher who had been so outraged by my Engels talk that time. Since then, he'd had it in for me, as we used to say, and it took me a while to understand that his acrimony was an honour as far as he was concerned, because debate and altercation presupposed equality. I was surprised that after the Engels incident he would occasionally come up to me and start talking about anything and everything. I enjoyed listening to him – he had a unique take on things. He once told me, for example, how in the '68 era, during the Springer protests, he cancelled his subscription to the newspaper *FAZ* and subscribed instead to *Die Welt* in solidarity with the Springer Group. That was really something.

Mr Vaupel wasn't just an RE teacher, or 'professor' as he liked to be called, he also taught Hebrew. He ran the extracurricular Hebrew Club, where 10th and 11th grade students could prepare for the Hebraicum exam. Participation was entirely optional.

As far as Mr Vaupel was concerned, there were only three topographies of note: Prussia, Greece and Israel. When he spoke it was either as a Greek, a Prussian or a Zionist. If as a Greek, then of course as an *Ancient* Greek. He had no truck with the contemporary Greeks – they were just lazy, according to this Prussian. Mr Vaupel could sing you a ballad of the times he'd been stitched up in Crete, where he was having a house built, 'or more precisely, a fortress, with thin windows like arrow slits, but in an austere minimalist Bauhaus style.' A fortress in a Bauhaus style? Even as a seventeen-year-old I could see this was certainly original.

As a Prussian, he extolled masculine virtues such as tenacity, discipline, bravado and presence of mind, and didn't seem impressed when his students took these at best as empty words, at worst as the kind of qualities you might need – as people said back then – to run a concentration camp. And as a committed Zionist, when it came to the crime against humanity that was the Shoah, he stood firmly on the side of Israel (always extending the first syllable and voicing the 's'). There could be no other place for a German, he insisted, than at Israel's side. He also admired the bold, militaristic nature of the young state. His vivid narration of the Yom Kippur War and the Six Day War would make your cheeks burn. And because he despised hedonism and luxury, he saw in the kibbutz a Prussian austerity which suited him well.

Perhaps 150 years ago Mr Vaupel might have been an educated and respected military chaplain in Moltke's army. We couldn't help wondering if he had a screw loose, but the fact that such completely different worldviews could coexist, that words and terms could be put together in combinations which were logical and yet so contrary – this was a revelation that was at once delightful and unsettling. But why not let Mr Vaupel put it in his own words? 'Everyone can speak Latin, the elite opt for Greek, but the elite of the elite use Hebrew.'

Of course, no student who was in his right mind took Hebrew in order to belong to the 'elite of the elite', and even to speak of it, as I said, would make you cringe. But Mr Vaupel had another, more tempting reward: a three-and-a-half-week trip to Israel in 11th grade, just before you had to start swotting up for the Hebraicum exam. And so I signed up for Hebrew Club, despite getting terrible grades in everything except for history – not that I cared.

I carried on sparring with Mr Vaupel, but that wasn't a problem for him. His rhetoric was staggering, his syntax sophisticated and absolutely infallible. He spoke in an absurdly constrained voice, munching his syllables like a wine connoisseur, but this idiosyncrasy, his guttural, nasal sound formation, lent a touch of magic to his speeches. So there he stood – wiry, his leathery skin tanned by the sun of Israel and Greece – in the Negev desert in the cave of En-Gedi, telling us how, right here, Saul fell into David's hands. Saul has already thrice sought David's life, and now David finds him here, in the cave, asleep. David's people reason with him that this is exactly the situation the Lord has spoken of: one day, He will hand Saul over to him, David, that he may do as he pleases with him. But David doesn't kill Saul. He spares his life and instead cuts off a strip from the bottom of the sleeping man's robe. When Saul sets off the next morning, David follows him and calls to him from afar: 'You see! I could have strangled you, but instead I merely cut off the hem of your robe. I would never lay my hands on the head of an anointed one!' We listened, spellbound by the drama the Old Testament had to offer. Nobody had told us these stories before.

We stormed Masada with Vaupel leading the charge, and anyone who couldn't climb the ascent briskly enough in the scorching heat of the desert was left straggling. Mr Vaupel had described the desperate struggle of the Jews against the Roman occupiers; they had barricaded themselves in the Masada fortress, but when it became clear that the Romans would raze the fortification walls to the ground with battering rams, the besieged preferred an honourable death to a miserable survival. The men drew lots to decide who would kill the others before giving themselves the mortal blow. Mr Vaupel was just explaining how all of this had been handed down through the writings of the Jewish-Roman historian Flavius Josephus when those bringing up the rear reached us at the summit, pale with exhaustion. Mr Vaupel only glanced at them – 'Ah, finally?' – as if they were exaggerating how tired they were.

We Vaupel students cultivated an ironic loyalty to him; we didn't share his views, but we defended him like an elderly relative. We studied him like ethnologists observing an endangered native tribe in the Amazon. He was a museum piece. But even as you think you value someone's views purely as an anachronistic curiosity, there is still a degree of intellectual contagion. No one recognised that better than himself, incidentally; if he hadn't been a Prussian and a Protestant, he would have made a very good Jesuit.

My rebellious phase was long behind me. From one day to the next I realised that I could get away with being lazy as long as I was affable and nimble enough. If the teachers liked you, you could get away with anything. This was a revelation, too, that life could be effortless and breezy. Maybe I wasn't a Tonio Kröger after all?

One thing continued to provoke the devil's advocate in me and that was the predictable, absolutely conventional moral judgments most teachers expressed about the world. If you wanted to make the teachers sweat, all you had to do was bring a broad spectrum of taboo names and terms into play, in an informed manner of course. The history teacher gasped when, with reference to Sebastian Haffner, whom everyone was reading at the time, someone remarked that there were doubts about the theory that the German Reich had been solely responsible for the First World War. This teacher, who was already harping on about a further lurch to the right (after the 'spiritual and moral turning point' of 1982, Poland was a prime target, so to speak), detected the whiff of revisionism.

When I read Sebastian Haffner's *The Rise and Fall of Prussia* shortly afterwards, I found myself armed with arguments with which one could genuinely defend the pomp and circumstance of Prussia: the rational state, the Enlightenment, the emancipation of the Jews, Frederick's correspondence with Voltaire, and so on. In addition, from Haffner you could glean that one of Hitler's decisive strategic goals in the days following 30 January 1933 was to shut down the Prussian institutions, to complete his *Machtergreifung*, his seizure of power. So, Hitler was not at all the logical extension and culmination of Frederick the Great.

These were all exciting new intellectual perspectives, and suddenly Mr Vaupel didn't seem so wacky either. What was so bad about being a *Prussian in spirit*?

Wasn't old Ribbeck von Ribbeck, whose pears had seemed so mouth-watering since I was a child, also a Prussian? In general, I was moved by the idea that something had existed that was no longer there. No longer existing was perhaps the most elegant form of being; it therefore also demanded the most respect. All the deceased who had once strived for something, forged something, were now gone, forgotten, and yet something remained. I read in Haffner that the Allied Control Council dissolved the state of Prussia with its resolution of 25 February 1947. And yet something continued to have an effect, something I found alluring. Once upon a time there had been a power and an idea that had stirred people's hearts and minds, at least there must have been something there, even if it was nothing but the memory of a pear tree. Or the great and terrible Katte Tragedy, the prince who had to witness his friend's execution. No wonder he later asked his soldiers, 'Dogs, do you want to live forever?' Suddenly I had an inkling why Tenno's nemesis Lothar was such a misanthrope.

And then Prussia, at first unconsciously, then coming more sharply into view, also emerged in my mind's eye as a lost landscape that I pictured as being a bit like the Baltic island that's the setting for Erich Kästner's *Emil and the Three Twins*. The Brandenburg sands, the pine forests. I then read Siegfried Lenz's *So Tender Was Suleyken* and found myself picturing the Masurian Lake District. These were places that had slipped into the hereafter not only geographically but also chronologically. And didn't we ourselves come from a lost territory of this kind, from Silesia?

Lately, Mama had quite often confided in me her frustration with friends and acquaintances not being comfortable when she mentioned the expulsion of our family from Silesia. Even the mention of the name Silesia prompted icy reactions at dinner parties, as if talking about one's own childhood were the first step towards dragging Silesia back into the empire. 'They're putting up a wall,' said my mother defiantly. 'It's too dogmatic for my liking.'

I had started to feel fond of Silesia. If there was nothing to tell about my paternal line, at least there should be some ancestry on my mother's side. I played with the phrase, 'We come from Silesia'. Not bad. More impact, though, with 'I'm Silesian.'

'You?'

'Yes. Well, my mother. Pilgramsdorf. Not far from Breslau.'

Mama and I both read a short essay by Wolf Jobst Siedler, whose *Walks between the Oder and Nowhere* was published in the elegant Corso series. Ah, the journeys to be taken on a glorious summer's night! Mama's favourite writer had always been Theodor Fontane, this spark now jumped over to me too, and the Prussia of my imagination was a strange conglomerate of Erich Kästner's Baltic island, Fontane's pear tree, Berlin's roaring twenties, Tucholsky's *Rheinsberg* and a family past that could be traced from Silesia to the Ribbeck Castle by the Beetzsee.

My mother was constantly reading, albeit slowly, and her favourite character was the old Dubslav von Stechlin of Fontane's eponymous novel. He seemed to her the ideal embodiment of wisdom, a sense of tradition and a kind, liberal heart, and his refusal to judge anyone else was entirely to her taste. This was how she herself behaved; it wasn't her place to judge. Whenever our acquaintances shook their heads and talked disdainfully of members' clubs – as they so often did because the whole 'obsession with clubs and societies' was considered the worst kind of German petty bourgeois hell among our progressive contemporaries – my mother would calmly emphasise the social value of such organisations for a small community like Dossenheim ('I'd like to stick to concrete examples here, too,' she'd insist). Now the Dossenheim Handball Club was not necessarily the same as the castle at Lake Stechlin, but she didn't recognise differences in social rank, she didn't even see them, and polishing an eight-hundred-year-old family coat of arms was no more or less valid than the traditions celebrated at the Kerwe parish festival in Dossenheim.

Was I Silesian, was I Prussian? Of course, it was all just a game to give free rein to my contrary streak and my longing to stand out.

Once my mother and I spent the evening with a couple we knew. Mama had always had a bit of a soft spot for the husband – a Greek man who was a senior consultant at the Heidelberg Eye Clinic – because he was such a sensitive cello player. That evening he said to me, as if he hoped to pass on some crucial experience, 'As a non-German you always have to be twice as good as the others.' While I felt honoured that he thought me worthy of such a conversation, I was also surprised things could be seen this way. It had never occurred to me that careers were decided on the basis of what someone looked like (or perhaps I had been half aware when I had worried about *The Winter's Tale*); that the Greek ophthalmologist and I were somehow in the same group was also a startling new perspective. I had never imagined that I would have the honour of belonging to a social group. I kept thinking about it, sensing the vague appeal of having it twice as hard as everyone else, even if nothing seemed to back this up. People didn't have obstacles placed in their way, surely? Or had I just failed to see them? In any case, the realisation that I might share a collective fate with others was as surprising an insight as when you read Marx for the first time and suddenly understand that society can be described as a class struggle.

Now it was time to start trying to make sense of it all.

# PART III

# African Americans

Nowadays, anyone who looks Arab is subjected to merciless stares, a prickly form of group prejudice I was never exposed to. After all, I wasn't a minority, I was a singularity. An individual who looked different because of an African father who otherwise played no role in my life. If my singularity was ever under threat, my reaction was to be mildly peeved.

In the seventies and eighties, apart from Nora, I only met one other person who also somehow fell into my category. His name was Kofi, he went to another school, and yet his name often came up. He came across as smart, self-confident and charismatic, and his father came from Ghana. We only knew each other casually, and I probably kept my distance, but once, it must have been around 1989, he came up to me and asked what 'my roots' were. I told him, and he told me about a club or association of some kind, I didn't quite follow, where Afro-Germans met, and asked if I would be interested in coming along? We had a shared experience, after all.

'Afro-German'. This was new to me. What was it supposed to mean? As I said, Kofi was a nice guy, in no way obtrusive, but the fact that he suddenly conjured up a term like this that was supposed to have something to do with me and my life – this felt like an encroachment, practically a threat.

Whenever I argued in defence of the rational state of Prussia, everyone nodded benevolently, especially since I was neither blonde nor blue-eyed and nobody needed to be alarmed that my paean was coming from the wrong corner. This was how I had positioned myself. And now here was Kofi offering me a completely different community, one where I didn't recognise myself at all. If people began to see me as an Afro-German, then I would no longer be who I had always thought I was, namely, German. What would I gain from that? Kofi's well-meaning offer was setting off alarm bells. No, this was not for me, there was no way I could get into this. I had to reject it outright. Kofi sensed where I stood and didn't press me on it.

When I told my friends what Kofi had said, they laughed, outraged on my behalf. Preposterous, they insisted. I was German, and skin colour made no difference. People like Kofi just hadn't got that yet! They were outraged, I now think, because Kofi's offer inexplicably presupposed a privation or a grievance; Afro-Germans would only join forces if they felt mistreated in this country. My friends (and I) didn't see it that way. No one had ever treated me as a non-German, not even behind closed doors. I had never been excluded. So, I didn't need protection as a minority.

It wasn't until years later that I found out that Kofi and his band, Advanced Chemistry, were one of the founders of German hip hop. Their breakthrough hit in 1992 was called 'Foreign in My Own Country'. I think the song was important in capturing a certain experience, and when I listen to it today, I'm impressed by how deftly Advanced Chemistry linked the question of being different with the murderous mob attacks on asylum seekers in Rostock Lichtenhagen, and the band's confident treatment of the sense of being a stranger in one's own homeland (and their scepticism that the radio stations would even play the track). But back then this simply didn't reflect my experience. I had never felt like a stranger in my own country. I had always felt I was in safe hands.

Or was I kidding myself? Was I imperceptive to the marginalisation I had encountered? Out of a desire for harmony? Had I suppressed unpleasant experiences in order to be able to live a happy life? Did I simply not want to perceive racism out of fear of bursting the bubble of my own contentment?

Sometimes people would say, 'There's no one as German as you!' An unspoken and certainly only half-conscious expression of the modern sense that being German wasn't in your genes, but in your mind.

Had I over-assimilated somehow, and become more German than any other German? An opportunist who had adapted to such an extent that my friends' conservative fathers were convinced that I alone would be responsible for the survival of our German cultural heritage?

Over-assimilation out of fear of exclusion – that was exactly the kind of schematic psychoanalysis I had an allergic aversion to, having grown up as the son of a psychotherapist. I dismissed this kind of tedious diagnosis, not because I felt it was wrong, but because it was too obvious to represent any real gain in knowledge.

Sometimes people would speak to me in slow, broken German, like the server at the bakery. 'You want bread?' I would then confirm, 'Yes, indeed, that's precisely what I intend to purchase, this loaf of bread...' My grammatically and phonetically ornate High German (with a tendency to a certain antiquity) was a psycholinguistic reflex, my language being my most tangible right of access to German society. Of course, it was not unlike Maggie Thatcher, who had battled her way up the social ladder from the world of her parents' grocery shop, but – as the old aristocracy noted with condescension – she tended to overshoot the mark in putting on her best Queen's English.

Life's a game, after all.

However, as with any game, you can only play the cards you've been dealt. And it was only later that I got to know of any black role models that I found at all likeable. Well, there was Eddie Murphy. He filled the cinemas in Germany, but it was obvious that he wasn't someone an ambitious young Thomas Mann reader would identify with. Indeed, if Eddie Murphy embodied blackness (and he emphatically did for much of the world), then I would have to take extra care not to have anything to do with it. The cringingly infantile voice used to dub him into German reduced this very masculine figure to a laughing stock. Was this what Mama had warned me about when she said black people risked only being celebrated for sports and entertainment?

Besides Eddie Murphy, there were Michael Jackson and Prince. They were all characterised by a strong physicality, something remote from the spirit, according to the Protestant ethic of my cultural upbringing. The oversexualisation of the black body was a racist cliché Germany had yet to get past, and it was one I wasn't keen to be associated with. In America, meanwhile, it was accepted and embodied in a way that was larger than life, always bigger and better. This may have represented a crucial freedom, but I didn't see it that way back then.

In short, I hardly knew a single black person besides myself. That only changed when I went to the United States for seven months after graduating from high school in 1990.

The first few days at summer camp were a disaster. There has perhaps rarely been a high school graduate who started working as a camp counsellor with such terrible English. (Did something go wrong in the selection process? Without a doubt. The American lady who interviewed me in Munich was very polite, but she noticed straight away that I could hardly string a sentence together in English. She smiled serenely and didn't torment me for long. Without it being said out loud, we both quickly realised that it would be best for me to abandon my dreams of the USA, and for us to end the interview there and part with no hard feelings. But I really wanted to see a play that evening at the Munich Kammerspiele, so as I was leaving, I asked her the way – slipping for practical reasons into German. I was heading to the Kammerspiele? She was surprised. This young man, who was a walking disaster when it came to English, wanted to spend the evening at the theatre? It didn't seem to stack up. She asked what I was hoping to see. *The Playboy of the Western World* by John Millington Synge. Suddenly we were in the midst of a conversation about theatre, and a few days later I received the letter saying I had been accepted.)

The summer camp was located on the sand dunes of Lake Michigan, just under an hour's drive from Grand Rapids. It was kept afloat by the region's wealthy entrepreneurs, with the intention of supporting 'inner-city kids', as they called them; they too should be exposed to sport, nature, fresh air, patriotism and discipline in a kind of Scout-like retreat during the summer holidays. They were picked up in buses from Grand Rapids and brought to Lake Michigan for ten days. (On the day of the return journey, ten days later, there were always a good dozen or so left stranded at Grand Rapids bus station; their parents had somehow forgotten them, and it was heart-breaking to have to take the children by the hand, take a cab to their home address and leave them with neighbours, because there was no one home.)

Each counsellor was responsible for a group of ten children. Since I wasn't up to much given my lack of language skills, I was assigned the youngest ones, the six- to seven-year-olds. And since it was, above all, about maintaining discipline (standing in line for the flag roll call, singing the national anthem with appropriate earnestness, sitting quietly at the table until the end of the meal, not fighting behind your counsellor's back, and, finally, at some point in the evening shutting up and going to sleep), it was – at least from the point of view of a European civilian – mainly a matter of imparting militaristic virtues. The ability to conduct a sensitive conversation with appropriate vocabulary played a subordinate role. That made my job easier. I just yelled 'Shut up!' when it got too loud at my table, prompting hearty laughter from 'my kids' at my funny accent.

Each dorm was shared by two groups of children. Adjacent to this was the room of their two allocated counsellors. My colleague Steve, an American, late twenties, actually a maths teacher, was the most experienced and mature of us counsellors, which is why the camp management had wisely put him together with me. Steve had a sanguine temperament, he could overflow with enthusiasm, but he also had an austere side. I really felt it in the first few days. Most likely because of my limited language skills, he took me for a complete idiot who had been dumped on him, of all people. He was helpful and conscientious in all practical matters, but he made no effort to hide his disdain for his colleague from Germany. I couldn't blame him, after all, I hated myself for my adolescent defiance, which had made me pay so little attention in English lessons. Now, though, it was a matter of soldiering on and salvaging what I could. In the evening, when the last boy had finally stopped simulating comedy fart noises and everyone had finally gone to sleep, I turned to the English books I had brought with me to learn from. I was totally exhausted by this time of day, of course, but that didn't stop me. I started quite naturally with *The Catcher in the Rye*, flicking through the dictionary and noting down every new word in my notebook, struggling from sentence to sentence. This linguistic diligence made Steve reconsider his opinion of me. He was also curious about the German books on my bedside table. We began to talk. When he found out that I had studied Greek, Latin and Hebrew in school, Steve reassessed his appraisal of me, because he was, as I learned shortly afterwards, an ardent papist. For him, the Roman Catholic Church was the body of Christ. In fact, he had three passions he was physically moved by, to the point of trembling, so acutely was he at their mercy: the Pope, Reagonomics, and beautiful women. Unfortunately, my English was too limited to understand his explanations of precisely how this trinity fit into a coherent system. Needless to say, he was a great sinner, and gave in to every temptation with quivering rapture; the ensuing remorse at cheating on his girlfriend yet again was no less deeply felt. When I walked through the town with him, his eyes would scan the streets like a radar, homing in on the backside of every woman who passed. He would then literally gasp for air when she was gone, in relief at being released from God's inconceivably seductive creation. He would speak very eloquently about the holy sacrament of marriage; for him there was a thrilling dichotomy in the tension between theory and practice, between what is and what should be. How bland life would be without a struggle with yourself and with the demons of temptation.

Steve also prided himself on his knowledge of ancient history, and so we talked late into the night about the Delian League and NATO. He introduced me to the concept of America, he taught me the national anthem, delighted to have an eager pupil, and lavished me with lectures on Reagonomics that gushed with pedagogical eros ('The Socialists think the cake is always the same size, so all they think about is how to share out this one fixed-size cake, but the point is, get this, the cake is growing, for everyone!'), and for every new word I learned, I was treated to a digression about the various nuances and connotations the word could have in different contexts. These lexical explanations were also a miniature course in American sociology. It was particularly important to him that I learned the word 'serendipity': rhythm, beauty, presence of mind and the arrogance of his mother tongue were all luminously combined within it. It was an intellectually lofty time in the counsellors' dorm at Grand Rapids Summer Camp. For the first time in my life I met someone for whom Ronald Reagan wasn't the devil incarnate, and it was only the second time, after Pfeifer-Papa, that I had encountered someone who adored the Pope with his ring of white hair. I didn't know what to make of it all. And yet I knew that rarely was anything more exciting than the very realisation that things could be viewed differently from my Heidelberg perspective.

In this way Steve became my cicerone to the New World. In essence, the foundation of our friendship was the humanistic grammar school. For Steve, I represented 'old Europe', an educated German who needed to have the socialist nonsense driven out of him, but also – in his mind – someone who could speak to the Pope in Latin if needed (hmm, about as well as I could speak English to Steve at the start of the summer). And I, on the other hand, had arrived for the first time in a country where there were black people, a country whose society was characterised by segregation through and through, where I was the camp counsellor for a group of poor, mostly black children, but I was seen by my protector as an almost picture-perfect embodiment of 'old Europe'.

However, at the time, I didn't notice this, for the simple reason that Steve treated me exactly as I was treated in Germany. At the beginning of my seven-month trip to the

United States, I couldn't yet see that in effect it meant he treated me like a white man.

I marvelled at the black kids in the camp (the oldest were fifteen years old). Their world was not mine. I knew nothing about hip hop. From time to time their rooms were searched and switchblades were confiscated. It was different with my own "sweet kids," and I would remember being fascinated because many of their faces reminded me of photos of myself when I was in primary school. Seeing my looks mirrored in others was an unfamiliar experience and it still is to this day. When I see children of my racial mix on the street, I still give them a complicit smile.

In early October 1990 (just as German reunification was taking place), I went to Chicago for two months to visit Yvonne. At the time, she was Executive Director of the Community Renewal Society, a powerful organisation founded in 1882, inspired by the Church and committed to overcoming racial and class boundaries. Whenever Yvonne spoke in public (and she could barely fend off the invitations – every congress, every celebration, every special church service seemed to rely on her as keynote speaker), she was treated as a celebrity, if this term is appropriate in a sphere permeated with theology, charisma, and the struggle for political emancipation. I heard her deliver a speech with great pathos, and while I sat there in the front row with goosebumps (I wasn't used to such emotion in political speeches back home in the Federal Republic), she gave me a passing wink as if to say, 'So, did I pull it off?'

In every article, toast or introductory speech, they always described her as 'The first black woman to...' Among other things, she was the first black woman to be ordained as a pastor in the United Church of Christ. Yvonne once said to me with her merciless irony, 'It's hardly surprising that I could always do what I wanted in my life – I'm always the first black woman, after all...'

Her ability to switch from intimidating austerity to delirious wit was breath-taking. 'Huh-huh-huh,' she laughed right from her diaphragm, clapping her hands in sync. She was a captivating storyteller and I loved listening to her. She was keen to share her experiences with me, but not to re-educate me, not to squeeze me into a schema. She accepted that my biography was different. After all, she knew Dossenheim, nestled amongst the lovely vineyards, and she knew that there was a milder view of the world over there.

I watched her with pride as she warmed up packed audiences with her expert delivery, and I thought: 'So this was the woman you had such a panic about going to the post office with as a child...'

Unlike Mama, her best friend Yvonne had come into bourgeois prosperity. Yvonne's apartment on South Park (with a doorman in uniform) had views onto Lake Michigan. As a child of the Navy town of Norfolk, she needed to be close to the water. I had a slight culture shock when I realised that the fireplace wasn't fuelled by wood; the ridiculous gas flames were supposed to simulate the atmosphere of a crackling open fire. America is a funny country. When Yvonne came home from work in the evenings, with frozen chicken wings to go into the oven and a quality red wine she had picked up for me at the "liquor store" (I wasn't yet 21), she would tell me about the time she spent with my mother 25 years ago in Cincinnati. This was an odd new feeling to hear about my mother as the protagonist in someone else's narrative.

If I visited Yvonne in her downtown office during the day to have lunch with her, we would often be accompanied by her lawyer. Yvonne introduced her to me as an intellectual. From the first second it was clear that we weren't going to hit it off. Small, wily, always in a trouser suit, when she smiled her face looked like she had just bitten on a cyanide capsule. She dragged every single thing anyone said immediately into politics – and that always meant racial politics. And it wasn't easy to escape these discussions once she'd got going. She saw through any diversionary tactics like a light-hearted joke and would thwart them right away. You could agree with her or not, but what she wouldn't tolerate was any pretence that there was a life beyond such questions. Our mutual antipathy was so strong that we both tried to act in a way that made it difficult for the other, and that's why I soon stopped reacting and instead made out that I was above it all, adopting Fontane's 'cheerful aloofness' and making a point of showing how little it affected me, because I knew my indifference would drive her to a white hot rage. To me, she seemed humourless and fanatical, someone who associated everything, and I mean everything, with race. At that time I still wasn't familiar with Brecht's poem 'To Those Born Later' and the sentiment that even when focused on injustice, contempt leaves its mark on the face.

As far as Yvonne's lawyer was concerned, there was nothing innocent in this world, everything was tarnished by racism, while from my Heidelberg perspective I had a much higher estimation of the innocence of the world. And so she treated me like someone who lacked awareness of his own social discrimination; I was refusing to open my eyes and see the truth about my life out of defiance, instead choosing to live in spineless complicity with my own oppressors. When she talked like that, I wondered if she didn't realise how ridiculous it was that she always wanted to be addressed as 'Dr'. I might be an Uncle Tom in her eyes, but at least I didn't have an inferiority complex. We exchanged cool glares, and the wise

Yvonne relished the discord, because she saw it as a good lesson, for the lawyer as much as for me.

This was a special case of mutual antipathy, but it was also obvious that the coordinates by which I was being assessed had changed since the summer camp. I had to face the fact that for the first time in my life black people perceived me as black. It was like how the Turkish greengrocers in Heidelberg used to hint in their body language at something we had in common, only here it was clear and far less subtle. 'Hey brother' I would hear on the street from African Americans – complete strangers. I tried not to give anything away, but I couldn't help feeling alarmed. 'Sorry, sir,' I wanted to say, 'but there's clearly been a misunderstanding!'

Since I was out and about in Yvonne's world, I was regularly asked, with warm sympathy, what problems the *black community* in Germany had to contend with. Or, if we had got to know one another a bit better, what it was like for me as a black person living in Germany. I sometimes got the impression that African Americans saw Germany as a tough kind of diaspora to have ended up in.

Once, when we were with her family in Norfolk, Yvonne and I went to visit a small rural community near Richmond, Virginia. It was a black congregation, the service was spirited, and Yvonne, who had been invited to preach, was so combative in her address that there wasn't a single dry eye in the chapel. After the service everyone shook my hand, and an elderly gentleman told me he still remembered my mother.

As Yvonne and I drove to Richmond after the service, she asked me if there was anyone I had had a particularly good conversation with. 'An elderly white lady,' I said. Yvonne frowned at me; there hadn't been any white ladies at the service. There was, I insisted – a very charming, dignified older lady, and I told Yvonne what she had told me. Oh, said Yvonne with a certain disapproval, she knew who I meant, but she was black. I was genuinely taken aback. Black and white were categories of pigmentation for me, and this woman had fair skin and facial features that were categorised in the somewhat brutal American taxonomy as Caucasian. That's not the point, said Yvonne, her background is what counts. And so I learned how the old, iron law of southern states racism – that one drop of black blood is enough for you and your descendants to be forever black – had now, conversely, become the proud core identity of the black community. At first I thought: what kind of ideological nonsense is this, where I have to describe a woman as black against all appearances? But the longer I thought about it, the more it made sense to me. People are bound together by a historical experience that persists even if their appearance, the external biological criterion that was once the basis of collective categorisation, has paled in colour. This woman must have had ancestors who got paler and paler from generation to generation, with more and more whites among her forebears, but in her conscious identity she had clung firmly to that line of her family tree that traced back to the slave ships, even if you could no longer read this ancestry in her skin tone.

Sitting in the car as we drove through the tree-lined, hilly landscape of Virginia, I reflected. Had Yvonne just told me off? The atmosphere was highly charged. And maybe, I thought further, she meant for me to understand something else from this: if this apparently white woman felt black, how ridiculous was it that I – so much darker than her – was presenting as white? Oh man, once you get into debating 'colour theology', there's clearly no end to it…

Here in the United States, I was drifting between two worlds. White people treated me as one of their own (and solemnly declared that BMW made the best cars in the world), and black people embraced me as if I had returned from the diaspora to the community of martyrs.

I then spent December with a friend of Yvonne's, Edward, a minister in Brooklyn. However, the only thing the Brooklyn of 1990 had in common with the district today was its name. This was Brooklyn before gentrification, and when I got back from Manhattan late at night on the D train and got off at Prospect Avenue to walk to Edward's little parsonage, Edward would be lying awake worrying about whether something might have happened to his guest from Germany. Edward was an early riser; whenever I got home he was always in bed. But he couldn't sleep until he heard the front door open. Then he called from his bedroom, 'Ijoma?' It was only when he heard me reply 'Yes!' that he could go to sleep.

Once he asked me if I read on the D train.

'Of course,' I replied. 'What else would I do?'

'Even at the stations?'

'I don't stop reading just because the train stops.'

'Well, you should look up from your book and keep an eye on the door so you can see who's getting on.'

Of all the subway lines in the world, the D train means the most to me ('This is a Brooklyn-bound D train!' – oh, the unforgettable voices of the New York subway conductors!). Whenever I stepped into a carriage at Columbus Circle, I would be the darkest of all the passengers, so everything felt normal, almost like in Heidelberg, just with a few more Asian people sitting beside me. The closer the train got to the East River, the more black people got on. Most whites left the D at Grand Street if not before; now the train crossed beneath the East River. Next stop: DeKalb Avenue. The passengers were now a mix of Latinos and African Americans. If there was still a white man in the carriage, I knew he would get off at the next stop, Atlantic Avenue, at the latest. Perhaps by some miracle he would stay on and not get off until Union Street. But, my God, he looked like a *freak*! By 4th Avenue I was by far the palest-skinned passenger, all the Latinos were long gone, and when I left the subway at Prospect Avenue, I was an alien element in the crowd. I was pale in a black neighbourhood.

As a house guest of the local pastor, it seemed to me that in a certain special way I belonged to the neighbourhood. When I walked the streets with Edward, he introduced me to the members of his congregation, who gave me a warm welcome. Each one had a little story that Edward would tell me as we walked on.

We were both classical music fans – and nothing creates more trust between people than a similar taste in music. Edward was a political person through and through, but there was always another side to him. I must have seen a particular integrity in this, also because a touch of sadness hung over him; his life as a pastor and his love of music existed in separate worlds. Now Edward saw it as his educational task to hone my awareness of colour. But unlike Yvonne's lawyer, there was something else for him besides this 'struggle,' something that could simply exist, with no pressure to prove its political legitimacy. You didn't have to define yourself solely by skin colour, you could also see yourself as a connoisseur of Schubert's Lieder. That was why Edward seemed to have something free and undogmatic about him. I didn't feel like I was clamped in a vice when he told me something about his lived experience as a black person. This made me all the more open to what he had to say. We had something in common that came before politics, a shared cultural homeland, and it was from there that he could take me by the hand and open my eyes to the ugly sides of American society.

In Edward's life there was the *vita activa*, the socially engaged life, the *community*, but there was also the possibility of withdrawal to the *vita contemplativa*, to isolation, an unassailable individuality, a kind of inner concert hall where he was mostly left to himself and his musical interests. I was so impressed whenever I saw how patiently he opened up the parsonage to visitors every day, whenever there was a knock at the door and a mother was asking for help because her son was yet again back at a police station. Whenever I saw him, in his thoroughly unsentimental way, considering what steps to take to help someone, and whenever he proudly introduced a teenager who would soon be graduating from high school to follow his path in life, it made such a strong impression on me, because at the same time I could see that Edward didn't give himself over entirely to his public role. He kept a small, closely guarded space within himself which he retreated to as soon as he had turned his back on the street, shut the door behind him and sat down to listen to Brahms's 4th Symphony. Within him was a combination of withdrawal into the world of ideal forms along with a sombre anger at the irradicable racism of white people.

He let others sense his affection as well as his distance. Joviality wasn't his thing. He was demanding because he was stubborn, and he knew it, but he saw it as a price worth paying. Why should something be easy? False harmony seemed pointless to him. If there was ever a touch of disappointment, even bitterness, he tried to undermine it with dry humour. If you only heard his voice, the tone and pronunciation of his English would make it hard to draw any conclusions about his skin colour; his way of speaking was a marker of singularity rather than of social ambition. Sometimes he sighed and said, in his elegant Bostonian accent, 'I like things white people do.' His tastes were those associated with white people. He might have also added, 'There's nothing I can do about it.' His predilection for museums, concert halls and French cuisine made him a loner, at least in the milieu where he moved professionally. But that only made his love for Brahms seem all the purer, because it certainly wasn't about striving to belong. When I went to the Metropolitan Opera with Edward, I couldn't help but notice a lot of people glancing our way. Their emotional and grateful smiles seemed intended to show how much they appreciated seeing two black people displaying an affinity for the aesthetic universality of classical music. Experiences like that annoyed Edward no end, while I took it with a smile. There was no denying that we were the only black people in the Met.

Many years ago, when Edward went to Washington, D.C. to study at Howard University, the traditional destination for African American students, his mother sent him off with a copy of *The Green Book*, a guide to the South for black people from the northern states. Black travellers could use it to find hotels that would offer them a room or where they could get a coffee. I knew about segregation in the southern states from the history books. Now I was living with a man, around fifty at the time, who had experienced it first-hand.

It was fortunate that Edward and I were both polemical by nature. Our process of mutual education therefore often took the form of teasing. 'Ah, here comes my Prussian guest,' he would greet me at the breakfast table. The best thing was that he was genuinely interested to learn about Prussia from me (and through me). If he told a story that was supposed to illustrate another case of everyday racism, and once again I didn't understand what he was getting at, then he would casually rub the fingers of one hand against the back of the other hand. 'Of course, yes, the skin issue,' I'd say, slapping my palm against my forehead.

Not being in Heidelberg at Christmas was harder for me than I had expected, despite the ice skating in front of the Rockefeller Center; Mama's Christmas rituals were more deeply entrenched than I had realised. On Christmas Eve, we were invited to an early supper with friends of Edward's, then he had to get ready for Christmas Mass. I sat in the front row at the church and watched him. He had a very different preaching style to Yvonne; he was more measured, more austere, more sparing with emotion. He was there for his congregation, but he didn't entirely commingle with them. The church was dark, candles flickered solemnly. Then, like probably every congregation worldwide, they sang *Silent Night, Holy Night*. But before they began, Edward said, 'And in honour of our guest from Heidelberg, we will sing the second verse in German.' Printed on the lyrics sheets that had been handed out was the German text, which the black community sang, with shaky pronunciation but with gusto.

Shortly after Christmas, I flew back to Germany (reunified in my absence) and for the first time I felt like I had somehow swapped experiences, taken part in a mutual dialogue with other people about that certain something that no one could fail to notice when they saw me. My time in the United States helped me feel I belonged to a community of experience that was previously unknown to me; no more than this, but also no less. Yvonne and Edward had trained me in a new kind of conversation. Who would I have spoken to about it before? My mother? That would have been absurd. Just because she had raised a half-African son, it didn't mean she had the faintest idea about such things. There are some things you can only explore with your own kind of people. My mother was my mother, and she had a strong sense of empathy, but she wasn't black.

# Nigeria

In January 1991, I moved to Munich, to a tiny studio apartment with an exorbitant rent, but it was in Schwabing – a good location. I had to do my national service, which was gratifying from one point of view: I had been drafted by the district recruitment office, which proved they considered me a fully valid German citizen. Voting was all well and good, having a passport was important, but both were rights granted to you. To be called on to perform one's duty in the army like everyone else, however, was a mutual obligation, a give and take, a genuine covenant. Even on this sovereign question, where blood undoubtedly played a role, there were no reservations about my person. I was treated like everyone else. The fatherland called and wasn't surprised when I responded. I was allowed to die for Germany. I was graded for medical fitness at T2 (I was slightly offended), but they didn't seem to think I would be better off with the Foreign Legion. Many interesting branches of the armed forces were open to me, the doctor confirmed. Once this point was established to my satisfaction, I opted for alternative national service – community service – instead of joining the military, and found a position at the Bavarian Red Cross.

Would anyone be surprised that I was doing national service? I wasn't sure I could rule out that reaction. There were enough narrow-minded bigots, after all, so to be on the safe side I braced myself for surprised looks. But there was nothing. Nobody asked, 'Why do you have to do national service? Are you German?' It was only within myself that this worry lingered on, albeit in miniature and locked away in the furthest, darkest and most irrational chamber of my heart. It was there all the same, still glowing like the embers the morning after a barbecue.

In 1992, I began studying literature and philosophy at Ludwig Maximilian University. During my first semester break in October, I had a holiday in Greece with friends. We went by car and ferry so we could take two surfboards with us. Three weeks later, when my friends dropped me off at my apartment on Clemensstrasse, I opened my mailbox in the foyer, in the joyful hope there might be letters awaiting me. The first thing I saw when I opened the mailbox door was an unusual envelope made of coarse, cheap paper, marked with 'Godwin Hospital' in bold. I had never heard of Godwin Hospital before, yet straight away knew this was from my father. I fished out the other letters too and thought, 'Damn. Here we go.'

I climbed the stairs to my apartment. I hadn't yet opened the letter, but I already knew what it said and what was in store for me. From now on, I had a father. I sighed. I felt dizzy. An unknown man from a distant country writes you a letter, and because he provided you with half of your genes, you have to comply with his desire to initiate a relationship, otherwise you'll be seen as callous. This is how it was, how it would turn out, I thought to myself as I unlocked the front door. This man was going to muscle his way into my life, and the fact that I had lived 22 years without him would no longer count for anything. Higher powers would come into play, robbing me of my freedom. I put my backpack down and closed the door. I took a beer from the fridge, lit a cigarette, and opened the letter.

I had never thought about my father. As far as I was concerned, he wasn't even a blank space. I had never once had the classic idea of searching for my long-lost father, and in the not entirely illogical assumption that there would be total internal symmetry, I had also not once anticipated him searching for his long-lost son. Why, after 22 years, should the status quo suddenly have to change?

This letter spelled the start of something new that I hadn't asked for. Simply ignoring it – return to sender, address unknown – wasn't an option. After all, it was in my interests that those around me saw me as not entirely heartless, and a normal, empathetic person would be expected to respond to a letter from his own father. Yet I had more right than Henry IV to say, 'I know thee not, old man.'

Wasn't everything just fine as it was? Hadn't I long overcome everything difficult and questionable in my life? Wasn't that proof enough that a fully valid existence was possible without a father?

I opened the letter. My father's handwriting was surprisingly legible. 'My dear son Ijeoma' – and I was taken aback. I could hardly insist that he had my name wrong, but on the other hand I wasn't about to accept that I had myself misspelled it my entire life. Had my first name lost its 'e' on its long journey from Igboland to the Heidelberg registration office? Or was my spelling a simplified version for international use?

I read on. 'I hope you will not be surprised to get this my letter. It is not usual for one to introduce himself to his child but in this circumstance I have to do it.' My father explained that he had had cause to come to Germany, and since my mother was fortunately still living in Heidelberg he had managed to find her in the phone book straight away. She had received his call very kindly and had given him my address. Of course, this letter wasn't an easy one to write. I must have often 'thought about it' over the past twenty years (he was wrong there), but that was the way things were. He had 'never, never' forgotten me. The distance and lack of an address made it impossible for him to get in touch. But blood was thicker than water, and he begged me to forgive him, because no matter how you looked at it, we belonged together. He added that he would love to hear how I felt about all of this and that he hoped that my feelings weren't bitter. Then he invited me to Nigeria. At this point he switched to a very fluent German, saying it would be fine to answer him in German, and adding that later he would 'introduce my contact in Germany' (which sounded a bit like the old world of the secret service, but it may just have been down to the fact that he was using a language he hadn't used for a while).

I can no longer remember my precise reaction to what was written in my father's first letter. I've told this story too often to be able to fully trust my current version. What I do know is this. Whenever someone asked how my father explained his absence for twenty years and his sudden reappearance, I would always quote that one sentence from his letter: 'Blood is thicker than water.' It was as if his entire letter had been reduced to that sentence for me. A sentence that I had a few issues with. I found it absurd. Appealing to a blood connection wasn't, in my view, a sensible basis for a reunion. Blood was an illusion; what counted were the relationships that I had cultivated – and here I thought of one of my mother's favourite phrases, one which used to bring me out in hives whenever she used it to refer to me. In my mother's eyes, everything that had value in life needed to be 'worked through,' with earnest concentration. It was socialisation, not genetics, that had made me who I was: my mother's love, not my father's seed. By invoking blood, he was in a way disregarding my personal history.

I hadn't even spoken to him on the phone and already it felt like I was arguing with him in my head.

But the question of how I felt privately about receiving my father's letter had no impact on how I responded. Like I said, I felt powerless somehow. It was perfectly clear that I would accept his outstretched hand; it was just as obvious that I couldn't reply with a critical analysis of the concept of blood ties. And besides, my mother was unambiguous about what she expected of me. Everything had fallen into place, and as far as she was concerned, this was the chance to finally get to know my wonderful father. For her, my father showing up was the most natural thing in the world, in fact, it was precisely what she had always expected. The fact that 22 years had passed before this most natural thing happened was a mere formality. It was almost as if she was bursting to ask, 'So, did I promise too much? He's a very fine man, your father!'

I don't remember what I wrote in my reply to this first letter, but I suspect that I played for time before finally sitting down to put pen to paper. If he was suddenly going to assume a paternal role now, so late in my life, then I wanted to keep his involvement and interference to the bare minimum. In fact, his next letter didn't arrive until three months later. My letter must have been cordial and amenable enough, because my father was in high spirits. In his second letter he told me who his 'contact person' was. I had four half-sisters, and the oldest, Ikunna, had recently started studying medicine in Heidelberg. He gave me her address at her student residence and her phone number: 06221... So my half-sister had the same area code that I had grown up with. He suggested I should get in touch with her; she knew all about me and couldn't wait to get to know her brother. His other daughters in Nigeria would jump for joy when they heard.

Good grief, I thought, wasn't it a bit soon to jump for joy? They didn't even know me yet!

Everything else in this letter was devoted to practical matters. It was all about getting me to my homeland as quickly as possible. My father didn't once seem to consider that his plans might somehow clash with my own. I was simply expected to be available. It made the most sense if I flew to Nigeria with my sister, he explained; as soon as Ikunna had visited me in Munich, he would buy the tickets. And he even proposed that I flew from Frankfurt, which struck me as a bit odd, as if I couldn't work that out myself. His suggested route: Munich – Frankfurt – Lagos – Port Harcourt. .

Not long after that letter, Ikunna visited me in Munich. On the phone, she told me that she had a friend, Michael, a fellow medical student whom she had met at the University of Heidelberg and who was also from Nigeria. She would bring him with her; he sent his regards.

I nervously waited on the platform. I saw them step off the train. It wasn't hard to recognise each other, in this crowd of white faces. Ikunna hugged me. I was amazed that she seemed not in the slightest bit self-conscious. Not at all shy or embarrassed. It was sibling love at first sight. At least from her perspective, which was so natural that I had no choice but to go along with it. 'My dear brother,' she said in her Nigerian accent. I sensed that her affection for me had nothing to do with any specific, individual characteristics, nothing to do with me personally – for that she would need to get to know me first. It was based entirely on my genealogical status; this was the only reason there was any closeness from the first moment. This was before any relationship had emerged, any authentic feelings. The possibility hadn't even crossed her mind her own brother might actually turn out to be a bit crap.

That weekend, we walked through the English Garden and the Isar floodplains, to the Flaucher river beach and the beer garden at the Chinese Tower – but no matter what I did or said, Ikunna always patted my shoulder and rolled her eyes as though nothing about me surprised her, as if she already knew me inside out, as if she wanted to say, 'Typical! That's just like him – my dear brother!' Sometimes her laugh also seemed to mean, 'How could he be any different!' – as if to say, he's a spitting image of his father, and yet also different, because he's untouched by his father's upbringing. 'You are *so funny*,' she said. I didn't know what to make of this at first. Yes, I had a cheerful disposition, I wasn't gloomy, but no one had previously identified me as having a special talent for telling jokes, so this 'funny' had to mean something else. I was presumably 'funny' because, without knowing it, I defied conventions that Ikunna might have expected of her father's son. Funny qualified the way that we differed despite our common origins, despite certain similarities. It is quite possible that with this qualification as 'funny' I was even granted a certain freedom within the scope of the stricter standards of Nigerian society. 'He is a little bit *funny*, but we love him.'

It was Michael who sometimes gave me a canny look, as if he recognised that this sibling intimacy demanded of me in an instant must have been out of the blue, perhaps because he wasn't part of the family, and therefore saw me not exclusively as the brother, but an independent person from Germany, for whom this new Nigerian way of seeing things might take some getting used to.

But there was also a hierarchical aspect to Ikunna's sibling love. She made it quite clear that although she would help me out if I was ever a bit lost with regard to the family and what was expected of me, in other regards she would happily submit to my command. She treated me not only as a brother, but as an older brother: *funny* in some aspects of his behaviour and perspective, but already blessed with the wisdom of seniority. As a firstborn you had more responsibility, more experience, more oversight. This was a status that came with the executive power to make decisions, but what was I supposed to do with that? I didn't even want to make any decisions.

Ikunna had a sunny disposition, in that we were alike. She had already been in Heidelberg for over a year and had completed a kind of foundation year. She had just started studying medicine. Her German was excellent and she enjoyed slipping in local Kurpfalz dialect expressions when she spoke. She didn't know what to make of the many books in my apartment, but she displayed a certain respect for them, seeing in them a sign of my intelligence, which, given the family I was from, didn't surprise her. She herself was hardworking and disciplined, and yet relaxed with it. She often did night shifts at the weekends to finance her studies; the money she received from her parents wasn't quite enough.

I admired her wonderful hair – such long, tight braids. She nudged me on the shoulder and laughed at me for being so naive. They were artificial braids that she hooked into her real hair which was actually short.

Did we look alike? Hard to say. All the same, Ikunna was thrilled about the resemblance between me and our father: I was his spitting image! I didn't have any opinion about it. In any case, it was enough of a struggle to overcome my inner resistance to her use of the phrase 'our father'. Had we already reached a point where this man, whom I still hadn't met, deserved to be called 'my father'? I pictured a Western European rom-com, where the girlfriend's flicking through an IKEA catalogue and the boyfriend says, 'Things are moving a bit too fast!'

In the following months, Ikunna and I saw each other a lot, sometimes in Munich, sometimes in Heidelberg. My mother was often there with us, too. Hell bent on making the most of this opportunity to establish an extended family at last, she invited Ikunna to dinner, to sing Christmas carols, to paint Easter eggs, to go to the opera. I think it was sometimes a little too much for Ikunna. Mama never forgot her birthday, she remembered every exam and showered her with the appropriate care and attention. Ikunna also had to get used to the abundance of postcards and letters my mother loved to send. It was years before Mama said to me, a little disappointed, that she got very little back from Ikunna. I didn't think anyone could blame her for that. As strong as Ikunna's family spirit was, and however much she liked my mother, she was just a fling from the past.

My mother was always keen to stress that my father was Igbo. But I didn't know what to make of the term. If words are used by others with awe, but fail to fill themselves with life, they sound hollow. This had changed since Ikunna came into my life; she explained for example that she could immediately recognise an Igbo in a crowd of other Africans, just as I could tell a Swede from a Frenchman. And I definitely looked Igbo.

Michael, her friend, however, didn't. Unfortunately, not only did he not look like an Igbo, he wasn't one either. Michael was Yoruba, and that was a problem. A marriage between an Igbo woman and a Yoruba man wouldn't go down at all well. Ikunna explained that there was good reason for it, although to me it seemed like a pretext. The Yoruba were traditionally not Christian and men would often marry several women. Polygamy wasn't prohibited there, she argued, so as an Igbo woman you never knew how exclusive your marriage would be. In truth, I got the impression that the Igbo considered their blood to be so noble that it shouldn't be mixed with anyone else's.

Michael was a Christian and as such was monogamous. But all the same, their relationship had no future, and they both knew it. Our father had met Michael during a visit to Germany in 1992, but it was clear that their relationship would only be tolerated while Ikunna was studying abroad. Our sisters in Nigeria had no idea about Michael, and Ikunna asked me not to mention him when I was there.

Over time I got to know my African family through what my sister told me. Brief introductory lessons. The Ezebuikes lived in Aba, she told me, in eastern Nigeria, where my father's hospital was also located. But life in the city was only one part of it; the village the father comes from is also important for a Nigerian family. That is where the family roots are. That's why the family always goes to Amucha, their village, at the weekends. I already knew that. When Mama explained to me as a child why my father went back to Nigeria, she always mentioned the village that had funded his studies abroad and that he wanted to give back what they had given him. When Ikunna added that our father was the chief of Amucha, this was news to me. Chief, I asked, amused; what did that mean? A local chief, who supported the village financially and had authority on important issues, Ikunna explained. Nothing to smirk about, apparently.

I also learned from her that my father had chronic kidney disease and therefore had to be hooked up to a dialysis machine every day, which was very exhausting. But above all, Ikunna talked about another strange illness I had never heard of, sickle cell disease. It was a genetic disease that only black people get, she told me, widespread mainly in West Africa. If both parents had sickle cell trait, then their children had a 50% chance of inheriting it, and a one in four chance of being born with sickle cell disease, which was fatal in almost all cases.

And this was the fate of our family. Both of her parents carried the gene and three of their children had suffered from sickle cell anaemia: my half-sister Nneka, who faced awful, painful recurring crises, and her two brothers Kezie and Ejike.

Kezie had died the previous year, in 1991, at the age of 11, Ejike nine months later at 10.

Ikunna added that I didn't need to worry. I was safe because my mother was German so she wouldn't have the genetic trait.

So I not only had four half-sisters, but also two dead half-brothers? My grief over their loss was perhaps better described as piety. I could hardly say, 'I've lost two brothers!' Their death lay in a past where they hadn't even existed for me.

But this left me, the firstborn, as the only son my father had left.

My father wanted me to travel to Nigeria over Easter 1993, during the semester break in March and April. This was the best time of the year in terms of the climate – dry heat, no rain. He tried to persuade me, but it was all going a bit too quickly for me, and I wasn't prepared to postpone my mid-term exam because of a trip to Nigeria. So we agreed on August and September.

And at some point I'd got a visa, my ticket to Lagos was booked, and I'd had all the vaccinations I needed, when my father called me. There was a change to the plan. He said he was just about to travel to Germany himself for a kidney transplant he had long waited for and which was now finally feasible. His sister would accompany him and donate her kidney, in an act of selfless solidarity. The advantage was that, given the genetic similarity, there was less chance of rejection. The operation would take place at the university hospital in Essen and he would have to stay in Essen for a few months for routine check-ups following the transplant. None of this should have any impact on my travel plans, after all, it was about finally getting to know Nigeria, he assured me, with him personally playing just a subordinate role. Everyone in Nigeria was ready and waiting for my visit. Before I set off, Ikunna and I should visit him in Essen, because he would arrive a week before our departure. We could spend the night in Bochum with an old friend of his, an Indian doctor whom he knew from his student days. It was all planned.

Was I excited? Certainly, but not in a drop-everything sense. 'Excited' is when you have expectations that might be disappointed, when something's at stake, when there's the risk that the woman you want to spend your life with might reject you. That wasn't the case here. Of course it's nice if you get on with your own father, but I wouldn't have been hugely disappointed if things had turned out differently. I wasn't on tenterhooks exactly. As soon as I was sitting on the train from Heidelberg to Essen with my sister, I felt like I had been fed into a family machine that was ticking over steadily and that nothing could put a spanner in the works.

Shortly afterwards, Ikunna and I rang the doorbell of a guest apartment at the hospital in Essen, and he opened the door. There he stood – maybe half a head shorter than me, but with a sovereign demeanour. His movements were measured, his eyes alert and sparkling. When he smiled it was warm, but by no means jovial. The sort of person you would approach gingerly, with respect. He would certainly have been a strict father. I couldn't help noticing his belly; it was round, as if he had a handball stuffed up his shirt. He later told me that this was a side effect of dialysis. His hair was receding. There was no mistaking that my cheek bones were from him.

He gave me a dignified hug. He welcomed me into a room that wasn't particularly cosy, but that didn't seem to bother my father. He laughed proudly and contentedly, as if to say, 'You're amazed, aren't you? How did I pull it off?' Then he pulled a huge present out from a suitcase, urging me to open it straight away. It was a white robe, like the kind chiefs wear on official occasions, with a kind of sceptre, a round shield made of white and brown fur that you held by a short wooden handle at chest height. My father wanted me to put the robe on there and then, and he got changed into one, too. Then we went outside in our matching outfits, and Ikunna took the first official photos of the chief and his son in the car park at Essen University Hospital. Like an emergency baptism, the contrast between the solemn significance of the ceremony and the prosaic backdrop underscored the urgency of the investiture. It was very important, my father said, that I take the robe with me to Nigeria.

We are both smiling in the photos, but I think we both had very different thoughts going through our heads. For my father and sister, the chieftaincy attire was part of a lived tradition, an expression of a genuine function, rooted in the social cosmos of Amucha. In contrast, I just felt like I was posing in fancy dress in the car park.

I think my father must have been so deeply convinced of the predominance of genetics that he showed not the slightest surprise or relief at being faced with a reasonably presentable son, who posed no obvious danger to the dynastic succession. He didn't pat me on the shoulder. Accustomed to frequent and profuse praise from my mother, I had expected at least a hint of it from my father, if only in the form of a gentle sigh of relief that his son wasn't a psycho drug addict. But for my father, such a possibility hadn't even crossed his mind. He could, so to speak, vouch for my sound character with his good blood. And he basically seemed to be counting on my gratitude for the precious gift of his DNA.

After we had changed back again, my father and I left Ikunna behind and headed to a dreary cafe near the hospital for coffee and cake. The idea was presumably to have a moment of confidentiality between father and son. But we didn't have too much to say to each other, which is hardly surprising given how little we knew each other. My father had a friendly, venerable kind of grin, which I was also quite good at (I had presumably got it from him), so we grinned at each other in our friendly and venerable way. It was all just as exhausting as I had anticipated. Could someone seriously come along out of the blue and make me dress up like a village chief?

Then we went to Bochum to meet my father's old friend, the Indian doctor, who had two tantalisingly pretty daughters my age. During dinner, as my father was talking to his colleague about medical issues, I marvelled at the daughters and suddenly wished my father was Indian. Out of nowhere I suddenly had an irrepressible curiosity about India. The truth was probably that at that moment any country in the world would have seemed less distant, more attractive, more familiar, more acceptable to me than Nigeria of all places. Brazil, for example. Why, dear God, why couldn't it have been Brazil? It would be a nice thing to be half-Brazilian. Brazil was all flirting on the beach and cocktails. But it was too late for prayers; our plane tickets were booked and Lagos awaited.

My somewhat acerbic mood that accompanied me on the Lufthansa flight from Frankfurt to Lagos set me up well for my first steps onto Nigerian soil. Ikunna was waved through at passport control, while the border guard withheld my passport, conveying to me with an expression of weary annoyance that something was missing. I didn't even have to weigh up the options. My mother had scrimped and saved every penny to help me, I wasn't going to blow it all on a bribe. If someone was going to be making demands around here, it was me! Wide eyed, I explained to the border official that my English was bad, unfortunately I didn't understand. Was there something wrong with my visa? If I'm not welcome here, no problem, I'll turn around and fly right back. Coming here wasn't my idea anyway! But clearly he wasn't in the slightest bit impressed by my excuse.

The man stared in my direction like someone who had experienced a certain amount of audacity in his career, but never an excuse as pathetic as a lack of language skills. Was this what he had served all this time for, worn down by his years of servitude? As if bribes were a question of grammar and not an internationally comprehensible language of their own, like a smile or a threatening gesture! For a moment the border guard seemed unsure about how best to put an end to this undignified spectacle. Then suddenly his expression was a mixture of authoritarian vexation and an all-round weariness with life, as if to say, with a groan, 'Enough fucking around. What's the point in dragging it out? You don't seriously think you'll get away with it?' We were at an impasse, and I was aware that, with the best will in the world, an official emblazoned with his national heraldry was hardly about to give in. This was about the honour of the Nigerian system, so to speak. For my part, I had no desire to play the stickler for principles, to carry it out to the bitter end, only to then draw the short straw; it was clear to me that the poor officer had little choice but to transform his tormented vexation into pure aggression the very next moment, if both parties were to be released from the paralysis of this absurd drama. In that moment, a young man, accompanied by a man in uniform, approached from the other side of passport control. The official gave a hand signal, and the customs officer sighed as though this was all he needed at the end of a long day, and promptly handed me back my passport.

The young man was my cousin, Reginald, who now welcomed me to Nigeria with a certain stiffness. Ikunna had already told me of his enormous wealth. He was in his mid-thirties and he was already the CEO of a Nigerian bank.

I had just a few weeks previously read in the *Frankfurter Allgemeine Zeitung* that the route into Lagos from the airport was particularly dangerous. There were frequent robberies, and the Nigerian gangs tended to make short work of their victims after they had handed over their valuables. Why would they leave a living witness? The article had said that embassy staff now only drove the route in convoy.

Reginald had an SUV and wasn't shy about putting his foot to the floor. It was after midnight. I could hardly see a thing out of the window. Ikunna was talking to our cousin, but it seemed he wasn't exactly a chatterbox. Eventually we turned into a small street that led to a row of mansions surrounded by high walls. My cousin's house was like a fortress: the property was surrounded by a tall wall, topped with barbed wire. He honked the horn, armed guards wrenched open the great gate, and with a screech of the tyres we turned into the interior of the citadel. Inside, the mild atmosphere of an oasis from the Arabian Nights, the unassuming elegance of a sultan's palace with numerous inner courtyards and bubbling fountains. Domestic workers scurried quietly through the corridors, and I wouldn't have been surprised to find two dignified gentlemen playing chess in one of the courtyards. The air conditioning buzzed, the diesel generator hummed an octave lower. In Nigeria back then the power went out almost every night, and if you didn't have a diesel generator you'd find yourself sitting in the dark. Continuous power supply was a status symbol of the Nigerian upper class.

I wasn't related by blood to my cousin Reginald. He had married Ugochi, my father's niece. She greeted me effusively. I went to take a shower, and was then served an evening meal. I smiled at everyone without exception, giving everyone the same heartfelt smile, because I didn't know who was family and who was staff.

The next morning, they let me sleep in a while, and then I met Ugochi's children. They had two daughters, who were four and six years old, and a son who was learning to walk. The daughters looked beautiful and very spoiled. Mostly they were dressed identically, in cute little European style dresses, in red or pink. When I photographed them, they posed in a skilful mix of bashfulness and coquetry.

Ikunna and I spent a week in Lagos.

While Ugochi was keen to make me, her new cousin, feel at home and show me Lagos, her husband kept his distance. He maintained a sphynx-like aloofness. I couldn't figure him out. We sat together at the breakfast table, CNN on the TV, him reading the *Financial Times*, and his serious face only lit up when his son was propped up on his lap. At that point, the nanny stepped back to leave the father and son alone for a moment of tenderness.

I thought the *Financial Times* might be a good starting point for a conversation ('You have to communicate!'), but

Reginald wasn't interested in idle chatter with me about global politics. If I tried to ask something about his work as a banker, he would react defensively, as if I needn't trouble myself feigning interest just to be polite. Sometimes he would accidentally tut to himself when CNN was delivering some breaking news, but when I myself commented on events, he would turn away with a smile. He treated me with respect but didn't ask me anything. Had he had a bad experience of opening up or getting too close, which, after all, always degenerated into shameless begging? It was clear that Ikunna and I were the poor relatives (Ikunna had already hinted that I had better not get used to the luxury of our cousin's house), but that wasn't the sum of it, because he was perfectly generous in his hospitality. It was as if he were ready to put his household at my disposal with all the conveniences it had to offer, but he had no intention of sharing his own thoughts or his inner life with me.

There was one occasion when Reginald received a large group of guests. The roof terrace was decorated festively and a buffet was served. The guests were radiant in their colourful traditional attire. This was a gathering of earnest men, all engaged in serious and important conversation. I was curious to get to know these people, so I attempted to approach, but although my cousin saw me out of the corner of his eye, he didn't ask me to join them. It must have been a very high-ranking and distinguished gathering, with a very selective guest list. I withdrew again, disappointed.

His wife Ugochi was as attentive as her husband was aloof. There was a schedule planned for every day, but she never told me beforehand what exactly she had planned, and even afterwards I was seldom sure what had been planned and what had happened by chance along the way. The principle of sightseeing didn't seem to exist. All planned activities dissolved into chance occurrences in the perpetual traffic jam of the megacity.

Lagos seemed to me like a city that consisted not so much of houses as of roads: multi-lane highways traversed by millions of drivers proceeding at a breakneck standstill. The congested labyrinths were like waterfalls frozen in winter, impossible to distinguish between motion and paralysis. The whole time I had the feeling that we weren't actually on a highway, but on a slip road, a feeder road, in an underpass, on a bridge or approaching an intersection. Every destination was swallowed up by transition.

Indeed, in this city of 14 million residents, the traffic was mostly mired in gridlock. From the car window, I saw overcrowded buses creeping along with passengers' upper bodies leaning out of the open windows. The stationary carriageways were transformed into a marketplace. Vendors buzzed around the motionless cars. You could buy everything from the comfort of your vehicle, from biscuits to books, handkerchiefs to crayfish (strung up in long chains while their claws still snapped open and shut sluggishly).

We drove to a golf club on a peninsula in the Atlantic Ocean where all the Europeans hung out. We had a soft drink and then drove back again. What was the purpose of this outing? To demonstrate that my cousin was a member of the golf club?

At the time, Lagos was considered the most exciting city in Africa. Connoisseurs raved about the music scene, though of course it wasn't exactly my kind of music. The city's nightlife also had a legendary reputation, and that was more what I was interested in now, but a detour to a bar or a club was certainly not on Ugochi's itinerary. And I wasn't allowed out alone; that was considered far too dangerous, and probably with good reason. I felt as though I were being carried around on a sedan chair, in forced passivity.

Only once did I sense a hint of something mysterious and exciting, the promise of adventure. We arrived at some kind of restaurant, basically a wooden shed crowded with guests, but the venue's improvised character was superbly staged and the swirl of guests seemed to follow a common rhythm, a kind of casual theatricality. We ate chicken pepper soup, the Nigerian speciality, which can blow the head off a European with its intense quantity of chillies. The restaurant must have been located in a district known for its bohemian nightlife; the streets were full of cheerful people walking past the open windows, a chaotic hustle and bustle. We drank beer from the can, I smoked, although my cousin looked on disapprovingly (whenever I smoked in Nigeria, people looked at me as if I had dragged myself out of the gutter), and for a moment I had the fleeting feeling that I was alive, that thrill of being in a new place. I would have liked to seek out adventure and come back here on my own, but of course that was out of the question; I wasn't allowed to go anywhere unaccompanied.

Another time we went to the Atlantic coast to have a picnic on the beach. We sat down on a large brightly coloured blanket, a good distance from the sea, because the shore was being pounded by huge ocean waves. We ate and gazed at the water, no different from the many other groups along the busy beach. The waves were noisy and beautiful. This was the same Atlantic that bordered the coasts of France and England and that washed around New York on the other side. A reassuring thought. I immediately felt less like I was abandoned on a strange shore.

My gaze rested on a dot in the surf. Something was bobbing in the waves. A branch of a tree, a plastic sheet? While the barely perceptible process of elimination had already settled on an answer, my optimistic mind was still reluctant to give up hope. *Oh no, please don't let it be a person!* But of course it was exactly that: a dead person, a drowned body, finally released from its amphibious ambivalence, now washed up on the beach. Everyone – my family and all the other picnickers on the beach – seemed to identify the situation at the same moment. The body lay there on the sand before us. All around me, everyone on the beach did the same thing: we got up, folded our blankets, sauntered along the shore out of sight of the dead man, and spread out our blankets to sit down again.

This wasn't to be my only encounter with death in Nigeria. A few weeks later I was on the road with Hippolite, another cousin, on a trip to the north of the country. We were on a country road when we saw a dead man lying in the carriageway. Hippolite had the presence of mind to swerve around the body. He didn't comment on the incident.

'Hippolite, there was a dead man on the street!'

Hippolite looked at me blankly. 'Yes, I saw it. I dodged it in time.'

'Are we just going to leave it there?'

'Why? Do you know him? Is it a friend of yours?'

I had to admit that my somewhat pompous sympathy was of a purely abstract nature.

The road to Reginald's house had very little traffic. It wasn't a thoroughfare, it only connected the mansions in the neighbourhood and there weren't many of them. And yet it was full of huge potholes, which Ugochi had to swerve around in her Lexus. Of course, in an SUV, she didn't exactly need to worry about a few bumps. But I couldn't understand it. The residents were evidently all filthy rich, so why didn't they get the road fixed? It would be entirely for their own benefit;

it's not as if it would even be a charitable act for the general public, since it was only residents who drove on it. It appeared as though concerning oneself with anything beyond the walls of one's private estate was unfathomable.

As a child I had always feared that I would be associated with Africa, the continent of famine, and now here I was and I had stepped into a world of wealth the likes of which I had never seen before. Was this the class that was plundering their country's rich resources? Was banking an honourable profession in Nigeria? How did you become a banker, anyway? Through academic excellence or because you belonged to the right family? Reginald was unfortunately no help with such questions, and Ikunna wasn't particularly forthcoming either. All she said was, our cousin was just really rich but, 'we're not, by the way. Just so you're not disappointed later.'

Once I was sitting at the table with Ugochi and Ikunna, with the television on in the background, when Ugochi yelled: 'My husband!' I looked around, but Reginald wasn't here. Finally I realised that her husband was on TV. In fact, the news report was about how he had just been appointed CEO of the leading Nigerian bank. The bright young banker! Maybe it had been a little naive of me to try and muscle in on that gathering of worthy gentlemen a few days ago. They had been doing business.

Despite Reginald's fame, it was clear that his wife's family, the Ezebuikes, were also highly esteemed within the walls of his compound. Education didn't necessarily lead to wealth or property, as in Heidelberg, but the propertied class showed a respect for education. Reginald had a Master's degree from the London School of Economics. Perhaps he had met the former director Ralf Dahrendorf, whose 'European Diary' I had been feverishly following in the Munich newspaper the *Merkur*?

But Reginald never spoke to me about his time in Europe, although it might have been the ideal common experience to kickstart a conversation. I found him unfathomable. For all I knew, his detached reticence might have been a spiralling double helix of LSE haughtiness and Nigerian arrogance. As if he were thinking, 'The European circles I move in are a few sizes too big for my impudent cousin. Best to keep quiet rather than embarrass him.' (Just like Swann in Proust's *In Search of Lost Time*, when he visits Marcel's parents and his aunts in Combray. They consider him an insignificant Jew, and he refrains from name-dropping his dazzling connections at the Paris Jockey Club, because he has moved in social circles so many levels above the world of his aunts that he doesn't care a jot if they fail to perceive the real him.)

I hadn't exactly imagined a straw hut waiting for me in Nigeria, but this was something else. What would it be like at my father's in Aba? More modest, of course. All the same, I wasn't indifferent to the question of money. I knew it was a base reaction, but sometimes when I thought of my father I remembered bitterly how Mama really hadn't had it easy. She had done everything she could to spoil me, generously supporting me far beyond her means, while my father had never paid a penny towards my upkeep. I was ashamed of even thinking this, also aware that my resentment wasn't justified, because my mother had always insisted that she didn't want anyone else's money, she wanted to be independent, it was all her free choice. But when I saw this sultan's palace and thought about the miserable carpet in our three-room apartment, you could almost see a cartoon-strip angry black cloud over my head. At the same time, I reminded myself it was nonsense. 'We're just guests here,' I told myself. 'My father has no access to this wealth.'

But there was another side to it. Since I had these new relatives all of a sudden, it wasn't so bad to realise that at least I came from what was considered to be a good family. In crude terms, my newly discovered paternal line represented a social step up in the world. What would Florian have to say about that?

Everything was new and exotic, and yet from day one I struggled with a kind of boredom. Part of that had to do with my lack of independence, but most of all I missed conversation. How thrilling it would have been to have someone to share my impressions with! Of course, there was always chatter and laughter, but nobody ever asked me about my life – what I was interested in, what I was doing in Germany, where I had been, what I thought of Nigeria. I almost didn't care what the focus was, I just missed the kind of discussion where you hammered away at a topic, swapping experiences and perspectives of the world – conversation as a means to get a better idea of who the other person is.

My cousin flew to London every two months to go shopping. I had been to London too, London could have been a topic of conversation, but she couldn't think of anything to say about the place. She loved London, that was all Ugochi had to say, and that was the end of the subject.

Yet I was the son of a mother whose core belief was the importance of communication! Why didn't anyone here want to hear my story? I felt like as far as they were concerned my life from birth to my arrival in Lagos was just a kind of extended stay at boarding school, over there somewhere near England, where my cousin went shopping. A genuine conversation was guided by curiosity about the other, you could talk about anything under the sun, but you kept on answering and asking questions to find out something about each other's personality, preferences and idiosyncrasies. You were supposed to talk and talk until you shared your broken heart or your marital problems; that was when you got to know someone – in the world where I was from, at least. I felt out of place, because I did not experience that mode of conversation here.

Another cousin of mine stopped by a few times while I was in Lagos. He was of slender build, wore elegant suits, and had a laconic wit. He was an architect. I was already jumping for joy inside: an intellectual! But even he couldn't quench my thirst for conversation. He had married a striking woman, who was, however, Yoruba. For his father, my uncle, this was a disaster. It was by no means hushed up, but it was mentioned with the terse defeatism with which you might accept a cruel stroke of fate. The conflict wasn't psychologically dissected, my cousin didn't say: 'Ijoma, I have to tell you something, so you'll understand me and where I'm coming from.' By the same token, he didn't expect me to say: 'Here's my shoulder, have a good cry!'

Let's put it this way. The approach to conversing and interacting with people didn't follow the laws of the psychological novel here, like it did at home. My family on my father's side lived in the genre of the epic: all action rather than sentimental journey. It was all pathos, not analysis; the focus on the dynastic, not the individual. Here, it was all about life's major plotlines, not about weighing up miniscule personal traumas on golden scales. Birth, marriage, death – those were the key elements of the plot, and whatever feelings, affectations, ruminations or melancholy simmered away in between, everyone kept all of it to themselves.

After a week in Lagos, Ikunna and I left my cousin's house and flew to Port Harcourt in a jittering plane with no seat reservations. I'm not afraid of airplane accidents, but I couldn't help thinking with a certain bitterness what grim irony it would be if I were to die in Nigeria of all places! The neurotic safety rituals associated with European airlines played no role here. Ikunna and I scrambled for two seats, and the plane rattled off.

Compared to Reginald's mansion, my father's house in Aba was a clear downgrade. This property was walled too, but the wall was lower and you could easily climb over with a leg-up. And where my cousin had an entire Praetorian Guard on duty, here there was just one old chap with a limp prowling my father's yard, who from a distance looked a miserable sight. He was kept on by the family out of the goodness of their hearts, although they could hardly expect he would be of any use in the event of a robbery. This spectre of a security guard would surely surrender to any intruders before he had even pulled out the gun like a fancy-dress toy lodged in its holster.

Aba, with its one and a half million inhabitants, is located in the southeast of Nigeria, in the Niger Delta. I never got much of a feel for the city, because here again it was kept out behind the walls of our home. A large, unpaved yard surrounded the house, which gave a nice impression of greenery with its many palm trees, if not a particularly cultivated one. There was a pitiful dog; it wasn't clear if its growl was one of lament or a threat. It spent its days in a cage on the side facing away from the entrance, also part of the Ezebuikes' not particularly sophisticated security concept. The house itself was spacious, with two storeys. My room with its own bathroom was on the ground floor, along with the kitchen and the large open-plan dining and living room. The most important pieces of furniture were the sofas in the living room, which you could flop onto at any time. The rest of the family's rooms were upstairs.

In the kitchen – and in the household in general – there wasn't a crowd of domestic staff at work like there was at my cousin's, where each member of the team had their own function without displaying any individuality. Here, there was precisely one good soul who at first glance was treated like everyone else, which is why – confronted daily with a flood of unknown faces who, without exception, introduced themselves as cousins – it was a while before I realised that she wasn't actually part of the family.

In fact, there would have been a simple identifier, but it was a while before I figured that out too. There are over 500 languages spoken in Nigeria. Because the country is a former British colony, English is the official language. The educated classes codeswitch between English and Igbo (or their other language) as if from one mother tongue to another, while the housekeeper spoke only Igbo. We spent the whole time wordlessly beaming at each other to express our goodwill.

The shower only had cold water, so every morning once I'd let her know I was up, the housekeeper would bring a large bucket of hot water and place it in the bathtub, and while I washed, she would prepare my favourite breakfast: a delectable combination of plantains fried in palm oil with scrambled eggs and chilli. The fact that I had already settled on a favourite dish, and that it was fried plantains, was met with applause all round, and on the third day, as soon as I sat down at the table in the morning, it was 'Ah, your beloved plantains again!'

I was taken in as part of the family. The high-octane antics of Lagos gave way to the quiet order of a morally serious, middle-class household. My father's wife, Joyce, watched over everything with a steady hand and astute serenity. She seemed to me an image of might and power, an elegant, stately woman, radiating life and energy in the graceful swing of her

African clothes. Her authority was inviolable. Depending on the situation, she could switch between seriousness and fun, not in the slightest perturbed that the split-second register change might not have been picked up by those around her. She had certain airs, but in Nigeria that's part and parcel of presenting yourself well. Her gaze was clear and sharp; you could see in her eyes that she saw through others' theatrics. She didn't have time for psychological drama either, but when I caught her eye, she looked back at me in a way that made me feel understood.

Otherwise, this iron grip of consanguinity still seemed a bit like a dark, sinister force. It was a relief that I wasn't related to Joyce by blood; that was precisely what made it easier for me to confide in her. There was less of the confused emotionality attached. In any case, Joyce was someone whose advice you would want, given the life experience and judgment that she radiated, while always looking both severe and serene at the same time.

But above all, my three other half-sisters took me under their wing. And how! Since there wasn't much happening and the time passed slowly, we were almost always together, unless I went off on my own to read. Even when I went out to the yard to smoke, they would follow me out, staring at my cigarette and shaking their heads, because they simply couldn't understand how their brother would degrade himself with such a lowly vice as smoking.

The greatest sacrilege I could commit, however, was to use the expression 'half-sister'. I quickly abandoned the prefix 'half' in the interests of familial peace. Inwardly, however, out of respect for the possibilities of language, I was of the opinion that the expression half-siblings, without being in any way derogatory, was more accurate because it took into account the undeniable fact that our common path on this Earth began not from the cradle, but later on. Couldn't the prefix 'half' be seen as more of a factor of distance rather than difference, I wondered to myself? Oh, my secret thoughts were of course pure pettifoggery and they crumbled, quite rightly, before the clarity of my siblings' love.

Ijeure, the youngest, was nine at the time, Nneka fifteen, and Ojugo sixteen. Ijeure had an immense instinct for play, her energy was inexhaustible, and her role as the baby of the family was so infectious that she soon put everyone in a good mood. Ojugo, on the other hand, was the serious, fearful and therefore responsible sister, who was always urging caution and would occasionally, out of her sense of duty, ruin a perfectly good game to avoid things getting out of hand and everyone blowing a fuse.

And then there was Nneka, whom my mother recognised as my 'favourite sister' as soon as I was back home and reporting back on my travels – and she was right. With Nneka, I had a feeling we were related not just in blood but also in soul, for the simple reason that she reflected on her inner life and tried to talk to me about it. That was exactly what I had desperately missed in Nigeria so far. There was something radical about Nneka, although also an air of sadness. She was well at the time, but the fate of sickle cell disease weighed heavily on her. She had suffered many crises in her young life and that may well have shaped her personality. You could tell that the role models available to her were all too stereotypical. She didn't straighten her hair, and that was still a statement at the time. Her skin was as dark as night, not unlike the wooden crocodile of my childhood; even among the family, she had a certain exotic enigma about her. She always tried to pull me away from the rest of the family and lead me off to a secluded spot in the garden. And I was happy to follow her. Then she'd say, 'Tell me, what do you think about...?' With her you could quickly launch into a philosophical discussion, and she was always ready to push conventional assumptions aside. She would roll her eyes in frustration at the ignorance of those around her if she didn't feel understood (isn't feeling misunderstood the beginning of individuality?), and in this way she stood in total contrast to everything I had experienced in Nigeria so far. She built a bubble of introspection around us where we could talk about anything, and I cherished every one of our conversations. We read Shakespeare's *Twelfth Night* out loud together. 'If music be the food of love, play on!' My English was pitiful, and she helped me. In exchange, I could share the things I knew about Shakespeare. And we were able to read the appropriately assigned roles; after all, it's a sibling comedy about separation and reacquaintance.

My relationship with Ikunna evolved when we got to Aba. As the oldest sister, she couldn't join in with this new brother excitement to quite the same extent as her younger siblings. With a nod to her status, she granted herself a certain authority to be in charge, a role that precluded too much silliness. This gave our relationship a more serious, in a sense more mature note.

I first noticed the change on a Saturday morning. The cook had bought a chicken at the market, which had since been held captive in the courtyard, its wings weighed down mercilessly with a large rock. As evening drew closer, Ikunna came to me with a rather blunt kitchen knife and asked me to cut the chicken's neck, a gesture comparable to the honour we extend to a guest in Germany when we let them carve the goose. Ikunna refused to accept my reluctance, my excuses ('I don't know how! I've never done it before!'). She insisted that I should stop making such a fuss, it was easy. I shook my head, horrified, as the hen twitched in panic. It's fair to say, the bird wasn't enjoying this conversation either; there was also something harsh about debating who would cut its throat, there in the presence of the one whose throat was being discussed. In truth, of course, it wasn't about the chicken, but solely about the question of protocol and whether I would live up to my duties as firstborn son. Breaking a chicken's neck was clearly one of those duties of honour.

In fact, I wasn't entirely averse to the idea in principle (I still find the decision only to eat animals you've killed with your own hands a compelling argument), I just couldn't deny that I simply couldn't bring myself to do it. I stuttered something about freezer shelves in the supermarket where chicken breasts came wrapped in cling film. At that moment, I could literally feel my authority crumbling away. Shaking her head disapprovingly – I wouldn't live up to my role, so she had to take command – Ikunna grabbed the chicken, hacked at its neck with the blunt knife for a shockingly long time, as though she were slowly massacring her unwilling (and incompetent, yes, and unworthy) *dear brother*, until finally she cut through and the blood began to flow into the scraped out hollow – not exactly bursting forth ecstatically, but dripping hesitantly, sluggishly, as though completely demoralised by our dispute.

The term 'cousin' has a very broad application in Nigeria, ranging from the greatest familial closeness to distant relatives without any emotional ties. Everyone is always a cousin. Hippolite was a close cousin, almost a kind of adopted son, part of the family, an admirer of my father. From the beginning he seemed to me like an imperial administrator, a loyal lord chamberlain of the House of Ezebuike, a man of honour and principles who, in the head of the household's absence, took hold of the reins only to surrender them – permeated by the magic of legitimacy – to me, as though this transfer of power fulfilled his entire conscience of duty. Hippolite had studied engineering, more precisely medical engineering, and was therefore firmly in charge of the technical side of my father's hospital. He was only slightly older than me, and from the way he interacted with me I had the feeling that he wanted to say, 'We're the future generation. This country will soon rest on our shoulders!' He was uncompromising in maintaining the sartorial style of an old-fashioned gentleman. He tolerated the women's chatter, but with a slight shake of his head he would indicate that, as men, we had important matters to discuss, alone. At such moments I wouldn't have been surprised if he'd said, 'Gentlemen, let us retire to the drawing room.' Unfortunately, he barely drank a drop of alcohol. A cognac would have suited him well.

In short, this was the family house. And ironically, the one thing no one mentioned, the elephant in the room, was how ridiculous it was that my father of all people wasn't there on my first visit to Nigeria. He had prepared the household in such a way that his physical presence during the repatriation of the son wasn't necessary. He sometimes called from Essen. He seemed delighted with how things were going. I always tried to say something to drag out the phone conversation, not because I felt the need to tell my father something, but because I was conditioned to find it embarrassing to ring off after a very brief call, as though we had nothing to say to one another. But in Nigeria it's not the length of a phone call that counts, but the fact that you take the initiative to call. The invention of the mobile phone and SMS messaging has been perfect for Nigerian communication practices; now you can send birthday greetings or wish someone a Merry Christmas with minimal effort and a minimal word count. The ideal is high frequency communication that's always as brief as possible. When my sister Ikunna occasionally called me in Germany later on, I would sometimes ask if I could call her back shortly as I was just about to head out. But that made no sense; I had misunderstood the nature of the call. It wasn't about a long gossipy catch-up, but a quick check-in call whose mission could be considered fulfilled after just three minutes of idle banter. Since Facebook and Twitter began their triumphal march through Nigeria, the frequency of communication could increase again, while radically slashing the overall effort and character count. The Facebook idiom in Nigeria consists of an extremely efficient and compressed form of English: 'How hv u bin? Thanx. Sori bro.' *And* becomes *n, are* is *r* and *see* is *c.* And the sound *th,* which is pronounced in English-speaking Africa with the tongue lingering briefly at the top of the mouth, means *the* is reduced unceremoniously to *d.* 'Luv d pics. Dey r so cute.'

In any case, my father, who had a not unpleasant way of muttering to himself in satisfaction, gave a little chortle on the phone, pleased that everything was going so well. Managers are always glad when things are ticking over nicely without them having to follow anything up. Everything was going according to plan. His operation, the kidney transplant in Germany, and my transfer to Nigeria were both proceeding without complications. My father's chuckle expressed that he was up to date with the news, that he had been kept in the loop, and had concluded from what he had heard that everyone in Nigeria was satisfied with me. At that time I wasn't yet aware of the wide-ranging plans he had for me.

How had I imagined it? What had I expected of this trip? I suppose I had hoped to get through the Nigeria chapter without offending anyone. I was touched by their warmth, the love with which they received me, but I knew that I couldn't return it to the same extent, that I would go back to Germany, and that I had no intention of changing anything about my life. At the same time, hardly a day went by without talk of my next visit to Nigeria. When someone pressed me, I pushed back in the friendliest way I could. As they say, 'I'd better check my calendar before I commit.'

I had already heard about the sickle cell disease from Ikunna. In Aba, too, the illness was mentioned again and again, not so much with regard to our brothers' recent deaths, but for the sake of explaining it all to me. They explained that if you had a German mother and an African father you could marry any African woman you liked, including someone with a predisposition for sickle cell disease. Your children wouldn't be carriers of the disease, because both parents need to carry the appropriate genes in order for it to be passed on. I nodded, confused. What was I supposed to do with this information?

The name 'sickle cell disease' comes from the way the red blood cells become deformed, taking on a sickle shape, and these cells clog the blood vessels and cause serious damage to the body's internal organs. On the other hand, the sickle shape makes it more difficult for the malaria pathogen to establish itself. This is how evolutionary biologists explain the emergence of sickle cell disease as an African phenomenon.

At the time of my trip to Nigeria, it was still really the beginning of the effort to raise awareness about SCD. There was only one protection against it and this was a genetic test. If both partners had the genetic disposition for the diseased haemoglobin S (instead of the healthy haemoglobin A), then you shouldn't have children together. Some Nigerian churches already required a healthy test result before they would marry a couple.

I couldn't ignore the fact that in Aba the question of marriage was never far from people's lips. They didn't push me, it was always mentioned in a light-hearted tone, but still they were keen to show me the opportunities. And in this context, because of my mother's genetic input, I had an indisputable advantage in that I could marry any African woman, regardless of her genetic disposition. No harm in knowing, right? Lucky you!

There was no consideration for the fact that it might have been embarrassing for me to be the object of these matchmaking efforts. The fact that my strong position on the Nigerian marriage market contradicted my own individual concept of and hopes for myself would have been taken for narcissistic arrogance. After all, what was life all about if not getting married, having children, passing on one's blood? It needed organising. Why waste time? I was clearly a good match, although I wasn't sure whether as an Ezebuike or as a German. Presumably as the sum of both strengths.

Whenever the question of marriage arose, I couldn't help asking myself, would my father have contacted me if his two sons hadn't died? My Nigerian family continued to exist in the genre of the epic, while I was the protagonist of my own psychological novel.

The days in Aba felt like a long, steady stream and I was definitely not busy enough. I was bored and even lonely. Despite, or perhaps because of, the affection I received from all sides, I felt lost in a culture that had welcomed me not merely as a guest, but was actively working towards my permanent naturalisation. There was the promise of a road trip to the north of Nigeria with Hippolite and Ikunna, but there were significant fuel shortages at the time, which is why our departure was continually postponed. And I still wasn't even allowed to step outside by myself. If I wanted to go somewhere, it automatically became a family outing. I also missed alcohol as a medium for sociability. As far as I was concerned, you only truly had a shared experience when you drank together, and how socialising was supposed to work without alcohol was completely beyond me at the time.

The most popular beer in Nigeria is called Star. In the evening I would enjoy a cool bottle from the fridge, although nobody joined me. When I had finished, I'd go to the fridge and get another. But once Joyce intervened. Quietly but firmly, she explained that she couldn't reconcile this with her duty of care for my person, and drawing on the example of a time-honoured chronicle of the past to set the standards for our conduct in the present, she explained to me that my father would drink *half* a bottle of Star in the evening, then put the cap back on the bottle and enjoy the other half the following evening. All good things in moderation. She seemed to think the needle on the dial was already in the red zone.

Not only did you have to socialise without alcohol, you also had to forego the freeing power of the night. In Aba, you received guests during the day. You sat together in the living room, in a large group, so there was always only one group conversation (with a Nigerian telenovela in the background, which you sometimes referred to collectively), and you didn't so much talk about specific topics, as enjoy the comforting feeling of being together. It was one round after another of laughter and giggles. I never had the feeling after a guest left that I knew them better than before.

At some point I realised that there were in fact two categories of guests: they were either cousins or potential marriage candidates. The latter could be reliably identified by the fact that they only laughed and didn't say anything – for fear that a wrong word might slip from their lips and be met with my disapproval. The thinking with regards to marriage was becoming ever clearer. They wanted to respect my autonomy and not exert any pressure, obviously they couldn't *make* me do anything, but they also didn't want to miss an opportunity to showcase at least the range of options. Take it or leave it!

The daughter of a toilet paper manufacturer was propelled into the race with a bit more of a nudge. My sisters explained that we had been invited to a wealthy neighbour's home, in the early evening for once. They didn't brush over the fact that the man had made his fortune from toilet paper of all things – on the principle, I suppose, that it's better to come out with it, than wait for me to stumble on the slightly disconcerting detail later. That was the only way to stay in control of proceedings and provide context, without which I might have failed to see that the dignity of the product was ultimately secondary to the question of market penetration, and once you've made it to the position of Nigerian market leader, nobody cared whether you got to the top thanks to the manufacture of personal computers or toilet paper. Incidentally, the neighbour had a daughter.

The toilet paper manufacturer conveniently lived in the house opposite. My sisters and I only had to cross the street. His house was also surrounded by a wall and behind the house was a green courtyard. We sat in a circle in their spacious living and dining room. The head of the house began a conversation with me, speaking with a slow creak, full of gravitas and devoid of vitality, as though dignity could only be achieved by a complete suppression of liveliness. His daughter and my sisters looked at us in silence and with bated breath.

Then isi ewu was served to mark the occasion. This very spicy soup is a Nigerian festive dish that uses every part of a goat's head – the nose, eyes, ears and tongue. It wasn't so much a shared meal as a symbolic act, where everyone watched the guest partake of the dish of honour. Again everyone was sitting in a circle, and the daughter of the toilet paper manufacturer said nothing, while her father served the soup. My sisters had hinted beforehand that it might be better not to overwhelm me with the potentially worrying anatomical details, but I wasn't one to miss out on trying something new, so they insisted: 'Go ahead!'

The problem wasn't so much the body parts included in the dish. The problem was that after just one spoonful of soup, I couldn't breathe. My face turned scarlet, my ears were burning, tears streamed from my eyes. I could no longer stay seated and jumped up from my chair, gasping, while the toilet paper manufacturer looked on baffled. 'It's hot! Hot! Hot!' I was about to faint. Now the house was full of commotion, everyone came running in with a different antidote. I was wiped out for the duration of this visit, and after about an hour, still weak and dizzy, I staggered back across the road. Everyone accepted that the prospects for a relationship with the toilet paper manufacturer's daughter didn't look too promising.

But, perhaps the dramatic excitement of my chili attack had in fact been a helpful diversion from the depressing fact that the daughter had sat there in silence throughout the entire visit? She hadn't exactly fluttered her eyelashes at me, either. Was it nerves that had left her speechless? Or had she assumed that this was how to most credibly qualify as a prospective wife? Someone who wouldn't cause her husband any trouble?

In general, I had the impression that women in Nigeria were relatively emancipated when it came to education and professional training. When it came to family planning, however, arranged marriages were still the norm. Marriage for the sake of love too often led to needless complications – my architect cousin and his Yoruba wife were a prime example of this. And of course there was Ikunna's boyfriend in Germany whose name couldn't even be mentioned. Their relationship was a sort of expat fantasy, bound by the pragmatism of the American motto, 'What happens in Vegas, stays in Vegas.'

My wonderful, very conservative cousin Hippolite was keen for me to be his best man. He wanted me to decide as soon as possible when I would next come to Nigeria so that he could start preparing for the wedding. I wasn't sure when I would come back to Nigeria, or if I would even come back at all. Either way, I didn't think this was the right order in which to do things. Wouldn't it make more sense to first find someone you wanted to marry, then have the conversation about who you'd like to be your best man? Hippolite shook his head, disappointed to hear such nonsense from a fellow adult. Finding the right woman was really not the biggest logistical problem; that would be easy enough once the time frame had been established.

Two months can be a long time when life unfolds entirely at home within the confines of the family. So little happened, and if something did happen, it was rarely anything to get me worked up or excited about. Instead, the time was dominated by lethargy, boredom and loneliness. If only there had been the occasional night out! I kept thinking of that evening when I met the daughters of the Indian doctor in Bochum. If my father had been Brazilian, then I'd have the same dark skin colour and I'd still find myself, as now, in a foreign culture, but we'd be heading out to Copacabana, where we'd sip rum cocktails on the beach and flirt with the bartender, instead of sitting in my father's house being subjected to a parade of mute marriage candidates. Or I found myself daydreaming about that bar in Lagos, where my pulse had risen because there was the promise of a party, a festive mood in the air... But now that establishment was out of reach, and I had been snatched from that place of vibrancy and vitality before I had even had the chance to savour it.

Was there anything like that in Aba? After all, one and a half million people lived here, so there had to be at least a small crowd of good people who knew how to combine those three special ingredients of night, music and alcohol into an explosive mixture. But the truth was I couldn't ask my family about it, they wouldn't have understood the question. What I was craving was something their language didn't even have a word for. At best, Hippolite would have braced himself and taken me to some harmless, insipid venue where we would share a beer between 8.30 and 10pm.

At a time in my life where the success of a holiday was measured by how late you got to bed, I became an early bird in Aba. It wasn't the end of the world, but I struggled a little with not having anyone to really talk to. Heart-to-hearts didn't seem to be on the Nigerian agenda. It would have been fun to joke about different cultural habits and get to know each other better. Unfortunately, Nigeria's cultural differences also included the fact that they were also off limits for conversation.

Were there other things that got people fired up? Yes: going to church every Sunday. Church, faith, Jesus Christ were major themes – not so much in my father's and Joyce's generation, but among my sisters and their friends. They didn't hold back on the religious lexicon. 'Praise the Lord' was an exclamation that came from everyone's lips several times a day.

If anything stood between me and my Nigerian peers, it was religion. I'm certainly not an atheist and I'll give anything a go when it comes to religious shenanigans, but hearing the same ecstatic refrains on a loop, the same expressions of infinite love for Jesus Christ that everyone was expected to utter endlessly, along with the insistence on having experienced the Grace of God that very day, was enough to drive me insane. All inward thought, all reflection on meaning was substituted by unquestionable faith; faith subsumed everything that I missed as a communication-obsessed navel-gazer. The only self-awareness anyone talked about was their story of epiphany, the moment when they become a born-again Christian. Hallelujah! In Nigeria, my familiar culture of reflectiveness was replaced by religiosity. While my father's generation were still good Anglicans, my own generation was firmly in the grip of the evangelical free churches. In the church of the ancients, Nneka told me, all they did was sing 'Holy, holy, holy' and she put her hand over her mouth as if to suppress a huge yawn. In her church, on the other hand, there was really something happening. There was no chance of being bored.

The free churches had thoroughly saturated life in Nigeria. Almost anything anyone said was lent emphasis with a mention of Jesus as your personal saviour and the immensity of his grace. And consequently, the Sunday service was a huge social event. Everyone dressed up to the nines. Everyone was up early to get ready, the ladies disappearing into the bathroom to put on their make-up. It was an exuberant display of magnificent colours and fabrics. Nobody held back on a Sunday. I even had to put on the white chief outfit. Then finally we were off, the mood heady as we drove to the church in the shimmering Mercedes. The fuss when we got there! The hugs, the kisses, the warmth of the greetings. You certainly didn't just slip in quietly without anyone seeing you. Ikunna had already warned me that they didn't get the service over and done with in the hasty, perfunctory manner you get in Germany; I should expect to be there for over three hours. The mood was exuberant, almost feverish, like the crowd was heading to a rave, not a morning at church. For all their festive mood, it was far from relaxing. To sit through three hours was no mean feat. The pastor had barely started to warm up before the first people were already falling into an ecstatic trance. What started as a dance, the upper body swaying, the hips circling, evolved into epileptic convulsions, heads tossing back and forth, arms waving in the air. The Holy Spirit was with them now. And because faith loosened the tongue, the spiritually gifted began babbling away, speaking in tongues, a murmur that was divine to the extent that it was free of human meaning, while the rest of the community cheered them on, praised them for their special connection to the higher spheres ('It's a gift,' my sisters explained to me afterwards). The whoops of support became ever more triumphant in tone because yet again, on this Sunday, the Holy Spirit had not failed to demonstrate his presence. You could rely on God. So many miracles were unfurling before our eyes; how could obstinate unbelievers continue to deny His presence? Whoever has ears to hear can hear the truth, whoever has eyes to see can see it! The congregation was now one heart and one soul. People leaned in, shoulder to shoulder, because the Holy Spirit transmits through touch, through this electrical impulse.

For three hours I was tense with fear, terrified they would read my dark thoughts from my furrowed brow and point me out as an unbeliever. Fortunately, Ikunna glanced at me reassuringly every now and then, like a prompter in the wings (*don't worry, everything's fine!*), putting aside her expression of ecstasy for a moment in favour of a down-to-earth comforting smile. She pressed her lips together and nodded slowly like a policewoman reassuring an alarmed citizen that the situation was by no means out of control. I gave her a grateful smile in return.

As described in the crudest Marxist criticism of religion, every political sphere in Nigeria had been replaced by religious references to the hereafter. As mentioned earlier, it was always a huge undertaking to get hold of petrol; if you went on a trip by car, you had to go traipsing around the black market in the hope of filling two jerry cans, and this could take forever. Once you'd filled up the tank, all gratitude was of course due to Jesus for not letting you down. The fact that the Bible instructs us not to use the name of the Lord in vain was apparently one of the less internalised maxims in Nigeria.

There was something so self-righteous about it. It wasn't enough to humbly thank Jesus for his act of redemption, it was a competition to see who could praise the glory of God and express their love of Jesus the most frequently and most loudly. It was like Kafka's beggar, who always glanced furtively to the side when he prayed to check who had taken note of his fervour. I couldn't understand how everyone else couldn't see through this obstinate excess piety, this inflationary praise of God, which in truth was barely veiled self-praise ('I'm so moved by the Holy Spirit, I must have been chosen!'). Were there really cultures where it wasn't considered unseemly to beat your own drum and show off about your inviolable possession of truth?

In short, faith didn't bring us together. But it didn't separate us either, at least not from my family's perspective. Anyone who didn't believe in God, or rather anyone who denied his existence, stubbornly refused to believe, was immoral and evil and would bring nothing but misfortune to others. By the same token, my siblings and relatives must have assumed that since their *dear brother* was obviously not a bad person, he must necessarily be pious and devout, even if he unfortunately lacked sufficient drive to shout it from the rooftops. It wouldn't hurt for him to be reborn in his faith, but for the time being that was a matter for the inscrutable counsel of God.

Once, my sisters and I went with Hippolite to a large market where there was a long line of stalls selling fabric. Since we were united by blood, why not wear matching clothes, we said to each other, and we went from stall to stall rifling through the huge range of patterns. Finally we agreed on a fabric: yellow suns on a light blue background. From there we went to a tailor, who took all our measurements. A few days later we picked up our voluminous robes with half-length sleeves that stopped mid-thigh. From now on we set out into the world dressed in our matching family outfits. Let everyone see that our family has come together, that we're now complete. In fact, the desire to present ourselves to the world as a picture-perfect matching clan was so strong that we started going on more frequent excursions. Let the world see us and admire us! We cruised through the neighbourhood in my father's old green Mercedes, and at every 'landmark,' at every view of a river, at every attractive stand of trees, we lined up for another group photo.

Finally Ikunna, Hippolite and I were ready for our trip to the north of the country. I was desperate to get going because Aba wasn't providing much in the way of adventure. Hippolite finally decided, right, OK, we're going to do it, despite the risk; there was still no fuel at the petrol stations, so we were going to have to turn to the black market.

Nigeria was sitting on huge oil reserves, and yet it wasn't able to supply its own population with petrol? It seemed that a lot had gone wrong in this country, which had been ruled by military dictators for decades, but Nigerians were great patriots and didn't like to talk about the problems of their beloved country. But when they can't get hold of fuel, that's when they lose their patience. It's the same as anywhere in the world – when it comes to getting around, enough's enough.

So off we went. The needle on the fuel gauge was closer to empty than full, but all the same, we hit the road.

The north of Nigeria around the city of Jos is very scenic – an imposing high plateau with broad vistas. There was a touch of the atmosphere of *Out of Africa*. In the national park, a monkey jumped in through the open sun roof when we weren't looking and got into the car, grabbed the bag with our biscuits, and in a few leaps he was back in the safety of his treetop. He seemed to relish our perplexed surprise as he munched away smugly on our biscuits. This monkey didn't just have a genuine awareness of guilt, he even – and this seemed to me the greater cognitive achievement – seemed to display true schadenfreude, a malicious pleasure in our annoyance. He indulged in a mimicked gesture of revelling in his triumph, which was in inverse relation to our frustrated defeat. Did he do it because he wanted to see our faces? More than anything else, I realised, it's in this malicious delight that you see the similarity to us humans.

We saw elephants, we saw giraffes. We ate coconuts and swam in beautiful freshwater springs beneath the palms. Then we were off again, and Hippolite seemed to be really enjoying showing me his country. He was a good tour guide, you could tell his heart was in it. And we always managed to get fuel supplies just in time, even if we had to pay the eye-watering black-market prices. I'd see Hippolite shaking his head bitterly as he handed the gas station attendant the naira notes, with an expression on his face that left no doubt as to how much he disapproved of this morally dubious situation (and the price).

When we got to Jos, we stayed with my architect cousin, the one I already knew from Lagos. He had invited about 16 guests for the evening, all men – young, very pleasant, cheerful, cultured types. People were chatting and telling jokes, and everyone was in a great mood. It was very relaxed and sociable – finally the kind of gathering I had been craving! After the meal, however, there was a change of tone. One of the men, who seemed to enjoy particular respect and seemed to be looked up to as the spokesman for the group of friends, turned to me in a way that suggested we had passed through various stages of confidentiality and had got to know each other, and now it was time for him to deepen the bond of friendship, so to speak. He said, 'I'd like to share the Lord's supper with you!' *But we've just eaten,* I thought to myself. What can he mean? Then the penny dropped. He meant communion. He wanted to celebrate communion with me and his friends! All the faces around the table were animated with joy. We were heading for the climax of the evening, everything else was just the warm-up. Unfortunately, I had to disappoint them. By telling them I wasn't baptised. The spokesman was only puzzled for a split second, this was a possibility he clearly hadn't anticipated, but the disclosure didn't seem to matter. On the contrary, a whole new perspective opened up for him. The usual official church baptism was a bit anaemic anyway, he seemed to think. A mere formality. And its absence was less a deficit than the ideal starting point for a clean restart. He spoke with winged words, 'Then let us baptise you!'

Whatever baptismal qualifications my cousin's friend had, I wasn't about to let him save my soul. But I also didn't want to offend anyone, so I kept my rage against the country's mass religious psychosis to myself. My hopeful saviour's eyes twinkled. At that moment he understood what a unique opportunity had presented itself for the higher glory of God. As the great Anabaptist he would complete the spiritual homecoming of the prodigal son! Everyone sat there expectantly. Solemnity is always an effective means of collective blackmail that makes it extremely difficult to break rank. The only way to counter this would be to brush it off with a casual bonhomie. I had survived the confrontation with the customs officer, I wasn't going to let this would-be Anabaptist intimidate me. I stammered, 'What? Now? No, no, don't worry about it!' It had to be possible to get out of a baptism without having to justify it with a theological denial (which would risk making things worse). 'Why not?' asked the acting Baptist, now with a hint of resentment in his voice. Then I had what seemed to me a flash of inspiration. I would beat him at his own game.

Adopting a solemn tone myself, I declared, 'I don't feel ready.'

'What do you mean?' he asked.

'Well, it's a very important step,' I said. 'Not something you do lightly, just like that!'

He looked at me in astonishment, also with a certain suspicion that I might have been having him on. Surely an invitation like this, that was after all a gift from God, wasn't to be rejected for such a frivolous reason? Why wouldn't you be ready? Didn't the Scouts always say, 'Be prepared'? He was presumably ready for a little resistance, but he didn't proceed to unleash his entire arsenal of persuasion. Perhaps there were mitigating circumstances. After all, as someone who had just returned from the diaspora, who was still reconnecting with their home soil, you had to expect a degree of confusion and uncertainty. He gave up. But he didn't hide his disgruntlement. It was like coitus interruptus. Shortly before the climax, I had switched on the neon light to kill the mood.

As soon as we got back from our trip to Aba, my mother called. Grandma had died. I had visited her in hospital in Calw, the week before I set off. She was 87 and I had flown to Nigeria knowing she might not survive the pneumonia. Lying on her sickbed, surrounded by her children and grandchildren, she had pulled my head down and whispered in my ear, 'Come back, won't you!' Her voice was already weak, but she was clearly serious. I despaired when I realised what she was worried might happen. 'Of course!' I replied, but actually I wanted to stamp my foot with indignation and shout, 'Why would you even imagine that I might not come back?' You really couldn't say that I was drawn to Nigeria, it was more of a commitment I had to fulfil to avoid hurting anyone's feelings. If I could choose where I wanted to be in my heart, it was right here, at my grandma's bedside, my grandma who had held my hand for 23 years. Here where I had spent my holidays as a child. My grandma who could travel for free on the Deutsche Bahn. Who would put her false teeth in when guests came (because with her there was a time and place for everything). We got along like a house on fire. And now Grandma was dying and was worried that my father who had shown up so late might drag me over to his camp? What, did she think I had always seen her grandmotherly care as a temporary arrangement? That the force that bound us together would expire the moment I heard from my real father? Did she see me – whose loyalty had always been beyond reproach – as a potential separatist? Did she really think the pull of a father would be stronger than that of a mother, she of all people, who had single-handedly brought her family to West Germany from Silesia? Or did she suddenly (or possibly not even suddenly) recognise my paternal inheritance as the predominant character trait, making her fear that, once I was surrounded by the Ezebuikes, I would immediately embrace them as my own kin? Did Grandma feel socially inferior? She knew my father from the early days – and as a well-travelled paediatrician with the allure of a chief he was, of course, despite the precarious exchange rate, a representative of a higher social class, while the Mangolds were, for all their warmth, of limited, modest and negligible means. (Just like the reaction when a relative marries up a class: 'He doesn't want anything more to do with us, he's probably ashamed of us.')

My sisters and Joyce tried to comfort me. They were very tender and compassionate. But nothing could allay my self-reproach. What kind of a terrible grandson was I that I wouldn't even attend my grandma's funeral? Why wasn't I standing by my grieving mother's side? Were these really my new priorities? At the same time, I redirected my anger at Nigeria instead of myself. So this country was the reason I was in completely the wrong place at this important moment? Instead of at the grave of my grandma, who had been at my side all my life, I was lying here crying under the roof of my father, who had only been interested in me for a year!

Then we drove to Amucha. A weekend in the country. There was always talk of Amucha, and now I was finally going to get to know the village where my father grew up, where he had long been the village chief. The mood as we set off was one of solemn excitement. I had a sense of the village as a kind of original spring from which everything flowed. Though the river of life might sometimes be murky amidst the battles of the world, it is purified by a return to the village. This was why no Nigerian lost touch with his place of origin and even residents of the megacity Lagos saw themselves as part of the village from which they hail. When a young woman gets married, however, she gives up her association with her original village and becomes part of her husband's village community, a process that is not entirely uncomplicated from an emotional point of view. The village is the bestower of identity, the keeper of tradition. Seen in this way, it's a huge leap that a woman takes when she becomes a wife. (What's a mother-in-law compared to an entire village-in-law?)

Of course, I had to pack the chief's robe and sceptre for the occasion. After the dress rehearsal in Essen, now it was time for the real thing, the home game, so to speak.

We set off in two cars. After an hour's drive we left the surfaced road and drove another hour on a dirt track through the jungle. It was the rainy season, so the potholes were full of muddy water. The clouds hung low, just above the treetops, no trace of the blue sky. Then the rainforest – which we had cut through on a road like a tall, narrow chasm – opened up and the first huts appeared.

The closer you get to something, the more the detail comes into focus. Monoliths of identity are the stuff of distance. Every microcosm becomes a macrocosm the closer you look. For a desert flea, every grain of sand might have a name, evoking the sounds, the memories, the mood associated with it, while for most people on earth at first glance it's enough to simply speak of the Sahara. In fact, I now learned, Amucha was the name for the broader community made up of some seventeen villages spread across the region. The Ezebuikes came from Umuokwara. While about 51,000 people lived in Amucha, our village Umuokwara had 5,000 inhabitants, but more than half of them, like my family, led a double life split between town and country. For major feast days, for weddings and funerals, for the annual assemblies of the village council and during the holidays, everyone returned in full splendour, ready to show the village their success and triumphs in the world.

My father, Hippolite explained to me, was the first medical student that Amucha had produced, so his title in Igbo was 'Ichie Dibia-di-ohanma na Amucha,' which translated as

'Venerable doctor of the people.' There are villagers who have never come into contact with any medical practitioner besides my father, who also provides the village with medicines. For this service, he bears the title Ichie; to translate it as 'chief' doesn't do it justice. Ichie is the highest rank of chieftain in the Igbo nomenclature and it's an entirely political role, which is why my father is also a member of the upper council of Amucha. The title is not hereditary, though; it is awarded on merit.

Amucha, as I continued to call it, because everyone else did, even though it was actually Umuokwara, was beautiful and tranquil. There were just a few concrete-built houses, the rest were huts surrounded by dense rainforest. At the centre of the village was a covered meeting place, the so-called obi, where public ceremonies and political gatherings are held.

The second we got out of the car, a crowd of children came running up, leaping about between the huts, clapping their hands with joy and watching us in amazement.

There were small hollow-ways cut here and there through the forest, where the village children ran back and forth, mostly to the river, which was a ten-minute walk away, a peaceful, inviting body of water. The earth had a strong red tinge. At six o'clock it was suddenly dark, as if someone had switched the lights off, then the village was enveloped in such complete, pure darkness, as if it were wrapped in a protective black velvet blanket.

The largest building was our house. It was huge, certainly twice the size of the house in Aba. The walls were cool to touch like concrete. It came across as rather stark and unlived in, as though it were waiting for future generations to make themselves at home. There hadn't been much emphasis on nightlife in Aba, but in Amucha we went to bed even earlier.

The next morning I wasn't given much time at breakfast. There was a nervous hurry, I was being shooed along. I was told to put on my white robe and I was directed to an armchair in our huge living room, which seemed to want to give a sense of dominance through its sheer size and emptiness, as if the feeling of being lost in a great hall evoked the necessary solemnity of the situation. Then about two hundred villagers, members of the extended Ezebuike family, walked before me in a long procession and each shook my hand in delight. Because they didn't speak English and I didn't speak Igbo, we ratcheted up the gestures of benevolence. Big smiles and waving.

Everything happened to me, passively. I don't remember my family warning me in advance what was in store for me, what happened at such occasions, or even asking for my consent. They sat me down, clapped and off we went. They were relying on me to be able to sit in an armchair for two hours. And yes, there are more difficult things in life.

But that was just the warm-up. The harmless warm-up. The main event was in the afternoon. Half the village gathered on the obi, palm wine was served. Everyone was dressed up for the occasion and seemed slightly tipsy. In the middle of the obi, I saw some tall men in dignified robes; they were the village dignitaries, the other chiefs who had come from the city to perform the ceremonial rites on behalf of my absent father. The villagers sat around them and listened respectfully. None of these men exchanged a single word with me, as I sat there dressed in the white chief's robe, sheepishly clutching the sceptre. There was no real need to talk to me, it seemed; I might have been the subject of their grandiose speeches, but the focus was entirely on them. As long as they were still at the helm, they weren't going to give up the spot as the central luminaries. They were flexing their muscles and basking in the limelight of their authority. Unstoppable in their boastful earnestness, they barked out their words like gun salutes. Mere platitudes on the whole, nothing of note. That is, until one reached the climax of his speech. Although grammatically it sounded like he was addressing me, in fact he was speaking about me rather than to me when he decreed in an incisive tone, 'Forget the name Mangold, you are Ijoma Ezebuike!' Clearly satisfied with the gravity of his words – could it have been expressed more succinctly? – he gave a contented nod as he spoke.

They believe in the power of blood, but it's only my African blood that counts.

I was at once affronted and rendered powerless. He was getting carried away with all the swagger and bluster, and it had gone too far. It was like a slap in the face for my mother. Total disregard for my story, my background. What I might think about it was utterly dismissed. I was to submit to their way of doing things. There was only one appropriate response: get up, turn around, and walk away. But where to? I was surrounded by forest, nothing but thick dense forest. I couldn't exactly dash to the bus station and get a ride to the nearest airport. I was stuck. Trapped. I had to grin and bear it. Except no, I didn't have to. This was the one miserable scrap of autonomy left to me: I might have to bear it but I didn't have to grin. Instead of a brave face, a grimace. It wasn't much, but it was all that was left to me, because the protocol hadn't provided for needing to secure my approval for this act of renaming. There wasn't any moment where I might have replied to the rhetorical question 'Do you want to live your future life as an Ezebuike?' with a defiant 'No offence, but I think I'll stick with Mangold!' All I could do in my impotence was simmer with rage. The power here was with the collective.

So this was the village? These men, who were concerned only with themselves, saw nothing of the anger on my face. The only person to see it was my father's wife. She knew what was going on inside me. I didn't have to tell her anything. She had sat at my side the whole time. When the official part was over and everyone got up off the floor, she spoke to me with great feeling, a tone of dismay in fact, because she was perfectly aware of what had gone wrong. 'Don't take these men too seriously. They are very reasonable people in the city, but when they go back to the village they just have to make themselves important. They don't mean anything by it!' It didn't make me feel much better, although it was comforting that she'd noticed I was upset.

It was a relief when we drove back to the city.

Now, at this point you should know that I like to sing in the shower. You can't hear how croaky your own voice is under the rush of hot water. That didn't work in my father's house in Aba, because you can't create a rushing Niagara soundscape with a tub of hot water and a sponge. I sang my favourite arias in the bathroom anyway, it helped with the feeling of being adrift. I felt a bit like Fitzcarraldo, who's desperate to build an opera house in the Amazon jungle. The dense forest feels more like home when Caruso's voice drowns out the screeching of the parrots.

At that time I was hypnotised by the *Rosenkavalier*, by the music of Richard Strauss as well as Hugo von Hofmannsthal's inspired libretto. Besides, at the time, Habsburg was close to beating Prussia to the top spot in my heart. I had been living in baroque Munich for three years, so there was little point in playing the ascetic Prussian. Besides, I had recently begun to react irritably to everything Protestant, while the Catholic double standards of acknowledging your sin and confession seemed to me a rounder, fuller expression of life. We were always driving to Austria from Munich, even if people slightly looked down on the Austrians, because in the early 1990s it was still a bit like the Balkans there, but on the other hand we admired their lifestyle, their cuisine, their courtly hierarchies, their sharp-tongued rhetorical skills and their uninhibited love of flirting. From there it was only a small step from the Hohenzollerns to the Habsburgs – especially if you were a chameleon like me, who liked to get into traditional identities and role models. Austria was like stepping into a costume department, a treasure trove of old words and old manners, and since I had become an obsessive reader I had fallen under the spell of precisely this kind of linguistic and cultural heritage. We were a people with a past, after all, and there had been a whole cosmos of manners and customs and forms that had perished, but which were preserved in books. It was in reading that you got an inkling of the grace and lofty fussiness of bygone times, and above all I was attracted to all that was ponderous and elaborate, the complex and intricate rites that were a chilly rebuff to all shabby pragmatism. I found that clinging to those outdated complexities, that stood in the way of our contemporary frictionless transactions, had something sublime about them, something that brought out the theatrical side of being human.

Interestingly, here in Nigeria I was surrounded by a great deal of ceremony and tradition, which ought to have been entirely to my taste. But I wasn't familiar with the social order that determined the rules of conduct, and I didn't associate it with sublime memories, subtleties and extravagances. Also, as I had just learned in Amucha, my own life was too directly exposed to the push and pull of these ceremonial rites for me to appreciate the pomp and circumstance, as an ethnological onlooker might, in purely aesthetic terms.

And so, here I was near the equator, longing for the world of the *Rosenkavalier*. There in the bathtub in Aba I sang the melody from the final duet: *'It's a dream; it cannot be true that the two of us are together.'*

Nothing could be further from the Nigerian reality than this Vienna of Empress Maria Theresa. But that was where I belonged! I felt a longing. And I thought to myself, what if someone outside heard me now and recognised the aria? How would they feel hearing me sing it? Surely they'd be surprised. They'd hardly believe their ears! So I sang a bit louder. Let it strike them like lightning! They would stop in their steps, spellbound. How can that be, they would ask. The *Rosenkavalier* in the middle of the jungle?! They'd approach our house, gingerly walk in until they had a glimpse of the singer (in the bathtub). Then they would join in the duet and we would sing Richard Strauss together in Nigeria, and we'd no longer be alone, and all would be redeemed.

# Love's Labour's Lost

When I headed for the departure gate at Lagos airport after two months and I saw the blue crane against its yellow background on the tail of the plane outside, a long sigh escaped my lips. I had survived. I looked deeply into the eyes of the stewardesses, my country folk. Two months was a long time. Finally, I was heading home. I sank into the seat, buckled up, and took a deep breath.

The first thing I did when I was back, though, was drive to Essen to report back to my father, who had responded well to the kidney transplant but would still be under medical care for some time. Joyce had also come to Germany in the meantime. So we saw each other again, at my father's sickbed. My father was wearing a black Adidas tracksuit, I talked about my trip, and the patient he was sharing a room with took photos of the three of us, me between Joyce and my father, arms on each other's shoulders. The whole thing had an outward ease about it, which as far as I was concerned didn't have much to do with reality. I knew my father was expecting more from me than I could commit to. It was only because I was so diplomatic about it that he had no idea he would be banging his head against a brick wall with me.

I went back to my student life in Munich. I had a lot of photos of Nigeria and even more stories that my friends were very curious about. 'So they wanted you to get married, baptised, and take a new name?" They thought it was wonderful that I had got to know my Nigerian family, but they also understood that I hadn't become a new person overnight, that I wasn't suddenly inflamed with adoration for my new fatherland. Ikunna was still in Heidelberg, and my mother started exchanging letters with Nneka, who complained that her brother still hadn't replied to her last letter. That didn't happen with my mother, who always wrote back. At Christmas, a huge batch of letters arrived in Heidelberg with greetings for me and Mama from all the members of the Ezebuike family.

In fact, there were three of us together at Christmas: Mama, Ikunna and me. When my mother asked her to tell us how Christmas was celebrated in Amucha, Ikunna kept her explanation brief. I could almost see the admonition forming on my mother's lips: 'Child, you have to *communicate!*'

I also saw Ikunna regularly when I was in Heidelberg. Once we went on a bike ride with a friend of hers who was also studying medicine, one of those Germans I had always avoided: well-meaning people with a fervent enthusiasm for Africa. (Sometimes this was doubtlessly unfair of me, as they simply knew a lot about Africa – unlike me.) This friend had recently got together with a Nigerian and was clearly very much in love. She didn't know, however, if his feelings were the same. He said he wanted to marry her, but who could say whether he only had his eyes on a German passport? She was keen to know how Ikunna assessed the situation.

Ikunna wasn't about to go out of her way to defend her compatriot. With cautious scepticism, she advised her friend not to rush into anything and under no circumstances to let love pull the wool over her eyes. Her friend nodded bravely.

Oh, she was completely torn! The guy was so wonderful, but on the other hand she had heard too many stories of Africans who ran away and left their German wives, and she didn't want to fall prey to the same fate.

The year after my trip to Nigeria, my sisters' pleas for me to visit them again were getting increasingly urgent. They were convinced that a new era had dawned for all of us, and they wrote to me that they couldn't wait to have me back with them again. Hippolite's marriage plans were also more and more explicitly dependent on my travel plans. But in the summer of 1994, I wanted to finally set off for my Promised Land – Italy. I was going to have a year abroad in Bologna, learning Italian, going to lectures on Semiotics with Umberto Eco, working on my culinary skills. I wrote back and explained my situation. As I wrote, I couldn't suppress the urge to depict my love for Italy as an existential passion, as though, in order to finally do justice to my own convictions, I wanted to imply that genuine love for a country was a decision based on elective affinities, not genetic inheritance. I wanted it to be clear that, for all my feeling of attachment, I wasn't ready to give up Italy for Nigeria. This wasn't an intervention in my life that I was willing to tolerate.

One way or another, I didn't go to Nigeria that year – or the following year or the year after that, so whenever my sisters told me how much they looked forward to my return, the expressions they used in their letters became increasingly formulaic. 'Next year in Jerusalem!'

In 1999, six years after my visit to Nigeria, I received the news that Nneka had died of complications from sickle cell disease. She wasn't even twenty years old. Her death really hit me. We were very alike, not just in appearance, but also in nature. Even so, the pain remained abstract; it was almost more like it took the form of a guilty conscience. Why didn't you go back to Aba to see your favourite sister? Why did you keep putting it off?

I saw my father another three or four times. Because of his kidney transplant, he had to travel to Essen for follow-up examinations from time to time. Then he would come and see me afterwards.

What was supposed to happen next? I could accept that there was a new situation to get used to, sure, but otherwise, I preferred everything to carry on as it had been before. I had no burning desire to go to Nigeria again, but neither did I want to be stubborn. I didn't mean to hurt anyone's feelings. I didn't want to feel like I was being tugged this way and that, so I told myself, OK, fine, two to three weeks in Nigeria every five years, that would work... But then the time passed and there was always something happening, and there was always another excuse. Straight after my trip to Italy, I needed to head to the United States to see Edward, and after that I had to concentrate on my master's thesis. In 1998, I moved to Berlin and started writing for the *Berliner Zeitung*, so I really had neither the time nor the headspace for a trip to Nigeria. And in 2001, I went back to Munich because I'd become the literary editor for the *Süddeutsche Zeitung*. Time was racing by, everything was exciting, and I simply didn't have any yearning to go to Nigeria, that all-important ingredient that makes a trip a priority. Nothing was drawing me there. It made me feel nothing but this vague lethargy. I didn't feel good about putting it off, but I was even more concerned that if I went back to Nigeria, there would be even more pressure to join the Nigerian family system.

It stayed that way whenever I met my father in Germany. Once we even met my mother in Dossenheim and had a walk together through the vineyards. It was so strange to see my father walking the paths that I roamed as a child. Nothing was so much my terrain as these vineyards; as a child I had even drawn a kind of treasure map of the hilly landscape with secret hiding spots, useful holes in the fence, semi-official abbreviations and the like. And now suddenly my father had stepped into my childhood landscape. It was like someone had cut and pasted him into the picture. There he stood, as the scent of the not yet fully ripe grapes tickled our noses, on the steep path that I had once sledged down in winter, over and over until my toes were icicles.

There was nothing more preposterous, nothing topsy-turvier, than seeing my father and my mother in the same place at the same time. How was I to make sense of it? But it was clear that there was no way around it. Just as there was once little I could do to avoid accompanying Yvonne to the post office, now there was little I could do to prevent this reunion. I can't even remember how it came about. My father always needed an invitation for his German visa (which was tantamount to having someone assume liability for him), and initially my mother did this until I myself had a reliable record with the tax office. I assume it was in this context that the two decided to organise a meeting of father, mother and child.

Father, mother and child. If you have never had this arrangement before, and you only know the Holy Family from Raphael paintings, you feel as awkward at a gathering like this as someone who has been in a tracksuit all his life and is suddenly made to wear a tuxedo. Or like me in a chief's robe in the car park of Essen University Hospital. Back then I was able to laugh at myself and see it rather ironically as a fancy dress costume, but here there was no room for irony.

My mother seemed excited but not excessively. She probably knew that the past was much too far away for us to need to talk things through, or at least that's how it seemed to me. To my amazement, she had invited some close friends (*meet and greet!*). I imagined they were supposed to act as a sort of buffer to soften the drama of our reunification, or perhaps she was motivated less by seeing my father again than wanting to close up a hole in our social cosmos. Perhaps she wanted to reveal the absent father, if only once, to prove his authenticity, like in cards when you reveal your hand at the end of a bold round to prove that you did have the king all along and weren't bluffing. Perhaps she also wanted to show off what an impressive man my father was, a man for whom unusual life decisions could be made.

The other times, my father visited me in Munich. If it was summer, we sat in the beer garden. We didn't talk about anything important. Once, I told him about my work for the *Süddeutsche Zeitung*, and he replied with solemn complacency that he used to read the *Frankfurter Allgemeine Zeitung*. Not the most sensitive answer, perhaps, I thought to myself, but, my God, you could have a worse fate than to have a *FAZ* reader as a father! We enjoyed our beers and I observed the sublimely dainty way my father managed to pick up and eat a pork knuckle. It reminded me that when I was a child, Mama always raved about how elegantly my father used to mould the Nigerian millet porridge into a kind of spoon with his fingers, to mop up the vegetable ragout.

Perhaps these encounters, as nice and cheerful as they were every time, were in fact like poker games where each player was busy with their own thoughts and strategies, behind a mask of calm. I can't say for sure. But one thing was beyond doubt, even if it only gradually became clear to me: my father had a secret plan. He kept his cards close to his chest, he only played one card per round, and if he couldn't make use of a card, he'd hold it back until the next time he visited Germany.

It was very simple. In this context, we should remember again that the defining Nigerian national genre is the epic, not the psychological novel. My father had lost two sons to sickle cell anaemia; now he only had daughters, a dynastically untenable situation. But only at first glance. A guy like my father is never caught on the wrong foot, he's always prepared and has an answer to any situation. He was playing the long game, looking ahead so that when the moment came, he could present a legally competent heir. He had Ijoma, after all, and no expense had been spared for his son's upbringing. Dear Ijoma had had a strong start at the Ulla Mangold boarding school, a first-class institution especially for the early childhood development phase; she was a *child and adolescent psychotherapist*, after all. And thus, when I was out of the woods, when I was good and ready, he had written to me, 'Blood is thicker than water.'

The trip to Nigeria had gone to his satisfaction. And the next time we met in Germany, he asked me to continue my studies in Nigeria; the university in Enugu had a very good German department, he insisted. I turned down his suggestion, not without expressing regret, and explained that my studies meant a lot to me, that I had a part-time job at the university, and that I was determined to graduate in Munich.

Every time we met, the conversation followed this pattern. We chatted in the most convivial way possible about trivialities. Then my father ratcheted up the conversation a gear and suggested that I could shift the focus of my life to Nigeria, and I put him off gently by promising to go back to Nigeria as soon as possible. But I haven't been back once in all these years. I suppose out of a certain defiant pride. Spending my vacation travelling to Nigeria would have meant foregoing a holiday somewhere else, and in my inner moral accounts, where I jealously keep stock of all debts and credits, the other holiday represented my real life. Why should I give up something about my own real life for this Nigerian life that had knocked on my door so late that I was unfortunately already fully booked? First come, first served: that's how I saw it in my internal bookkeeping, which I would like to stress is flawless, pedantic, and – in the pettiest way possible – always accurate.

Once, my father assured me that he had already spoken to the Nigerian authorities and that nothing stood in the way of dual citizenship. The embassy would issue me with a Nigerian passport at any time. I hemmed and hawed, until he finally dropped the subject. I would have liked to have made him happy, but I also didn't want to bend over backwards for a not insignificant act of symbolism when my heart wasn't in it. You don't marry a woman you don't love just because it's what she wants.

Another time I received a letter from him where he informed me that he had now transferred shares in his hospital to me. As a co-partner, I was invited to participate in all decision-making processes. I read his letter and shook my head. I was a literary scholar in Germany, not a hospital workflow optimiser with a branch in Aba.

When we last met, it must have been 2004, my father played his last card. If this tactic didn't work out, he'd call off the whole offensive. But I only realised this later. We were sitting in the Paulaner Bräuhaus pub on Kapuzinerplatz in Munich, where the Pilsner is particularly refreshing, even citrusy. By the way, I have a tiresome habit of being able to endlessly wax lyrical about food and drink. And because we never talked about anything particularly urgent or personal, I was just about to explain to my father what I found so delicious about this Paulaner, when he pushed his plate of pork knuckle to one side (which he did gladly) and gazed into the distance like a commander, before staring at me with a philosophical smile. 'I want to leave you my hospital,' he said. 'You're my heir.'

I knew right away that this was going to be exhausting. And that I would refuse. After I had taken a deep breath to compose myself, I realised to my relief that I could easily justify my rejection.

'You know that I want to stay in Germany. I'm not going to move to Nigeria.'

'You don't have to move to Nigeria. It is enough if you come by once a year and check that everything is going well. You'll own the hospital, but you don't have to do anything. You can take most of the important decisions from Germany.'

'But that would be crazy. My specialism is literature (even if you don't seem to notice me telling you, like it's some mildly irritating background noise that will stop again once the engine's warmed up). I have no idea about hospitals. You need a specialist.'

'No, that's not necessary.'

'I don't get it. Sign the hospital over to Ikunna, that would make much more sense. Ikunna studied medicine and she's your oldest daughter. She's perfect!'

My father shook his head as if I didn't understand.

'Or Hippolite. Sign it over to Hippolite! He's always been part of the family, he knows the hospital inside out, he's been working for you for years, he admires you, and he's got the technical mind you need. You *need* technical expertise in a hospital. Today more than ever. Hippolite and you, you're the perfect team!'

My father directed his gaze into the distance again. His smile had given way to a resigned melancholy. The way he listened to me was like humouring a small child, letting them speak, even though clearly they're too young to see the bigger picture.

In retrospect, I do sometimes think that if I had experienced a stronger culture of dialogue in Nigeria, if my father had involved me in a genuine conversation, if he had shared with me his vision of the future, his dreams and desires, if he had listened to my vision of the future, my dreams and desires, if he had simply given this big thing a bit more room, if he had drawn me into his thoughts, if he had tried to make the whole thing the slightest bit appealing, if he had tried to entice me with talk of an income, if he had somehow shown any empathy or recognition of my German life, and tried to explain how it could have been reconciled with a Nigerian life, if he had sketched out the attraction of a double life in an era of globalisation, if he had said anything, anything to try and persuade me, maybe I might have softened, maybe I might have ended up agreeing after a long discussion. But such a discussion wasn't in my father's nature. All he could say was, 'I want to leave you my hospital.' He couldn't make a story out of it. It was supposed to be self-explanatory, I was supposed to just see it exactly as he saw it in his head. He wasn't anticipating having to wrangle with me over it. The fact that reality emerges during conversation wasn't part of his worldview, and when I didn't respond to his suggestion, he didn't launch into a second attempt to persuade me, he didn't pull out all the stops. He simply accepted it. And so there we remained, stuck at the point of my rejection.

I was offered a second life and I turned it down. From the chief's sceptre to the hospital, I have never taken what was offered by my father and made it my own. In retrospect, I sometimes regret it. And I wonder, would it really have been so bad? After all, who nowadays is ever satisfied with just one life? Surely everyone would like at least two or three lives! After all, migration is no longer just a phenomenon of poverty, but a question of lifestyle, something that enriches your quality of life. Those who are unlucky enough to come from an ethnically and culturally homogeneous family choose at least to marry into other worlds. Seven-year-old grandchildren are put on the plane by their mothers in Berlin-Tegel to spend the Easter holidays with their grandmother in Toledo, and those who don't have a culturally mixed family know they're missing out on experiencing a much-loved topic in the bestseller section.

I turned down this offer of a second life. I think because it was too much for me, because it demanded too much of me. Where do you get the strength to live two lives? If I wanted to do one well, I wouldn't have the energy left over for a second. In theory, I'm in favour of dual citizenship, but in practice I wasn't able to serve two masters or dance at two weddings (unfortunately, I've had to live with my conscience about not even dancing at Hippolite's wedding). Sure, I turned down the chance to have an enriched life experience, but under the circumstances it wouldn't have brought me anything better. Especially as Nigeria stood before me as a country where the customs officer at the airport wouldn't let me through because I wasn't prepared to pay him a bribe, where my life was always in danger because the streets were dominated by organised crime, where no one built bridges through conversation or storytelling, and where, at every inconvenient opportunity, all my relatives of my generation like to remind me that Jesus was our personal saviour.

The next I heard from Nigeria was the news that my father and his wife had adopted a son. Eleven years after he wrote to me, hoping to get me to move to Nigeria, my father had found a new heir. He had given it time, he had been patient, but now he wasn't going to indulge any more false hopes and would accept the fact that he wasn't going to get anywhere with me, that I wasn't going to play the role he had intended for me. He had relied on the power of blood, a factor that can bide its time, confident that it has the leverage, that the access it's granted is more fundamental than any superficial cultural influence. That's how it is: the power of blood relies on natural instincts, just as Henry IV relies on his son becoming aware of his duty to his family in their hour of need, that it's time to leave behind his dissolute life at Falstaff's side and, as it were, step up as a late arrival into the family business (and the next time he meets Falstaff, who looks at him with doting eyes, he claims, 'I know thee not, old man!').

And I would also say that blood is strong. But not strong enough to build a rough and ready bridge over the abyss of two decades of absence. So, anyway, my father managed to resolve the issue of his line of succession in an almost modern, enlightened way through adoption. His chosen solution, however, remained baffling to me. How could adoption be a solution, I asked myself, when the dynastic tradition was so archaic that daughters didn't count and only male blood could continue the family line? When that's the context, how could a son who wasn't related by blood be installed as a full heir? From that day on, I still got the occasional Christmas phone call and birthday greetings from my father (he did actually like me), but he no longer had any plans for me. A force that had been tugging at me for eleven years suddenly went slack, and there were no bad feelings. Perhaps my father also realised that his family politics and my upbringing simply couldn't be reconciled. I don't know. I've been receiving very respectful Christmas cards from my new brother since he was old enough to write.

After studying medicine in Germany, my sister Ikunna settled permanently in England. Hippolite also relocated with his family (at some point he had given up waiting and married without me as best man) to London, where he teaches at Imperial College and develops cost-effective medical equipment for Nigeria. I see both of them when I travel to London. We're always happy to see each other, but we never talk about what I've written about here. Maybe because it's too obvious to waste words on it. Here too maybe, I don't know.

In the hallway in our apartment in Dossenheim, the schedule for the Heidelberg City Theatre was always hanging up next to the calendar marked with the school holidays. I know I was fascinated for a long time by a play that must have been on at the Studio Theatre because I can picture myself standing there staring at it, puzzling over the dark, mysterious and completely meaningless combination of words, 'If only you had said something, Desdemona'. My mother always liked to talk, and I talk a lot too. But talking, it seemed, wasn't always that easy, even if it might have saved Desdemona from being strangled by her husband.

My mother died in October 2010 and this was the greatest caesura that my life could have had. When my father passed away a year later and on another continent, I found myself incapable of any more pain. I didn't go to his funeral.

The official memorial brochure that celebrated my father's life also included a photo of me. I was wearing the chief's robe in it. When I saw it, I thought to myself, perhaps I did miss out on something good. If rather superficial. I was the one who hadn't allowed it to go any further.

# Obama

So, I never went to Nigeria again, nor did I become the proprietor of a hospital, and I turned down the role of heir to the chief. Nevertheless, ever since I had met my father and visited Aba, my life had changed. If someone asked me about my father and mother, I now had a story to tell; a blank space had been filled, an embarrassment resolved. Of course, it doesn't feel great when the person you're telling asks in disbelief, 'And he never got in touch with you again?' and all I can do is nod.

Something else was different, too: the country around me. It was only in retrospect that I could see the turning points and the change in atmosphere, gradual shifts over the course of time that are too minute to see up close.

For most of my life I had viewed my otherness as a personal fate, its challenges and pitfalls something I had to deal with alone. I owed my existence to a very individual constellation, so it could hardly be generalised or seen as a common task for society. I didn't want to project my fate onto society. When Kofi approached me in upper school with his offer of solidarity among Afro-Germans, my reaction was indignation – as if I was being collared for having something in common with them. I didn't want to have anything in common with anyone else, I was happy being distinct, unique.

Besides, I didn't perceive the difficulties associated with my starting position as threatening or discouraging, but rather as quaint. Of course, there were people with ugly prejudices, and some might have hateful thoughts in private, but nobody had really said anything insulting to my face. I felt I could rely on this level of civilised behaviour. So, by and large, I saw no cause for complaint. Everyone in this world had their burden to carry, and mine seemed light compared to many. Of course, since reunification I didn't feel quite as comfortable in the new federal states as in the old ones, but to complain that people didn't correspond to the Enlightenment ideal seemed to me to misunderstand the way of the world, and to blame German society for some people's potential experience of disadvantage didn't correspond to my concept of honour, you might say. Under no circumstances did I intend to be seen as a victim or as needing the support of well-intentioned polite society. I wanted to be a citizen, the same as everyone else. Sometimes I thought of the Greek ophthalmologist and what he had said about how as a foreigner you always had to be twice as good. Was he right? I was still sceptical. As a self-description, it seemed to me too egotistical, but if he was right, I intended to see it as a matter of kudos to be competing in the most demanding performance category. Perhaps having a fancy name and a title and a fortune isn't all it's cracked up to be? Don't people with all that inheritance and privilege have it too easy to really stand out?

When I was asked – in the nineties as a student, in the noughties as a journalist – whether I had been disadvantaged by my origins or my appearance, I replied, 'No. The opposite, in fact. It's opened doors for me because it attracts attention; people are curious and come up to talk to you.' With a little coquettish irony, I would add that only certain high offices were closed to me, because of course there would never be a Federal President who didn't look German.

That was how I saw it in the nineties, now of course such thinking is clearly outdated. But there was no bitterness in it; it just seemed to me a pragmatic assessment. Fate hands everyone different cards and we should decide without resentment which game we can play with them.

Of course, when I spoke positively about Germany in this way, I was aware that some of my friends and acquaintances were quietly humouring me. 'Yeah, yeah, that's what he always says. But surely he's suppressing something. The world can't be as rose-tinted as he sees it! He just doesn't want to admit it because he wears his optimism like a badge of honour.' Yes, maybe I genuinely didn't want anything to ruin my innately optimistic view of the world, which was why I would rather classify a curious look directed at me as confused rather than racist.

And I took precautions. For example, I had a tactic that became so innate that it was only much later that I became aware of it. Whenever I approached someone who didn't know me, if I needed to ask for directions in the street for example, I instinctively knew that I needed to say something the moment I came into the other's field of vision, so that the familiar sound of my words could soothe the underlying unease inspired by my looks. And since the reassuring effect of my words always set in pretty quickly, I never blamed people for that first moment of fear. After all, this initial pang of fear was something I also knew well enough.

On one of my first trips to Italy (it must have been in the summer of 1989), I was in Umbria, in the medieval town of Città della Pieve. I had just bought an ice cream. As I was leaving the ice cream parlour, a carabiniere rushed towards me, a machine gun slung over his shoulder. He ordered me to accompany him to the police station. We walked silently side by side. I tried to smile so that we wouldn't paint too abject a picture to curious bystanders. It must be a misunderstanding, I explained, but the carabiniere wasn't ready to tell me the reason for my arrest. At the station he handed me over to his superior. He had an all-points bulletin for a wanted man. I took a step towards him so I could stand at his side and sneak a look at the bulletin myself. Top right: a photo of a young man who looked North African. There was no resemblance to me whatsoever. The carabiniere dismissed me with a gloomy expression after taking down my personal details, as if I were not entirely innocent in this mix-up.

This wasn't nice, no question about it; in an ideal world you wouldn't be summoned to a police station just because you looked African. In an ideal world, however, there would be no criminals and therefore no carabinieri with their stop and search criteria. Experiences like this were the exception (it was only after September 11th that I was perhaps asked for my ID by the police on the train a little too often to stay good-humoured about it), and I wasn't prepared to derive from that a reason to condemn the entire world.

I had never experienced Germany as a racist country, not even as a place that held me back. So I had no reason to develop a counter-identity. I was a somewhat eccentric German, ethnically unusual but, for that, all the more dyed in the wool, culturally speaking. When I saw *The Master-Singers of Nuremberg* for the first time at fifteen, I could only smile in agreement at Hans Sachs's lines in the final act:

*What is German and what is true*
*No one would know*
*Were it not for the German Masters!*

In those years the West German bourgeoisie was just about to discover hedonism and culinary refinement in Tuscany, returning home from their holidays full of smugness about how progressive they were compared to the barbarians who still hadn't discovered *la dolce vita* (the fact that from a Roman point of view we were all barbarians, was, however, one of the central tenets of the German grammar school, where a thorough knowledge of Latin and Greek could lead to a kind of inner-worldly salvation). In this new context, I perceived a gap in the market that seemed to be especially made for me: if the Germans were struggling with their history and with identifying as German, if they were keen to see themselves as good Europeans, who, if not me, could tell them 'what is German and what is true' without anyone needing to fear they were being subjected to a history lesson from an incorrigible racist? 'Wherever I am, that is Germany,' Thomas Mann had said in his Californian exile, and as a student I admired this excellent turn of phrase, smug as I was back then. It was something I could play with.

No wonder people were soon saying to me, 'You're more German than any German.' When they said that they saw me as an easily explained case of compensatory over-identification, someone who wanted desperately to belong here.

But I was never convinced by such psychological explanations, ('You're being defensive,' Mama used to say), so I was always mulling it over. Thinking about the term assimilation. Was I a naive case of over-assimilation?

The term had already come up in history at school with respect to the alleged German-Jewish cultural symbiosis. From this perspective, assimilation as a social tactic hadn't exactly worked out well. It was in Germany, after all, where Jews were more assimilated than anywhere, that the Nuremberg race laws were passed. That the Jews renounced their fathers' faith, left behind the Eastern European shtetl, and not only absorbed German culture but also brought it to light in the first place, not to mention fighting and dying for Germany in the First World War, and the fact that the first conductor of Wagner's *Parsifal*, Hermann Levi, was himself a Jew – none of that had helped their cause. Gustav Mahler however had to convert to Christianity in order to become head of the Vienna State Opera; life wasn't the same after that. Of course, apparently not wanting to do things by halves, he also married an out-and-out anti-Semite, Alma Mahler-Werfel, who mocked her little Jewish husbands and, of her children, the only one she thought was pretty was her daughter, whom she had had with an Aryan, Walter Gropius.

Did the term even apply in my case? Assimilation means discarding your inherited culture in order to adapt to the cultural code of the environment. I hadn't inherited anything that I could throw overboard. I had grown up without a father, so I didn't have any African influences to reject (except for our black crocodile). Besides, I definitely didn't want to be one of those people who was never satisfied with their lot, who saw everything as a sign of exclusion. I knew some real masters of the hermeneutics of racism who, with the self-assurance of the aggrieved, see discrimination wherever they look. Things never went well for long between me and people like that. First there was the usual affection, the jovial openness you get when two people meet who are conscious of not looking like other Germans, which tends to lead to a connection and usually to a good mood, to a certain esprit de corps, just like two people who went to the same boarding school tend to understand each other implicitly, even if they were there at different times. But with people who feel perpetually aggrieved, it was quickly clear that our temperaments weren't a good match. We may as well have been from different planets. Always with a long-suffering frown, these were people who wouldn't let it rest with Germany. No matter what happened, they always brought it back to their skin colour. It was inconceivable they could be denied something for any reason other than racism. I didn't want to deny their experience, every experience is genuine, but secretly I thought, 'If you were just a little more personable, maybe people would be nicer to you too!'

In any case, it isn't easy to clearly identify cases of racism. The affected individual has the most nuanced sense of it, of course, but it can't be entirely up to the person concerned to judge whether something is a matter of racism or not. If people asked me – and Germans love to hear stories like this – whether I had encountered everyday racism and I told an anecdote that illustrated xenophobia (naturally I had few up my sleeve; it wasn't like I hadn't experienced any), I noticed that my words were perceived not as my assessment but as fact. There was a communicative asymmetry here: nobody contradicted me (that was never the case in other contexts), because after all, as a German, you couldn't even imagine what it felt like to be exposed to racist harassment. I had a privileged access to the truth, apparently. But it isn't really a balanced conversation, is it, when one party has the power to rule what constitutes valid empirical truth?

If I was relaxed about things, though, it didn't mean I thought I was just like everyone else. I was always conscious of what set me apart from others. It was always clear to me that there was one final difference, one final realm of not-belonging. I didn't want to be naive or starry-eyed about it. My dark skin colour had long been in the process of becoming a generally less conspicuous characteristic, but out of pure anthropological pessimism I had to reckon with the fact that it could be reactivated at any time as a basis for discrimination.

When it came to National Socialism, I couldn't stop wondering how it was that so many Jews had stayed in Germany for so long after the Nazis had seized power, in spite of the harassment and gradual disenfranchisement. Why hadn't they realised earlier what was going on, what was coming their way? How do you know when it's time to pack your things? In any case, I told myself, perhaps best not to get too invested in your own homeland, because love makes you foolish, and you can keep one last *reservatio mentalis* if you don't get too distracted by Goethe, Lessing and Heine and keep an eye on what's setting the tone on the streets. But you shouldn't get too cosy with the Zeitgeist; keep a step back to avoid nasty surprises and the risk of rejection later.

At the same time, I had always held myself back from taking a stand 'against xenophobia'. It seemed absurd to be against xenophobia on moral grounds when it was obvious that I had a personal motive, a personal advantage, from living in a country that was as unxenophobic as possible; the explicit condemnation of xenophobia, which was nonetheless reassuring for me, was reserved for 'bio-Germans.' On the other hand, anyone who is a potential target of a xenophobic attack, whether real, perceived or anticipated, doesn't condemn it morally, but weighs up the chilling practical consequences. Better to stay or to leave? I've never been indignant about xenophobia – it seems to me an anthropological constant. I simply told myself it could be good to have a second passport, an American one, just in case. Even a cursory glance at world history shows that the civilised nature of any state structure can't be relied on in the long term.

But I had no cause for specific concerns. The opposite, in fact. Life was getting less and less complicated, and as I got older I felt like my most difficult phase was behind me.

I had got used to my specific circumstances, and I had developed routines to deal with risks, while at the same time I could see the country around me becoming more and more heterogeneous; I no longer stood out so much. When I looked around me, I had to admit that I wasn't so unique anymore. As a teenager, little children in strollers had stared at me. By the 1990s, they had lost interest in me and I no longer noticed those curious eyes peeping out from strollers. (When I see kids who look like me, I still like to throw a complicit glance as if to say, 'Hey, brother!' But they don't seem to get it anymore.)

I went to Tuscany with friends once in autumn 1988; this was before the summer trip to Umbria. We were sitting in an osteria in Cortona. The food was good, as was the wine. I tasted my first Brunello and understood what it was, above all, to be German: a love of Italy. The landlord was a cheerful type and he came over to our table, patted me on the shoulder and said, 'Ah, Maradona!' Diego Maradona played for SSC Napoli at the time and was worshiped like a god by the Italians. The landlord's appellation for me was clearly meant as camaraderie. Of course, I didn't look in the slightest like Maradona unless the whole world was divided into white and 'everyone else', or 'the West and the rest'. In that case, I suppose, I belonged more in the Maradona camp, but then there was the question of which side the rather dark-skinned Tuscan restaurant owner would have been on.

Ten years later, France was hosting the FIFA World Cup. The beloved star of the Brazilian team was the striker Ronaldo with his crooked teeth and slight paunch. Now people joked, 'You look like Ronaldo!' That was perhaps closer, but it was still a pretty imprecise comparison.

But then, another ten years passed and everything was different again. There was a black man who everyone seemed to be talking about – or was I just imagining it? A young Illinois senator was a contender for the Democratic presidential candidate. When speaking about him, you had to be careful not to accidentally say Osama bin Laden; sometimes in the early days he was introduced with his second name, as well, Hussein. Whereas just a few weeks into the presidential race, it already seemed absurd that anyone could ever confuse the names Osama bin Laden and Barack Obama. But I was flummoxed. This man was black, but he wasn't from showbiz or sport – a rare individual who fulfilled my mother's stipulation of old. All the same, I was biding my time to see what would become of it. Was there now going to be a black man who was constantly the topic of conversation? There had never been anything like it. Would this have consequences for me? Would it spell the end of my invisibility that had helped me feel secure? Would it affect me personally?

At the time I was working as literary editor for the *Süddeutsche Zeitung*. A colleague of mine, a smart and likeable chap, and a proven connoisseur of the USA and its literature, who only occasionally stopped by the editorial office, stuck his head around my door one day. He had a meaningful expression on his face, but also looked a little anxious that he might be crossing the line of what was appropriate. In his heavy Bavarian drawl he said, 'Isn't that Barack Obama a spitting image of you!'

It was clear by now that I really wasn't going to be left out of it. OK, deep breath, this was going to be fun. Were people now going to stop seeing me as German and instead as someone who had something in common with an African American politician from Chicago? I had to take a closer look. No sooner had my colleague gone than I started googling photos of Obama. He was a bit darker than me, but I liked the look of him. I had no objections about the comparison. After all, for the first time in my life, I was being compared to someone who had a similar educational background to myself, closer at least than Maradona and Ronaldo.

This was progress. I had just been to Tantris, to a meal hosted in honour of Germany's first three-star chef Eckart Witzigmann. An eighteen-course amuse-bouche menu. A lot of his apprentices had come to mingle with the Munich PR set. The champagne was flowing and we were all a bit tipsy when a cook from Vienna slurred, 'So, who do you play for then?' That didn't feel great. Fortunately, a vintner from Styria gave him a severe rebuke. In my embarrassed shock, I was lost for words.

The moment I started googling Obama, I realised scenes like this would soon be a thing of the past. Obama was my man. I would have much to gain personally from his presidency. And besides, I had also succumbed to his charm like millions of others. But my inner glow wasn't kindled so much by the Black Obama as Obama the Intellectual. Wasn't the fact that such a smart, highly educated man might move into the White House more astonishing than the, admittedly, historically unprecedented fact of a black man potentially becoming president?

But it seemed to be only me who saw it that way. The way I thought about it was again most likely due to my tendency to downplay the skin colour issue and turn it into a social question – 'the skin issue,' as Edward put it, whenever he didn't want me to evade the topic.

However, one thing was obvious: this Barack Obama didn't fit the image the world had of a black American. He wasn't a king of bling, or a comedian like Eddie Murphy, he wasn't an activist and preacher like Jesse Jackson. This was a third possibility opening up, between hip hop street cred and civil rights activism, something new. I thought of Yvonne's lawyer and the Brecht poem, but Obama's features weren't marked with contempt, his voice wasn't hoarse, and yet he talked about inequity and injustice. Unlike Yvonne and Edward, Obama hadn't personally experienced segregation, especially as his childhood and teenage years were spent in Hawaii and Jakarta, far removed from the struggle led by people like Yvonne. Obama had been spared the many humiliations that Yvonne's lawyer would never forget; his struggle for black rights wasn't determined by his environment, and that lent him something free and universal.

In fact, as I found out, he wasn't actually an African American at all. His background was really more like mine: his father, who was from Kenya, had met Obama's mother while studying in Hawaii, but soon after their son was born they had both gone their separate ways. Obama was ten when he last saw his father. As a child, he moved to Jakarta with his mother and her new Indonesian husband, and he spent his high school years with his maternal grandparents in Hawaii. His first contact with the African American community was when he first moved to Chicago in the mid-1980s. Having grown up not an active Christian, it was here in Chicago that he joined the United Church of Christ – the church for which Yvonne had worked all her life.

When Obama became president of the *Harvard Law Review* during his postgraduate law degree, he was described as the first African American to hold this post. But wasn't the important thing that he was, in a sense, a later immigrant, a blow-in? An African-American in spirit, like I was a Prussian in spirit? In any case, there was an ambiguity about him, about how he carried himself, that made him irresistible. He seemed to hover above, not rooted to one place. He transcended his environment. He wasn't confined to representing one group. He was so free.

And like me, he had half-siblings in Africa. I couldn't help but love him.

After Obama won the presidency, I wrote an article about skin colour for the first time in my professional life. It was titled 'Two Shades of Black.' In the first part, I considered Obama's poise and the extent to which he could change the public perception of black men. In the second part, I switched to the first person singular and conveyed my own experiences, especially how my perception of myself had changed over the years.

The next day, a young colleague from the Sport section congratulated me on my essay. I was working in the Berlin editorial team at the time, and our offices were next to each other so we saw each other all the time. He had read it with great interest, but had been surprised when suddenly there was talk of 'me'. He seemed utterly baffled by it. It was only then that the penny dropped. 'Oh, of course, Ijoma is black!'

The sports writer, fortunately, and not the Viennese chef, was the general rule in my life. But perhaps what I've experienced can be more precisely defined: the Viennese chef reacted the way he did because he only saw me from the outside, while my colleague knew me, knew how I spoke and thought. It's always been like this, since I was a child. I was called 'the chatterbox', especially at my athletics club. Today I realise that the reason I talked so much was so that no one could mistake me for a foreigner. I talked in defence of my Germanness. And as long as there was no black crocodile in the room, it tended to work.

A few years later, I had a girlfriend who wasn't German and for whom I was decidedly too German (she thought Germans needed a bit more oomph, a bit more fire). She insisted, 'The more African you look, the better!' I used to shave my head every three months, when my hair got to about one and a half centimetres. Then from very short it grew back to the same length and I'd start the cycle again. I had never thought of doing anything different with my hair since that time when, at thirteen, I had failed to convey my vision of Udo Lindenberg to the local barber.

But now, when I was ready to reach for the clippers, my girlfriend was saying, 'Let it grow!'

'Really? How's that going to look?'

'Like Basquiat.'

'Who?'

'Jean-Michel Basquiat, the artist. Friend of Andy Warhol.'

She googled him and showed me photos. Great guy, no question about it, but the idea that my hair might look like that one day was pure fantasy. But since my girlfriend was very assertive, I didn't have much choice. A good year passed, the metamorphosis was gradual, but eventually the time had come: my hair had grown into dreadlocks. I had grown into a new me. It was an overwhelming success. Everyone loved my new look. Honestly, people loved talking to me about my hair. They clapped me on the shoulder and congratulated me as though – after such a long incubation period! – I had finally broken free. They thought it was fantastic that I was finally accepting it. 'You've changed too, haven't you?' I now had an afro, that much was true – but whatever this 'it' was that I had supposedly finally accepted, they seemed to ascribe me a lot more self-confidence about it than I really felt.

Of course I knew what they meant by 'it,' and I gave a resigned nod, because resistance was futile. I liked my new rasta look, but the idea – insinuated by my compassionate friends and colleagues – that it was a long-awaited expression of my long-denied inner essence seemed to me a not particularly desirable process of naturalisation. The body, after all, is at most an aspect of theatrical staging, not of deeper truth.

As far as I was concerned, my new hairstyle was me playing with my identity, not its biological substrate being revealed. In fact everything about identity is a game, really, and isn't it almost barbaric to see it differently? The Prussia of Ribbeck's pear tree, the Habsburg empire of Hofmannsthal's *Rosenkavalier*, the spectre of my forebears' Silesia – that was all toying with identities, costumes we clutch at to throw over our naked bodies. But all uniforms, all identities, are just invented traditions to cling to with our nostalgia, and it's best not to have any illusions about their divine creation. In the end, 'what is German and what is true' is an effect created by Wagner's music, and in a similar vein I saw my new hairstyle as nothing more than playing with my own appearance.

Of course, biological fate also sets certain limits on what we can do with our bodies, it is not entirely a social construction. And if people wanted to see in my new hairstyle an affirmation of this inescapable inner truth, if that's what they were getting at, then it wasn't very modern, but maybe not entirely wrong. In any case, I wasn't going to put up a fight.

In the summer of 2013, Edward visited me in Berlin. We had always stayed in touch; until Facebook came along, he sent regular letters. In 1997, I had spent another two whole months with him in Brooklyn. But by now he was a worthy old man of seventy-five, living in Chicago, since the Brooklyn where I had visited him no longer existed, and with his minister's pension he had been priced out by gentrification.

Edward and I knew each other's every quirk, every obstinacy. Even blindfolded, we could tell what the other was thinking. Sometimes Edward shook his head at me, before I had even said anything, having caught me thinking something he didn't approve of. After two days in Berlin, I noticed him grinning a lot, a mock suppressed grin that you'd do well not to ignore. He also started rubbing the back of his left hand with his right thumb, that gesture I would never forget. 'The skin issue'... Eventually, he said, 'I won't say a word. I won't say a word.' (Edward loves to sing his English in his wonderful Boston drawl, sometimes uttering a phrase twice just to savour the melody.)

'What?'

'The people here are staring at me!'

Typical Edward, I thought, of course he thinks everyone's looking at him. I've lived as a black man in this country for forty years, and the last time children stared at me from their strollers must have been in the early '90s, but Edward comes to Berlin and after two days he's convinced that people in this multi-ethnic city are staring at him!

That was how my thoughts rumbled on when another voice came through in the background. 'Take a closer look,' I told myself. 'He's right, it's true. You've already noticed it, you just didn't want to admit it. People really are ogling at Edward, and it's not subtle.'

On our next walk, Edward pointedly looked up at the blue sky when he felt people's eyes on him, as if to show that he could choose to ignore it if I preferred.

'Fine, you're right,' I said. 'But I don't understand. They don't look at me. Is there a sort of tolerance for colour deviation, up to a certain shade? Is it that my cappuccino tone is still within the tolerance range, whereas you're just too dark not to stand out?'

Edward thought perhaps that was it, but he didn't want to presume to judge in a country he didn't know. Anyway, he was reassured that I at least saw what he was seeing.

The next day we sat outside in the sunshine at Café Savigny in Charlottenburg, surrounded by the casually genteel, cultural bourgeoisie. And yet I felt the eyes on the back of my neck. If I turned around, everyone beamed as though they had seen the Holy Spirit in us, and when I was about to take a selfie of Edward and me, I had barely reached forward with my iPhone when someone from the next table jumped up and offered his services. There was something jarring about how keen he was to help. Edward's expression was like a barrister in a courtroom drama. 'No further questions, Your Honour!'

Los Angeles is the only place I know of that I could describe as being 'colour blind', and I can't deny that there was something refreshing about being there. Something was different. Something in me. I felt different. For the first time, I no longer had to do something that I hadn't even realised I had always done: that sharp intake of air, that combat readiness that went with every encounter, that extra dose of presence of mind before going into any situation, just to rule out any misunderstandings. I no longer had to anticipate the other person's reaction in order to be able to influence it in my favour, because here nobody inferred anything about you from the colour of your skin. An automatic response that I had relied on all my life didn't need to click into action. It was like pedalling hard on your bike thinking you're in the highest gear, only to find you're in a much lower one than you thought. You're pedalling in vain. There's no resistance, your energy is wasted. In LA, this energy could find another use.

This was not at all the case in New York. The city is ethnically and culturally diverse like no other place in the world, but I will never forget how, when I visited Edward in the 1990s, all the guests in a restaurant would glance up when a *mixed couple* walked in. It was only a brief, essentially respectful look, people were even embarrassed, but they couldn't help it, it was too tempting to wonder which particular circumstances had brought them together and what special cultural experiences had shaped their lives since. That may be a thing of the past, but not that distant past.

All the same, New York hasn't stopped seeing colour, quite the opposite: it's become oversensitive to it. Your ethnic phenotype is part of your social appearance. You carry your ethnic identity with you like a veteran wears his old war medals. The way you present your background, the way you use your appearance, emphasise it or downplay it, is all part of the performance of your identity. This has its positives, but – like everything in New York – it takes a lot of energy.

In contrast, the California phenotype is genuinely post-ethnic; the typical Los Angeleno looks like a cross between a Korean and a Mexican, a new, emergent universal look that no longer tells you anything about someone's origins, but only about some third thing, something about California perhaps. Being mixed is the norm, and you can mix very different shades of colour with a similar result.

Many friends, especially Americans, have insisted I was wrong to speak so warmly about LA, contradicting me like Mr Kaufmann with his orthodontic practice in Ludwigshafen. My perspective was limited to the affluent milieus I had hung out in; of course, money was more important there than race. It's an objection that can't be dismissed out of hand, but those who contradicted me lived in the same milieu. I suppose even in this one social group, the extent to which people notice someone's skin tone can vary. So I wouldn't contradict my friends outright, but add perhaps that while Los Angeles might not be how you'd imagine an ideal world, it's at least some progress that, for once, money is more important than race. It's not the end of the journey, but it might be the beginning.

As a child and as a teenager I always lived in the fear that someone might shout something offensive at me, something racist. It never happened. At some point I let my guard down. I knew that the syllable *neg-* would never be followed with *-er*, always with ... *-ative*. But history favours the circle over the arrow. Everything always comes back round again.

In 2014, a book was published by the writer of feline crime fiction Akif Pirinçci called *Germany Gone Mad: The Mad Cult of Women, Homosexuals and Immigrants.* The book was nothing but an orgy of disinhibition. A tirade of hatred and profanity. My review pulled no punches. But I don't think I was ready for the outrage it provoked. On the website *Politically Incorrect,* they were seething; what could you expect from a filthy 'left-wing' journo? And there was me thinking all my life that the only thing further right than me was the wall, but the spectrum of opinions around me had evidently shifted so much that I, a disciple of Mr Vaupel, was now on the left. I could live with that, but it was a shock to suddenly have this utterly unabashed racism rain down on me. This was new. Well, the half- '*neger*' and 'German darkie' would say like that, argued the trolls. Another commentator shared a photo of me with a comment that I had probably been 'airbrushed lighter with Photoshop'. Another insinuated it was beneath his dignity to engage with me. I had experimented with my rasta locks, after all. After my hair's enormous success story compared to my Dossenheim years, now for the first time it was being used against me.

Another example? To quote in full: 'I suggest we extend some sympathy to our culturally rich asset to the arts with his high pigmentation parentage. For our dear mixed-race German, banging the drum is in his blood. What can he do but bang on? And that's fine – at least you know what to expect.'

Akif Pirinçci was asked about my review at a reading in Bonn. His reply – which you can read in *Frankfurter Allgemeine Zeitung,* 12th May 2014 – was that Mangold can piss off back to Africa, back to the bush.

I couldn't help thinking how smug my friends would all be. They had always said that I saw the world with rose-tinted spectacles.

What was it Hans Sachs sang in the *Master-Singers*? 'Who will say its name? It's nothing but the same old madness.'

# PART IV

# Mama's Death

My mother had never been to Venice. So, in November 2009, we flew there together. I can't go two years without seeing Venice. This time, it was pouring with rain and, as always in November, a thick fog lay over the lagoon. At night the vaporetti's navigation lights flickered in the milky soup. A muted foghorn sounded.

The rain added to the atmosphere of the hazy, ghostly light. It was never far from one church to the next. We strolled through the Scuola di San Rocco admiring the Tintorettos on the ceiling – without getting sore necks, thanks to the mirrors we had brought with us. At the Accademia, we lingered in front of Giorgione's *Tempesta*, wondering, as one should, whether it isn't actually a depiction of the exodus to Egypt after all. At the Frari, we had a good look at Titian's *Pesaro Madonna*, and I told Mama about my dream of writing an illustrated book one day about patrons, those shady types who feign humility, vain busybodies who are fixated on art, pious yet with an eye on status and reputation, devout and yet narcissistic. I waxed lyrical about those masters of Catholic grandstanding, uninvited spectators to the Salvation who, thanks to a purse full of money, have muscled their way into so many paintings where they gaze out provocatively, in half profile, two heads smaller than the Apostles, proud yet humble at the same time, benefiting from that immortality that only the arts can grant. I knew that my mother's heart would race when she heard my enthusiasm for these art world benefactors. She had never had money and had absolutely no time for the honorifics of the establishment; everything boastful was alien to her. She was religious in a quiet way, like a Franciscan monk who sings with the birds and, to her, seeing a status symbol in art was an empty delusion. This was the last thing she would have thought of, the idea of succumbing to the glamour of patronage. But she was never dogmatic, she was who she was, without ever wishing to set herself up as an example. Anything or anyone that was different from herself could count on her sympathetic curiosity, and that was why she enjoyed seeing this, and why she was giggling with pleasure at the sight of her son – who always craved distinction while fretting about standing out – apparently striking out in a completely different direction, expressing his penchant for worldly (and spiritual) pomp, and raving about patrons of all people. Mother and son were made of the same cloth, but cut to a very different pattern.

Just two months later, in January 2010, Mama was back in hospital. After ten years, her cancer had returned. Back in 2000, she had had a successful operation and radiotherapy, but this time the prospects were bleak. The cancer had spread. An operation would have been a serious procedure, and the prospects of it extending her life were uncertain. My mother decided against it. She didn't want to fight again, she would rather surrender to her fate. When we asked the doctors how much time she had left, they estimated between two months and a year and a half. Mama was given a stoma and could return home. Once she had got used to it, after the initial fear, it seemed like we were entering the final act of our life together. The previous acts of the play of our life had been lovely, but those last few months were the radiant summation.

We wanted to have one last trip together before her final journey, which she would have to make alone. Our destination was Rügen. Ever since my mother had taken me there on bike tours as a child, I knew she had a pull to the north. She was fond of the mild-mannered, open people of Heidelberg, but she always had a longing for the north. When I was a child, when my long summer holidays began and the humidity in the Neckar valley became oppressive, we would always head up to Hamburg by train. We would have our bikes sent on ahead. Cycling through Holstein Switzerland, we would present our passports at a godforsaken border post near Flensburg, greet the bleak expanses of Jutland where we'd struggle against the eternal north-westerly to reach the Skagerrak, before heading east into the softer landscapes of Zealand, until we finally came to the small Danish island of Møn. There, on a clear day, standing atop the chalky cliffs, you could see the Baltic island of Hiddensee on the horizon. That was always a sublime moment, because we were as close as we could be in those days to the topography so beloved of my mother, the Fontane reader: the landscapes of the Mark Brandenburg and Mecklenburg-West Pomerania of her childhood. Holstein Switzerland was beautiful, but in truth it was just a substitute for an inaccessible landscape, from which we were separated by the Iron Curtain, but which actually belonged to the world of a more distant past. Silesia and Brandenburg were places of her childhood that were beyond reach in the present. Lost topographies, and that's why the East, in its irreality, was able to awaken such an overwhelming longing. The more closed off the land, the more fertile it was for flowering fantasies.

I feel sometimes like my mother's personal mythology, which passed seamlessly down to me as a child – Silesia, Brandenburg and all the landscapes of Fontane – blurred into one partly historical, partly literary, partly autobiographical place of yearning. Even as a child, the song *Maikäfer, flieg!* *(Fly ladybird, fly!)* would move me to tears, as if this lament was about my own family chronicle (it actually refers to the Thirty Years' War, but I only learned that later, as a student). *'Der Vater ist im Krieg' (Your father's off at war):* that must have been about my grandfather, who died on the Eastern Front. *'Die Mutter ist in Pommerland, Pommerland ist abgebrannt' (Your mother's in Pomerania, it's all burned down):* for me that was the name of the world from which my Grandma had fled with her children. In my imagination, the burned-down Pomerania, Silesia and Brandenburg merged into a fairytale world that could only be rebuilt by reading Fontane.

As soon as the wall came down, in the summer of 1991, Mama and I drove to Hiddensee. We rented an apartment that had once been the home of the great GDR opera director Walter Felsenstein. The fall of the Berlin Wall opened up unexpected access to the world of Fontane, which had been lost to a decades-long Sleeping Beauty-like slumber. The restaurants had signs saying, 'Futtern wie bei Muttern' – *Good food, like mum makes* – and the food was really shockingly bad, but in our readiness for nostalgia this fact only reinforced the feeling of being on a journey back in time.

Much later, in 2008, two years before her death, Mama visited me in Berlin. I rented a car so we could travel around. We had already been to Chorin Abbey and Rheinsberg one morning when I saw my mother absorbed in studying the map. 'Shall we go to the Beetzsee today?' she asked. 'I've found the place where we stayed with the Ribbecks on the map. It's called Bagow. Here!' Her finger pointed to the tiny lettering on the map.

How often I had heard the name Beetzsee as a child, but I had taken it for an imagined place, a sacred fiction, so to speak – the sort of fantasy you don't subject to a reality check out of respect for your mother's feelings. And here she was asking, 'Shall we go to the Beetzsee?' I looked at her as if she had just announced the train times for the fictional Lummerland from *Jim Button and Luke the Engine Driver*. In my head, the Beetzsee was every bit as mythical as Atlantis. I took the lake and the mansion of the von Ribbeck family to be a poetic fantasy my mother had clung to in consolation over the loss of her home, a transitional object, the stuff of legends and not somewhere you could physically drive to from Berlin. And now here was Mama sitting on my balcony, pointing to the map, and it really was marked 'Beetzsee.' Northwest of Potsdam. I was on the verge of a defiant retort like some intractable officer of the law, 'That doesn't prove anything!' As if the main thing was to resist distracting illusions at all costs. But instead I said, 'Sure, if you think that's your Bagow, we can go there.'

We got to Potsdam quite quickly and everything was normal enough up to that point. But as soon as we turned onto the country road which, according to the map, would lead to the Beetzsee, I felt like we were driving against a backdrop that had been painted onto the landscape just for the sake of my mother's fantasies. After about fifteen minutes of her looking out of the window in silence and concentration, Mama said, 'The village is coming up ahead.' And indeed, after the next bend, and as if from a distance of 64 years, the sign appeared welcoming us to Bagow. Mama continued, 'Drive up to the chestnut tree over there, then turn right. There should be a dead end that leads to the house.' So we turned right at the chestnut tree. A street sign confirmed it was a no-through road. Another two hundred metres and then there it was on the left: a large stately home. Schloss Ribbeck.

Nothing had changed. The GDR had respectfully preserved my mother's childhood memories. Everything was exactly as Mama had described it. The Schloss, or manor house, had been leased to the local community (the Ribbecks, from whom it had been expropriated at the time of the Soviet occupation zone, bought it back after 1990), but it had lost none of its dark and mysterious character. A renaissance château with a steep pitched roof and a side extension from the baroque period added later. The surrounding parkland lay open before us, exactly as Mama had described it. It was bordered by reeds and through them a narrow boardwalk led to the River Havel. The idea that Mama had as a child lived somewhere where you could jump straight into the river had always seemed so implausible to me, a child of the seventies, when all German rivers were so polluted that swimming was out of the question. But here we were. This was where she had learned her love of swimming.

It was a quiet moment. Mama didn't have tears in her eyes nor a flowing stream of words, but at that moment everything fell into place. For me it was also a moment of finally making amends. So all this really existed. This place I was seeing had only been a brief stopover in her family's life, and yet mother and son were now standing in the grounds of Schloss Ribbeck as though we had come full circle; the refugees had come to rest. And suddenly I had the feeling that our trip to the Beetzsee was the one and only thing I needed to achieve in my life. And yet just a few hours before, I still had no idea that the one thing I absolutely needed to do in my life was to take a trip to the Beetzsee with my mother.

I can't say why this place meant so much to both of us. Nothing else came of it. After about an hour we got back in the car and drove back to Berlin, but we were happy. And when we got back to my apartment in Pankow an hour later, it seemed just right that I lived here (and not in beautiful Munich), so close to the lake, the Beetzsee. So was I a Brandenburger after all, even more than I was Silesian? My goodness, what a lot of parts of me there were!

When Mama was discharged from hospital in spring 2010 with instructions from the doctor that she should spend her remaining time in as nice a way as possible, we decided to go to Rügen in the summer. In July, I came to Heidelberg to pick Mama up. She was in good form, full of confidence that heading north one last time was the right thing to do. She was relaxed, almost in high spirits. The next morning we took the regional train to Mannheim, but before we had even reached our first stop, my mother turned pale as a sheet. She was trembling. There was no way we could continue our journey. I wanted to call a taxi at Mannheim train station and drive straight back to Heidelberg, to the hospital, but my mother gathered the last of her strength and protested. 'No, let's try and keep going.' So we changed trains in Mannheim. I took our cases while Mama struggled on with shaky steps to the platform where we would catch the Intercity Express to Berlin. I manoeuvred her into 1st Class. All the passengers and the conductor could see our distress and the irresponsible nature of the situation, but no one asked us to do the only sensible thing, which would have been to get off the train and seek medical help. They respected my mother's last wishes, if you will.

On this trip she told me a secret. Well, can I call it a secret? At least, something she hadn't told me in the forty years of my life. Perhaps it was the proximity to death that got her talking, or perhaps she realised that in this exceptional situation I wouldn't be able to stop her from talking about my father; I had never been a particularly willing audience for my mother's Ozurumba stories, but how could I stop her now? In any case, there on the train from Mannheim to Berlin, sitting in 1st Class, she told me for the first and only time that when I was five years old, she sent a letter with photos of me to Nigeria. She wanted to let my father know that I was fine so that he could be happy for his son. A German couple who were friends with my father and mother worked in Enugu, the university town near Aba, so she sent the letter to them. The couple confirmed that they had delivered the letter. But she never received a reply.

That was the first time I had ever heard my mother say something negative about my father. His lack of response, the fact that he had nothing to say to his son – it pained her, she said. She didn't say she felt 'hurt,' but that 'it pained her'. Everything was as she always said: she had loved my father, she knew he would go back to Nigeria, she had accepted it and could live with it because it had been her decision, the path she had consciously chosen. But the fact that he hadn't replied to her letter containing photos of his son – that hit her hard.

My mother spoke slowly, fighting her exhaustion. Sometimes her pronunciation took on that strange accent that belonged to her like a dark secret. I listened and didn't say anything. I had to accept that the people sharing the train carriage with us could overhear our family history; this time, feelings of shame were secondary.

We didn't make it to Rügen. In Berlin, we went straight to a hospital. When my mother was discharged three weeks later, she was thin, shrunken, emaciated. She could only eat the tiniest bites. Going back to Heidelberg was out of the question. So I decided that we would stay in my apartment in Berlin. She had to accept it. She didn't like the fact that she had left her home in Dossenheim without being able to say goodbye. Rituals of departure and arrival had always been important to her. But there was no other way.

There were two more months, and they were intense. But the mood was never gloomy. Friends came from all around to say farewell to my mother. Nobody beat around the bush or avoided the reality. Soon, Mama wouldn't be here anymore, so the remaining moments had to be used courageously to establish that closeness one last time through talking, and Mama's most precious conviction that life is about communication was demonstrated to impressive effect.

It was a golden October day the week before she passed away, and the farmer I go to at the Saturday market had some small yellow pears from Werder. I bought a kilo and ran home, thrilled. 'Mama, these pears are from Werder, and Werder is Havelland.' By this point she was eating almost nothing, but she mustered up all her strength to chew and swallow at least one slice of the Ribbeck pear.

A week later, on the Sunday, the sun was shining again, and the time had come. Mama hadn't spoken for two days and her eyes remained closed. When I held her hand and spoke to her, she squeezed mine. At lunchtime, her breathing changed to a different rhythm. Her breathing was loud, rattling, and there was a long pause between each intake. I was surprised by how unmistakable it was that death was there at the door. I sat by her bed, helpless. Should I try to drag her back to life? Should I cry as I meet her death? I lacked the composure to sit there as a passive witness, so I got up and fetched the great Conrady, an anthology of poetry. I needed to do something ritualistic instead of praying, something that gave me stability. I opened the book and flicked through the pages, with nothing specific in mind. It fell open onto Theodor Storm. Of course, the one about Husum: 'On the grey beach, by the grey sea / A town stands to the side.' It was one of Mama's favourite poems. Whenever our bike tours took us to Husum, she would always recite Storm's verse and we wondered how he could describe this town of all places, with its colourful facades, as grey. Now I read the same lines to my mother again. Her breath rattled on in the now familiar rhythm. I turned the page. Theodor Fontane! How had I not thought of that? I read *Herr von Ribbeck auf Ribbeck im Havelland* aloud to Mama. During the second stanza, which begins with the line, 'After a number of years had gone by / The noble Herr Ribbeck at Ribbeck did die,' Mama took her last, rattling breath. I read our poem to the end.

In the days before, I had worried that I might be afraid of her dead body. But then the opposite was the case: when her soul had drifted away and her lifeless body lay in the bed before me, I waited over two hours before I notified the doctor. When he came, he approached the deathbed in the most delicate way, like you glide across the parquet of an old stately home in those felt slippers they give you. He cast a pious look at my mother, before going back to the living room to sign the death certificate, less an official act of signing than a gesture of devotion. He might almost have lit a candle too.

After the doctor left, I hesitated again before calling the funeral director. The idea of having to part with my mother once and for all suddenly seemed too much; as long as she was still here before me, everything could go on as before. She had barely eaten in recent days. I choked up as I looked at her body. It now seemed like my mother had laden all the pain of her illness onto the shoulders of this dutiful workhorse of a body; she had shrunk under the burden, while becoming light enough to transcend to the hereafter. Her struggle was over, and what was left of her seemed transformed into a mummy, this ideal form of existence for the incalculable time between this world and the next. No need for a pyramid, my bedroom was just fine. I was in the process of accepting the new situation: Mama would be dead, and yet still be here.

When the two undertakers finally came, I sobbed like a Sicilian mourner who throws herself on the coffin and refuses to let go. They wrapped the body in a black shroud and carried it out of my apartment forever.

When I visit my mother's grave in Dossenheim, I'm now one of those people I hated seeing as a child, those stooped old people traipsing to the cemetery on their pilgrimage. Instead of paying homage to life, they clung on to a dead person, their minds focused on something that no longer existed and which nevertheless seemed to have a ghostly power over them. Back then, widows still wore black, and they wore headscarves when they visited the cemetery; I could see the entrance from our apartment. Pensioners would bring a watering can with them, fill it at the tap and drag it over to the grave, panting, to water the flowers.

When I stand by my mother's grave today, I can actually see the balcony of my childhood bedroom, at least when there's no leaves on the trees.

The three birch trees in front of the house have now been felled. My mother's practice used to be in the basement, our apartment on the first floor. When I got home from school, Mama was with a client. But I never used the key, I'd always ring the bell. When the door opened with a buzz,

I'd call downstairs, 'It's me!' And Mama would call up from the basement, dividing the syllable into two pitches: 'Ye-es!' Then I'd head upstairs to find my lunch, no longer hot but still warm, waiting for me on the hob.

Every day for an entire childhood.

'It's me!'

'Ye-es!'

# Self-doubt

How many books have I reviewed as a literary critic where catastrophe could have been averted if the protagonists had simply spoken even once about the trouble brewing, about the conflict that blows up in their faces at the end? It's always when it's already too late that the questions are asked that should have been asked long ago, and suddenly everything opens up, light streams in, the wall of silence is broken. Don't ask me. As a critic, I usually come out in hives at the clichéd motif where a novel's characters don't dare talk about the inner heart of their existence. It seems to me like an off-the-shelf literary device that has long gone out of date. *If only you had said something, Desdemona.*

As a psychotherapist, it was my mother's job to get other people to talk in such a way that they were made to relate to their mode of living. The truth sets you free – a big statement, sure, but as a child I could often observe what was meant by it. Everyone who had a conversation with my mother seemed to leave with renewed spirit, their hearts relieved under her guidance. After Mama's death, I received letters from people whose names I had never heard before, who wanted to tell me how much clarity, strength and courage my mother had brought into their lives. Terms like blocking and repression were familiar to me from an early age. I always hated it when my mother justified behaviour she didn't approve of as a 'completely normal defense response' or when she interpreted my reluctance to talk about something as an act of suppression.

When I was older, I took comfort in Nabokov's ridicule of Freud. In this I had found myself a theoretical foundation for my rejection of psychoanalysis, although I knew full well, of course, that this rejection only confirmed the central Freudian tenet of defense mechanisms. But that was exactly what always annoyed me about psychoanalysis: that every rejection of it was interpreted as an unconscious confirmation of its deeper truth. When I read about Karl Popper's concept of self-immunisation, I thought: ha! Psychoanalysis is immunising itself against any rebuttal, by interpreting all counterarguments as symptoms of the very disease that it believes it, and it alone, can diagnose...

'Why are you being so defensive about it?'

'I'm not being defensive, I just think it's a load of rubbish.'

'Why are you getting so worked up about it?'

'I'm not 'worked up'!'

'You should listen to yourself!'

'I'm just saying, quite calmly actually, that psychoanalysis is a hermetically sealed system of thought.'

'I think you're suppressing something.'

Why should the power of repression be so strong? Why couldn't its spell be broken? What actually got in the way of asking the most crucial questions?

And here we come to another classic cliché. We only start delving into the past when the other people involved are dead, so then we have to speculatively reconstruct what until recently could have been revealed by some very basic questions. Why are we so reluctant to ask when the people concerned are still alive? Why is it not until they're silenced forever that our thirst for knowledge is awoken? As if there's a kind of reluctance to interrupt the lives of the living, while we will happily shout thousands of questions at a grave without hesitation. I suppose we don't like to speak to people we love about something that might be difficult to face.

I spent the first months of 2015 in the United States.

I was visiting professor at Washington University in St. Louis, Missouri, on a sabbatical that gave me plenty of time to write. I was sitting in my little apartment one evening, snow falling outside in the dark, as I searched the web for information about the sickle cell anaemia that had taken the life of my sister Nneka. The websites of American medical schools were particularly enlightening in helping me better understand the disease.

Then I remembered that Joyce, my father's wife, had written a book about it, *Coping with Sickle Cell Disease: A Mother's Own Experience*. Now I thought about it, I could picture her pressing a copy into my hand when I was in Nigeria. So I googled her name and I got several hits. Among other things was an article in the *Premium Times*, a Nigerian newspaper based in Abuja, from 2013. It described the dangers of the disease, mentioning how some churches refuse to marry couples if the bride and groom are of the same genotype (I already knew that), and giving voice to people who had dedicated their lives to fighting SCD. Joyce was also interviewed as the author of this book. And to give readers the context about how she had lost three children to SCD, the article outlined her life story.

Hardly a single noise penetrated my apartment from outside, the snow had dampened everything. Snowflakes fell swaying in small loops through the light of the street lamps, briefly rising again before they floated down. I read that at the age of 22, she left Nigeria to marry Ozurumba, a medical student she had never met. The people of his hometown, Amucha, had raised the money to send him to Germany to study. 'When the time was right, they felt it their responsibility to send him a wife too.'

Sparse words which weren't written for me; the effect was all the stronger for it. When you read something you can't believe, people like to say you can't believe your eyes, but in this case it was the other way around. I knew immediately that what my eyes were reading was absolutely correct. That was how it must have been! And it meant I needed to adapt my story to a completely new reality.

In the philosophy of science there is a guiding principle that there are always at least two possible theories to explain a phenomenon. If in doubt, it made sense to choose the simpler and therefore more elegant hypothesis (which needed fewer additional hypotheses), and the newspaper version of my family history was unbeatable in terms of its simplicity, elegance and clarity. The entire Nigerian epic in a few brief words: 'When the time was right, they felt it their responsibility to send him a wife too.'

It was 1972 when Joyce arrived in Germany. Here, too, the article is authoritative in its precision. And I was born in 1971. So I wasn't two years old, as I had always said, when my father left us, but much younger, and he didn't go back to Nigeria, his future wife came to join him in Germany. It wasn't he who had gone back to his village. The village had pulled the emergency brake and intervened in his life, selected a wife for him and sent her to Germany, and he had submitted to this decree. What the article didn't know (but the village, I could imagine, must have known and that was why it resorted to these frantic countermeasures) was that 'Ozurumba, a medical student' was already a father. Namely mine.

My eldest sister, Ikunna, born in November 1972, wasn't born in Nigeria, but in Germany, in Bochum to be precise, where I saw my father for the first time in 1993 and where I, at the age of 22, had formulated the assumption that he must have met his likeable Indian colleague during some stage of his medical studies before the Heidelberg period. Mama had only ever talked about him studying in Heidelberg, but didn't mention at which stage; I was the one who had told myself that he must have started his studies in Bochum. First Bochum, then Heidelberg, then Nigeria.

The correct order was first Heidelberg, then Bochum, then Nigeria.

So the village elders had chosen Joyce as my father's future wife (an excellent choice, by the way, for such an atavistic institution; perhaps we shouldn't underestimate the wisdom of arranged marriages), and the article mentioned this fact to explain why my father and his wife – both medically trained – hadn't discussed their genetic dispositions at the time. At the end of the day it was simply an arranged marriage, and in spite of the village's usual caution, this aspect wasn't considered. And so my father didn't go back to Nigeria to start a new family there, but stayed in Germany where his future wife came to join him. He in Bochum, his son in Heidelberg – no more than five hours away by train.

But what shocked me most that night in St. Louis was another discovery. The realisation that I must have always known this, I just hadn't wanted to admit it.

I had always imagined repression as a subtle process occurring deep beyond the threshold of my own perception.

By no means did I envisage it as something as undemanding, as crude and tangible as closing your eyes, refusing to listen, pretending no one had said anything, deliberately not processing or suppressing information.

In fact, my behaviour was nothing if not active falsification of evidence. Whenever someone had asked me how old Ikunna was, I had made her out to be younger because I *knew* that her being born in 1972 (plus the nine months before that) couldn't be squared with my version of events that claimed that my father went to Nigeria in 1973, 'when I was two.'

And not only that, Ikunna had herself never made a secret of the fact that she was born in Bochum. If she had mentioned it, I must have given her such a blank stare that she didn't feel comfortable to go into it. And now I also remembered that my father had himself written to me in one of his first letters that his daughter's German was excellent, no doubt influenced by her early childhood memories from Bochum.

When I read that article in the *Premium Times*, it was 10pm Central Time, which was 5am back home. I had to talk to someone about my discovery, I couldn't be left alone with this news, but all my friends in Germany were asleep. So I called Edward, who I had visited in Chicago just a few weeks earlier. In any case, there was no one better to talk to about it. Anyone who has worked as a pastor for four decades knew a thing or two about pastoral care.

'I told you that I've started writing about getting to know my father. And I also told you about Sickle Cell Disease. I've just been trying to find out more about the disease, and that's when I came across an article about my father's wife. It says my father didn't return to Nigeria when I was two years old, and the village, Amucha, sent his wife to live with him in Germany.'

'Ah yes, the village,' Edward interrupted in a warm voice, 'I remember it well. Where your father's the chief. I always liked this village cohesion, this solidarity.'

'And that's precisely the point. They chose a wife for my father in his absence and sent her to join him in Germany! I presume at pretty much the exact moment when they could no longer ignore the fact that he had fathered an illegitimate son with a German woman.'

Edward began to lose his usual composure. 'Are you okay?' he asked firmly.

'Just a little confused. You know, it's only about five hours from Bochum to Heidelberg by train. While I was growing up in Heidelberg, he was living in Bochum.'

'For how long?'

'I don't know. Maybe two or three years?'

Edward commented that he could well imagine how painful this late realisation was for me, but while he was expressing his sympathy, I realised that that wasn't the point at all. It wasn't that I felt betrayed or any less loved by my father, because he was so heartless as to live around the corner without coming to see me. I was just shocked at my ability to repress the seemingly obvious.

'I'm mainly just amazed at myself. I should have known all of this. When people asked me about my father, I've always said that he went back to Nigeria when I was two, but I really don't know where I got that idea from. Maybe Mama told me that, or maybe not, and now I can't ask her. In any case, my version was always that it was two years. But something I've never thought about, something I've never noticed, at least not in a way that would have called my version of the story into question, is that my father doesn't appear in any of the photos of me as a two-year-old in a stroller being pushed through the vineyards of Dossenheim. There are photos of my father in a jacket and tie, carrying me in his arms, but the baby he's holding is no more than seven months old. After that he had already set off for Bochum.'

'I can well imagine how upsetting this is. That your father was really close by, but didn't contact you.'

'No, you're focusing on the wrong thing. It's not Bochum that's upset me, but my limitless ability to suppress it. I'll tell you something even worse. I've always made my sister out to be younger than she is. And at the same time she's never made a secret of the fact that she was born in 1972.'

'Why was it so important to you that your father didn't leave until you were two?'

'It's embarrassing, to be honest. All my life I thought that the later my father left us, the less it seemed like it was my birth that was the problem. The less shame there was. The more proper things seemed.'

'Shame? What do you mean by that?'

'A father who runs away a few months after the birth of his son is a scoundrel. And a mother, who can't keep hold of the father for more than a few months – well, that doesn't look great, either. But a father who, after two years, feels the burden of responsibility for his village weighing heavily on his shoulders, and returns to his homeland alone because the mother of his son can't imagine moving to Africa – that's a father who still isn't a perfect embodiment of normality, but at least he's not just a one-night-stand. You know, as a child I was always uncomfortable when someone asked me whether my father was a GI, because I imagined a GI as someone who would get a German girl pregnant and then scarper. I preferred the Amucha story to that. The idea that he struggled for two years, giving family life together a good shot to see if it could work out, and then, after my mother and father had listened to their instincts, coming to the difficult decision that he would return out of a sense of responsibility for the village he comes from. To give back to his people what they had given him. An almost noble character trait.'

'And wasn't that actually the case to a certain extent? Your father was part of Amucha's moral system, and that's why he had to act that way.'

'You could see it that way.'

'Do you think your mother knew that he went to Bochum?'

'I don't know. I don't think so. I don't even know if it was Mama who told me about the two years or if I came up with that myself. All I know is that she always said, "your father went back to Nigeria out of a sense of responsibility for his village." I don't think she knew about Bochum. My mother wasn't someone who would say anything other than the truth. But I'm not sure.'

Outside, the snow continued to fall, and all I could see was the black sky, the white streets, the wobbly electricity pylons that looked even more crooked than usual under the burden of snow. The night was silent. The few cars that pushed their way along the street were also covered in snow, their roofs white, as if they were just moving bulges in the soundproof skin of snow that smothered the world.

'How are you feeling now?'

'I'm just amazed at how much I could fail to see.'

I hung up and gazed out of the window at the falling snowflakes. Now I remembered that Joyce once mentioned that she had lived in Bochum for two or three years. She had absolutely not made a secret of it. But this suggested that Mama must have known. And if my father presumed my mother knew, then twenty years later he had no reason to keep it a secret. In her gently determined way, my mother would have seen a higher meaning in the outwardly brutal nature of it all. It was only from the outside, she might have said to herself, that it looked like an ugly authoritarian act where my father was pulled away from his illegitimate son by way of a hastily arranged marriage, but if you thought your way through the cultural context, then things looked a little different, and what had happened to her and me at the time was the inevitable harsh side of an altogether responsible community decision. It was Amucha that counted, not Bochum. Bochum was external. The true essence of the story was Amucha. And it was this story alone that was to be communicated to the son, its allegorical significance – give back to your community what it has given you – trumping the prosaic reality of the situation.

My mother had always told me that my father was a paediatric surgeon, but now I had to assume that it was in Bochum that he had trained in this specialism. So did that mean she knew about Bochum? Or did she assume that he had returned to Nigeria to get married, but then came back to Bochum to specialise? Perhaps she had found out about it from their mutual German friends in Nigeria, through whom she had tried to contact my father? Did she know and not find it important?

I don't think she knew. It wasn't like her to be secretive. At the very least, she would have mentioned it on our last train journey from Heidelberg to Berlin. In any case, it made little sense to tell the story of the letter that was never answered but then to leave out the Bochum episode. Or did she assume that I already knew about it because, after all, Ikunna had spoken about it quite freely? Or was the turn of events – an end to emotional intimacy that wasn't enforced by geographical distance – simply too painful for her that she blanked out the idea that her son's father was only five hours away by train, and could never quite bring herself to speak about it? Or was it actually fine by her, but she was just blanking it out for me? That is also conceivable.

I tried to imagine how they might have parted. Did she take him to the airport in Frankfurt and then, after one last hug, instead of going through security, he left the terminal and hopped on the next train to Bochum? Or was my mother the one who acted in cold blood? She wanted this man's baby, and she knew from the outset that she would raise the child alone, just as she knew that he would go back to Nigeria. Maybe it was precisely what she wanted: to be a single mother, to love her child's father from afar. Then the agreement would have been so unambiguous from the start that my father wouldn't have felt any moral obligation to say whether he was moving back to Nigeria or heading to Bochum. And it's at this point I notice that all these hypotheses only ever come as close to life itself as a reconstruction of a crime in a trial based on circumstantial evidence.

Nobody wants to be forced to become someone different than who they're used to being. Best not to go digging into the past, perhaps, best to leave it be. I was two when my father returned to Nigeria, and if the truth was different, well, so what? Who actually benefits from the truth? It was only writing this book that forced me to take a closer look, I realised. Did it mean I needed to construct a new image of my mother now? No. I wanted to cherish the image I had always had of my mother who had accompanied me and sheltered me for 44 years.

At the same time, that night in St. Louis, I remembered what was in store for me when I got back home: the boxes waiting in the basement of my Berlin apartment. I had to laugh.

What a crude literary motif – in the end it's always boxes! Six boxes filled to the brim with letters. That was all I had inherited from my mother. Her life as an epistolary novel. Unfortunately, her side of the correspondence was missing, of course. But with her customary foresight, she had used the last months of her life, before we set off on our trip that ended up in Berlin, getting her paperwork in order. She had thrown away anything that wasn't significant, and had tied up all the important letters thematically into bundles. She wanted me to read through them one day, and she realised that it would help if she cut paths through the thicket for me, otherwise I wouldn't know where to start with the impenetrable abundance.

When I was back at our Dossenheim apartment after her death, I briefly opened the boxes and had a glance inside. I saw there was a bundle labelled 'Basilios,' for example. Another marked 'Yvonne.' Another: 'Ozurumba 1968–1971.' I didn't get any further than that. I carried the boxes out to the removal van and stacked them up in my basement in Berlin.

When I told my friends about them, they were incredulous. 'What?' they asked. 'You've got your father's letters to your mother, and you haven't once looked at them?'

That's right.

And even after I got back from the United States, it wasn't like the first thing I did was run down to the basement and haul up the boxes. A few months passed by. I was happily working on my book, and only occasionally thought to myself, 'I hope I won't have to rewrite everything when I read the letters.'

At some point, however, I was ready to go down to the cellar. The boxes were pretty dusty after sitting there for nearly five years. As I pulled Mama's boxes out, I also stumbled upon some boxes of my own letters, and I figured that as I was digging into the archives, it couldn't hurt to have another look at my father's letters to me. So far I had relied on my memory when writing. It was high time to compare what I remembered with the sources.

I started with my father's letters to me. It wasn't difficult to spot them. They were in white envelopes that had yellowed more than the others and they were marked 'Godwin Hospital' in large lettering. There weren't many of them, but more than I remembered, sometimes in English, sometimes in German. I was a little ashamed to be reminded how beautiful his letters were; dignified and sensitive. He wasn't at all as tongue-tied as I had made him out to be. He had indeed written the sentence 'Blood is thicker than water,' but it was by no means as central as I had remembered it. I was utterly bowled over as I read one letter – stunned in that way that prompts a sudden feeling of remorse. It was a letter from 10 June 1993, written three months before my trip to Nigeria. In my previous letter, I must have told my father in detail about my holiday in Greece in the late summer of 1992 (when I had a near fatal incident when windsurfing. A violent storm came out of nowhere, and I couldn't pull my sail up because the wind kept pushing it back down to the water again, while at the same time driving me out to sea. All I could do was cling to the board while the waves crashed over me, under a dark, menacing sky, until two hours later I was rescued by some valiant neighbours with their motorboat...). I must have given my father a colourful description of my distress at sea. Whatever I had written, he had been impressed by the letter. Very impressed. He had shown it to his wife, he told me in his reply, this time in German (his German was still surprisingly good), and then he actually wrote: 'My wife read it too and she said that boy's going to be a writer.'

How could I forget all of this? Why hadn't it entered my mental image of my father? Why did I have this enduring impression that he only ever talked about medicine and had shown little interest in my life?

It continues in a way that a novelist would never get away with: 'But my reply (to Joyce, that is) was that I can't say precisely. We're just beginning to see a good example. Your composition on your trip to Greece was so interesting, perhaps the trip to Nigeria will be a book or an entire series!' If I had taken his letter a little closer to heart back then I might have made notes during my trip to Nigeria, which I would be very grateful for right now...

'You're funny,' he goes on to say, before apologising that his letters are so short. 'You know, medical professionals are sparing with words, but big on action (...) In other words, we medical professionals are not distinguished for our literary skills, that's why we study science from the outset.' He tells me how happy he is that Ikunna visited me in Munich. And then: 'Iku must have told you that she came to Nigeria with us when she was four. Until then she could even speak the Bochum dialect.'

I put the letters aside. For the first time, I missed my father.

The letters from the time after the trip to Nigeria were clearly determined by an obsessive pattern that we could no longer extricate ourselves from. He would constantly send me greetings from people I didn't know, supposedly everyone was desperate to know when I was coming back, they all missed me when Ikunna came home to Aba for Christmas without me. I recalled how indignant I was when I read this for the first time. How callous could he be, to imagine that I could possibly spend Christmas anywhere other than with my mother? Or he would suggest, why didn't I come to teach German at a Nigerian university? It would be good for my CV, my international links, etc... Letters from him were always like a reminder from the tax office: constantly wanting something from me that I didn't want to give. Answering his letters constantly meant giving him the brush off.

In retrospect, I have to say, my behaviour was cowardly. I never pushed it too far, so I couldn't be accused of anything, but I was so passive I must have been exasperating. I was so apathetic I was practically catatonic. When, on my first trip, they were already talking about the next one, I never promised I would come back. I just smiled amiably and never committed to anything, neither in person nor in my letters. I would outline the reasons why I couldn't right now. I never made any firm commitments to my father, my sisters or my cousin Hippolite; I didn't sign up to anything. Touched by the affection that came my way, I tried not to offend anyone, but neither did I take the initiative or ever respond with much enthusiasm. When the ball was in my court, I didn't bother tossing it back, I just left it lying there. I had responded to my father's approaches with such pliant passivity that he finally gave up. That it worked out this way was almost certainly because we avoided talking openly, because we never laid our cards on the table. If we had, I'm sure I wouldn't have been able to maintain my diplomatic Teflon-coated slipperiness, but we never advanced to such dramatic frankness. There was never a moment where we shifted from the epic genre to the psychological novel.

Perhaps there's also a simpler and more basic explanation, perhaps it wasn't a question of affection; it was love. On every postcard, Ikunna wrote, 'My brother, I love you very much.' And maybe that was too much for me. So much love in one fell swoop, which you then have to live up to. I didn't reject it, but I padded myself with a kind of shock absorber, to translate the exuberance of this love into something more manageable, something that didn't ask me to change my life.

Then I opened the other box, the one with my father's letters to my mother. They were handwritten, but they were still legible even after 40 years. They began in 1968 and ended in the summer of 1971 with a letter from Nigeria, where my father sent greetings from his family to Mama and me; everyone was happy to hear that the boy was fine. And he reports that he has already found an apartment in Bochum. So my mother knew about Bochum. It seems likely that she also knew about Joyce. But I don't know. And that's all the letters tell me.

It had been half a year since St. Louis, time for this new knowledge to settle. My old life story had turned out to be fictitious. In the meantime I had replaced it with a new one, and by now I had got used to it enough that the question of who had known what was no longer of such burning interest to me. Whatever the truth was, life was good. Perhaps it had been productive to examine my deluded self under the spotlight...

What had bothered me more was finding another letter in the box. It turned out, the collection didn't end with my father's final message in the summer of 1971, but with the copy of a letter Mama had written to my father in 2004.

The very existence of these pages was a surprise to me. Apparently, she had written them when my father visited her again in Dossenheim – a visit I hadn't known about. When he had left, she had given him the letter with the request that he waited until he was on the plane to read it (the letter was typewritten and she had made a copy for her own archive, marking it with the comment in pencil: 'Read on the plane'). It was a love letter. It opened with a quote from a 1910 sermon by Henry Scott Holland – then the canon of St. Paul's Cathedral in London. A philosophical and religious reflection on transience. 'All is well. Nothing is past. Nothing has been lost.'

My father must have travelled on from Heidelberg to see me in Munich. He didn't tell me that he had just been to Dossenheim, so I was under the impression that the two of them had only seen each other once in the past few years – that time when we had a walk together through the vineyards. I was wrong. The "grown-ups" clearly had their own lives, as it suddenly dawned on me.

After the opening lines from Holland, Mama reminds my father of the first letter she received from him 36 years ago. Those first letters were signed 'Levi'; she had asked him at the time if he also had an African name. That prompted him to tell her the story of how his mother had given him the name Ozurumba, and because of this beautiful story, which the letter itself doesn't recount, it had been 'no stretch at all' for her, my mother, to name me Ijoma.

She went on. She had dug out his letters again when he made contact with me in 1992, but she had only had a quick peek at them, 'because I was afraid, afraid of myself.' In her letters, my mother tended towards a pathos that made my toenails curl, but at this point I couldn't blame her. Now, however, her letter takes an unexpected turn. She writes that she once sent me one of his letters, adding that I was 'impressed and touched and also full of respect for the way you write and tell a story.' I have absolutely no memory of this, but clearly I've already squandered my reputation as a credible witness. At the time, my mother goes on to say, she thought about giving me the entire batch of letters, but eventually decided that it wasn't yet the right moment. That must have been in 1993.

And this time, when he visited her in Heidelberg again – this is 2004 – she thought again about giving the letters to him to bring to me in Munich. If she had, she reflected, it would have been 'something of an act of initiation.' But then she says something puzzling: 'But it wasn't such a good idea after all, because nothing came of it.'

It isn't clear from her letter why nothing came of the idea. Another declaration of love follows.

At this point, I must insert that my mother was humble in many ways, but one way in which she certainly wasn't was that she had no doubts whatsoever about her authority with regard to human interactions. She was always confident that she knew the right thing to do – thanks to a special sensitivity to the trials and tribulations of every individual life. In this respect, she saw herself as a proven expert. This was the fabric of her life, woven from the countless conversations with individuals who felt that she understood their difficulties, doubts and longings, and took them seriously, in spite of how harsh she could be at times. And as I read her letter again, I wondered whether there wasn't also a hint of megalomania in it; her letter, written in 2004, was almost more addressed to me than to my father, and she must have been firmly convinced that her message would reach me in due course. But not before its time. She had anticipated everything with such minute foresight. She was sure that after her death, one day I would turn to her epistolary legacy, following the order in which she had arranged the correspondence, and that I would therefore read my father's letters from between 1968 and 1971 before coming across this letter from 2004, where she remarked that back then, in 1993, it was still too early to show me the bundle of letters, and in 2004 – for whatever reason – the right opportunity still hadn't come up. I imagined my mother tying the letters into a small bundle shortly before her death and thinking, 'This is how it should be. When I'm dead and buried, that's the time for him to read these. Then he'll also read this letter of mine to his father and know that Ozurumba visited me again and that I always loved him.'

That must have been her last will, and implausibly enough it did indeed turn out as she would have wished. She had counted on her version of the story reaching me, her preferred way of resolving things. There was something a bit pushy, presumptuous, about her know-it-all way of pulling the strings in my affairs (from beyond the grave!), I thought with a certain irritation (well, sons will be harsh with their mothers). And it was by no means the case that I had had a burning interest in this story earlier or that I had pressed my mother with questions about my father and their time together. On the contrary. Nevertheless, I couldn't help but see something manipulative in the deliberately tied bundle of letters. With the best of intentions, of course, as with most manipulations. And at the same time I asked myself whether I had perhaps already felt this as a child. After all, what do children register more strongly than manipulation, even if they can't identify it as such, perceiving only the cognitive dissonance around them? As a child, didn't I have my doubts about my mother? A scepticism that wasn't so much about her tireless unconventionality, but more about the self-confidence with which she decided what knowledge and awareness were best for her son? A childlike distrust, which, even if my hypothesis was correct (I'm not sure), I could hardly articulate, precisely because my mother was so widely recognised as a good person, who was always there for others, who never forgot anyone, who would happily go along with whatever was happening. Perhaps what I had always considered to be my personal weakness, my not wanting to know anything about the relationship between my mother and father, was in fact just a reflection of their meticulously planned information policy?

Perhaps as children we already know everything, we just don't know that we know it.

It was in this context that I went to Heidelberg to speak to a friend of my mother's, Monika. She was a little younger than Mama and was also a psychotherapist, a specialist in dyslexia. She had prepared for my visit and had already drawn up a list of the qualities she particularly valued in my mother: 'her ability to listen in such a way that an experience became something of value,' for instance, or 'her readiness to fight like a lioness,' or 'her skills as a party host.' My mother also had characteristics that Monika struggled with, her incorrigible refusal to accept help when she was in financial difficulties, for example (though I knew from Mama that this wasn't entirely true, and that Monika had herself often helped her out). We sat at our old dining table that Monika had taken after Mama's death, a farmhouse table made of cherry wood that had a warm glow to it. I knew the dark knotholes that adorned its tabletop like the back of my hand. As a displaced person, Monika said, my mother felt like a nomad all her life. Hence her reluctance to hoard things. If you gave her something, she would pass it on, not without mentioning this chain of giving, because the real meaning of the gift lay in this story which formed a connection between two people, creating a network. But for Monika, something else was more important about my mother: her obstinacy, inflexibility even. Her list of Mama's points that annoyed her included 'her refusal to let you challenge her.' I knew immediately what she meant. Although my mother was known for getting people to talk, there was, Monika now told me, a part of herself that she kept closed off, where she got tetchy and defensive, fending off any criticism and keeping any discussion of herself at bay. You couldn't exactly put your finger on it, it wasn't so much a specific topic, more an indistinct zone. If you touched on this zone, my mother stiffened like a deer frozen in a car's headlights; there's nothing you could do to get her to budge. Monika said her cancer was one of them, as well as human biology in general; these topics she repressed with every ounce of her being.

And now Monika reminded me of something about my mother that really stood out, the way she sometimes spoke with a strange accent, so that in certain situations her German no longer sounded like it was her mother tongue. Yet it wasn't a foreign accent exactly. She stretched the vowels, gave them a slightly different quality, her voice became nasal and mannered, and even her grammar seemed to stray beyond what was normal. This accent always emerged at emotional moments, at times of euphoria and enthusiasm, but also when something felt uncomfortable. If she had to speak to an answering machine, it would always be in this voice (and before she hung up, she'd close with 'Mama' – as if she was signing a letter).

I barely noticed it as a child, it was only as a teenager that I could no longer ignore it, because my friends asked why my mother sometimes spoke so strangely. Everyone noticed it. My mother didn't deny that it was so, but could only comment on it as though it were something she only knew from hearsay. If everyone said so, perhaps it was true… As a psychologist, she knew that any divergence had to have an explanation (preferably something in early childhood), and that's why she suggested tentatively that perhaps her way of speaking went back to the year in Silesia when she lived among Poles and wasn't allowed to speak German in public. But she didn't seem to be convinced by the explanation herself.

Monika, who worked a lot with young people with dyslexia, had a term for it: 'psychogenic disgrammatism.' But even she had no explanation for the phenomenon.

As a child I had reservations about Monika for a long time. I associated her with a birthday party that Mama took me to when I was five or six years old. Perhaps it was Monika's birthday. In any case, there were a lot of adults there, they must have been in their early thirties and they were a rowdy bunch. There was asparagus from Schwetzingen. Asparagus is a tricky vegetable for children with its bitter flavour and fibrous structure, but I liked it, though I had to concentrate when I ate it. I remember there was a large open-plan kitchen and dining room, and some people were sitting at the table while others were standing around in a group. My head was level with their hips. I managed to squeeze in at the table, with my plate of asparagus, when an adult turned clumsily and knocked over a glass of orange juice. The orange juice flooded my asparagus. I was shocked. This combination was unbearable. I was shaken. Adding to my disgust and horror was a feeling of abandonment, because at that moment I couldn't see my mother. Nobody seemed to understand that something terrible had happened. Everyone just thought, not to worry, it's just a bit of spilled orange juice, someone get the boy a new plate.

To this day I don't know why I was so upset by it. But I remember that I told Mama how I felt. I couldn't explain it, but Mama took me seriously. People should be allowed to get upset even without a cause, she thought; not everything needed an explanation or a reason.

From then on, as a child, Monika belonged to that world where reckless adults spill orange juice over children's asparagus.

'Your mother always wanted to protect you,' Monika told me. My childhood hadn't been as rosy as it had seemed, but Mama did everything she could to keep unpleasant experiences at bay, including the racist remarks that had indeed happened. She shielded me. Monika told me two stories. I was already vaguely aware of both, and in both cases I could picture them distinctly in my mind's eye without being able to say why these two incidents had emerged so clearly from the fog of my memory.

However, in my memory, these stories lacked their core essence; the decisive passages, without which the stories had no real meaning, were blacked out by the censorship authority, i.e. my mother. I only got the harmless version. Mama hid a few things from me, like any mother putting her hand over her child's eyes when there's a scary scene on TV. The child then doesn't see what happens, but still remembers the moment when everything goes dark.

One story was the one about Pastor Meerwein, who didn't want me in his Protestant kindergarten – allegedly, as Mama had always told me, because I wasn't baptised. But now I learned from Monika that my missing baptism wasn't the heart of the issue. In truth, Pastor Meerwein had said something racist about my origins. Monika didn't know exactly what. Or perhaps it was something derogatory about the fact that Mama had had a child with a black man. In any case, the tone or demeanour must have been so drastic that Mama spoke of him with contempt for the rest of her life.

The second story was one I could still remember perfectly well. I must have been six or seven years old when a young couple lived above us, Mr Köhler and Ms Bracke. It was when trim trails were big in West Germany, and because they didn't have any children, just a cocker spaniel, whom I was very fond of, they always took me with them to do the trim trail. There were light blue signs distributed around the forest telling you what sequence of movements you were supposed to do. You jogged from one instruction sign to the next, pausing for a bout of pull-ups, squats, that sort of thing. After the workout, we would go to the local pastry shop and I was allowed to choose my favourite cake: lemon cream.

But although I enjoyed our Saturday excursions with the Köhler-Brackes, one day they were called to an abrupt end. And I didn't know why. Mama told me I was no longer to have anything to do with them because they were bad people. So I avoided them both, and from then on my friend Volker and I changed Ms Bracke's name among ourselves to Ms Kacke, *Ms Shit*. But we didn't know the reason why.

I had thought about it every now and then, but I couldn't figure out why our nice arrangement with the cocker spaniel and lemon cream cakes had suddenly come to an end. 40 years later I got the answer from Monika, who had heard the *whole* story from my mother. At Christmas, Mr Köhler and Ms Bracke had said to her in a snide tone that Ijoma could be Caspar, one of the Three Kings, as at least he wouldn't need to "black up". Whatever the tone in which it was said (they seemed to like my company on our Saturday outings), a red line had apparently been crossed for my mother and all contact was broken off. But because they lived in our house for a good year after that, from then on I always listened at the door of the apartment to see if I could hear any footsteps in the stairwell before I went out. I didn't want to have to look them in the eye after they had been so nice to me.

My mother was a protective filter shielding me from everything bad. The fact that she succeeded in this must also have something to do with the fact that there wasn't really much to battle on this front. Whenever we think about our lives we look for what we don't know; compared to knowing, ignorance is the more complex variable. For a hundred years, the supreme discipline exploring ignorance was the unconscious; there has to be something in our soul that is beyond easy reach, a restricted area, somewhere off limits where the really illuminating stories unfold. But isn't that just more psychobabble? Not because there's no repression (I can hardly keep on denying it!), but because talk of repression has itself become a myth with its own momentum, marching on like a machine, full of buttons the patient needs to press for it to keep on ticking over by itself. You're hardly considered a complete person without your fair share of repression these days.

People plunge into their repressed subconscious like jumping into a fountain of youth, hoping to emerge from it again with a renewed identity. But with every new incarnation, you're just the same old you.

They're convinced that when they have named and blamed the trauma, the original, unharmed, intact self will re-emerge. But life is never without harm, there is no unharmed integrity, and there's no need to take ourselves too seriously. As soon as we open our eyes and let a piece of the world into our inner self, our ego is no longer intact. Yes, I think perhaps it is this concept of intactness as origin myth that repels me so much about the whole enterprise of Freudian therapy, because existing in the world necessarily means being vulnerable or harmed in one way or another, and besides, most traumas are overrated, or worse still, everyone is on the look-out for their trauma because they don't feel complete until they've unearthed one. It's hard not to have the feeling, however, that the psychoanalyst placed the trauma there to be found, like a parent putting out extra eggs for the Easter egg hunt, so no one feels excluded from the wonderful ritual where everyone finds their own prefabricated Easter egg and yet is convinced they've found something of their own that is incomparably personal to them. However, this trauma may be hidden elsewhere, somewhere that's not even on the psychoanalyst's map – or worse still, it turns out there's nothing that's incomparably personal, and we just pay the analyst to flatter us by feigning trauma. In any case, it always made me suspicious that this thing about me that was supposedly so painful to uncover, this thing that everyone else assumed I was suppressing, was in fact so patently obvious, which was why everyone was so fond of patting me on the shoulder – a gesture so hackneyed it was almost folkloric – and asking, 'Why do you reject Africa? What are you repressing?' But a repression that is so obvious that the suppressor himself would not even deny it (he would only say, it's not a matter of repression, just disinterest, which is explained by the fact that Nigeria is as far from my realm of experience as Tierra del Fuego!), well, such a repression doesn't deserve such a grandiose term.

And as much as I resent Dr Freud, I know of course that he is far smarter and more sophisticated than my caricature of him, and so the reason I didn't suppress things in the subtle and complex way that he earned his immortal fame describing was perhaps nothing but the fulfilment of a personal need for revenge, but in the manner of a child who covers his eyes with his hands and is convinced that no one can see him.

My chosen Easter egg is orange juice spilled over asparagus. It was a shock, and it's a proud trauma, because it stands for nothing. It isn't a parable or a metaphor, nor is it a code for something else. It is simply orange juice, annoyingly spilled over asparagus.

# Family

W hen I didn't go to Nigeria for our father's funeral in autumn 2011, my siblings were disappointed. They couldn't understand it and kept asking why I hadn't come. But they didn't turn against me. They seem to have limitless patience with me. And while their lives are dictated by the Nigerian epic and they find it a shame that I don't comply with the rules of their genre, they don't hold it against me. Perhaps they think to themselves, there has to be an outlier in every family, and he grew up in the diaspora, so it's hardly surprising.

In fact, I've had much more regular contact with my siblings since our father's death. I've also been showing initiative for the first time. When you lose both parents, you appreciate more what you still have in the way of family. Ikunna once made the cheerful comment, 'Ijoma you're so German!' Something relaxed inside me, because I finally knew that they weren't expecting me to be Nigerian. And I was actually happier to be Nigerian without this expectation weighing me down.

Ikunna now lives in Essex with her husband, a psychiatrist, also Igbo, and their two children, Zara and Ezra. I'm very fond of my niece and nephew, and they're a little bit like a reflection of my own life – yet another combination of origin, looks, culture and mannerisms. They barely know Nigeria, but the country and its culture are of course ever present via their parents. At the same time they live an English life, go to an English school, have English friends and neighbours. They differ most from their parents in their approach to communication. They're still children, but they'll chat with you for hours about everything under the sun. Their uncle is particularly glad to note their fascination for history; they're well informed about all the schemes and stratagems Wellington used to defeat Napoleon and they had a lot to say on the question of whether Brutus's murder of his adoptive father for the sake of saving the Republic could be morally justified.

My siblings were of no help in writing this book, though. Again and again I asked, 'Tell me what you remember about my trip to Nigeria!' Well, they remember they were very happy. Anything more specific? Did anything surprise you? Not really, and now, over twenty years later, they couldn't remember exactly. They had noticed that I smoked. 'So, when did you finally stop?'

I asked Ikunna if she was nervous when she found out that she had a brother in Munich? What about when she came to visit me for the first time?

Nervous? Why? No, she was delighted. After all, she was still in shock after losing two brothers, so it seemed like a blessing that another brother had appeared out of the blue.

But, I replied, what if she didn't like this new brother?

'Oh no,' she said, laughing and shaking her head at my naivety. 'We have the same genes, why would I not like you? There is a saying in Igbo: the child of a snake can only be long. Which could be interpreted to mean, it's obvious that, as a child of our father, you'd be okay.'

'You don't have to explain the figurative meaning to me, I understand. But I don't find the saying very convincing when you're talking about anything more than superficial characteristics. In Shakespeare, there are often siblings who are very different. One brother is malicious, the other is kind – just as in real life.'

Ikunna was a little surprised. She had never looked at it that way before.

Ijeure, my youngest sister, came to visit me in May 2016. The last time I had seen her was when I was in Nigeria, when she was eight or nine years old. Now in her early thirties, married, she was the mother of two children and a hat designer; hats play a bigger role in Nigeria's social life than in sartorially stripped-back Germany. I knew Ijeure's hats from her Facebook page, they were extravagant and anything but inconspicuous. A peacock's tail would be subtle compared to them. Nigerian style is anything but understated! And neither is Ijeure. Ikunna had warned me that our youngest sister can be incredibly, infuriatingly late, and that she spends two hours a day in the bathroom doing her hair and make-up, and there's no chance of a short cut. But to make matters worse, if you want to leave at 12 o'clock, you'll have a hard time getting her into the bathroom at 10 o'clock. She can't handle time, it's better to just accept that from the start.

Ijeure had visited her sister once in England, but apart from that it was her first trip abroad. So I tried to make her understand that traveling was a psychological challenge, that it was emotionally taxing, that it's not unusual to feel exhausted and long for the peace and quiet of home. I suggested she shorten the trip and that instead of the three weeks she envisaged, two weeks would be ideal for everyone concerned. Of course I felt a little heartless when I wrote this to her, but as an older brother you have to let your siblings share in your own life experience. Ijeure didn't respond to my email at all (this being how she generally dealt with disagreements), but booked her flights for three weeks as planned.

I picked her up at the airport in Tegel. She had become an impressive woman, of uncompromising extravagance, filling the room in the sense of the African ideal of beauty (as I had already noticed on my trip to Nigeria, only the men had lanky figures), but I recognised her face immediately. She pushed a luggage trolley laden high with two absurdly large suitcases; it looked more like nine weeks than three. I knew from her Facebook photos that she was a very fashionable woman. Almost every day she posted photos of herself showing off her hat creations, these flamboyant theatrical productions, colourful and lush, hyper-real in the way she styled them, and the exact opposite of the German cult of naturalness. Her use of make-up was also resource-intensive. When she stepped out of the security gate, she was still a little crumpled from the long flight, but I knew that she would transform as soon as she unpacked the contents of her suitcases.

As soon as I had heaved her luggage onto the bus, she launched into two lines of enquiry. It was clear she didn't intend to beat around the bush. Why wasn't I married and why didn't I believe in God? The truth is, I do believe in God, but when someone takes this approach, I take the opposite standpoint on principle. There we were on the bus heading across Berlin. This was a foreign country to her, I wanted to point out what you could see through the window, but she wasn't interested. She hadn't come to get to know Berlin, but to get to know her brother. Why in God's name was I still not married? What was I waiting for?

'The perfect woman? They don't exist, nobody is perfect,' she insisted, as though this was incontrovertible truth. She had clearly come to Germany on a mission, and visiting

Museum Island wasn't on her list of priorities. She was already opening up photos of her friends on her smartphone. 'Do you like her?'

My God, this was embarrassing, everyone on the bus could hear us. I lowered my voice in the hope that Ijeure would, too. *What will people think?*

Ijeure followed a binary logic. 'Are you so nasty that the women run away? Or so soft that they take advantage of you?' I didn't recognise myself in either alternative, and I found it mind-boggling that Ijeure could reduce the multiplicity of human psychology to two basic types: either a man was too good and was consequently at the mercy of the evil within women, or he was too evil and for any good woman he was consequently a bit too much. I on the other hand wasn't at all under the impression that things were going badly for me with women beyond the normal dose of bad luck, so I suggested that things were perhaps more complex than that (when people disagree with something they always say things are *more complex*), but Ijeure had a smile of superiority on her face, the smile of a believer who won't allow herself to be pushed into a corner by a wily atheist. At the end she just added without any irony, 'Does she have to be German?'

'Ijeure, why do you think I even want to get married?'

A silent pause, a defiant silence, as we drove through the district of Wedding. This was her first time in Berlin, but she didn't notice anything about the city because she was so focussed on getting me married.

More pictures of beautiful women were called up on her phone, mostly showing off Ijeure's hat creations. Admittedly, they were pretty good looking. Ijeure shook her head, exasperated by this point. 'I can't explain this to my friends any more. They think I'm deliberately fobbing them off because

I don't want to share my brother with them.' So that's what this was about. As long as I was unmarried, people in Nigeria thought I was still up for grabs. We were silent, both frustrated.

Then she responded with another question – and we still hadn't got to my apartment. 'Why didn't you come to Papa's funeral?' I said we both had very different relationships with our father. 'Don't you feel part of Nigeria?' I tried to explain that Nigeria was a foreign country to me. Home is where you grew up and where you feel at home. She nodded, more in resignation, as you nod in recognition of the sophistry you face, knowing that you have no chance against such sly counter arguments. Then she announced triumphantly, 'You and Papa, you look so similar!' I nodded. She replied, 'Blood does not lie!' From the expression on her face, I wouldn't have been surprised if she had headbutted me in frustration like a stubborn child who still doesn't know how their times tables.

She would repeat the same phrase many times over the next three weeks. 'Blood doesn't lie!' The longer I thought about the sentence, the creepier it seemed. When someone specifically emphasises that blood doesn't lie, does that suggest that something else is lying instead? Did Ijeure think I was denying the truth that I was my father's son? I wouldn't get very far with that line; the facial similarity clearly gives me away. 'Blood doesn't lie,' after all.

Finally, we reached my apartment. Because the suitcases were too heavy to drag up the stairs, I got another empty suitcase from the cellar and we split Ijeure's things into three. It really was only clothes and shoes. And while I mulled over how exhausting the next three weeks were going to be if we had to constantly work out our differences like we just did on the bus, for Ijeure it seemed to be a perfectly normal sibling interaction and nothing to worry about. And

I remembered that I used to think – as the only child that I once was – that the great thing about siblings was that unlike with friends you could really let rip, no holds barred, without the risk of losing them over it. At school, I always envied brothers who could give each other a merciless bruising. Ijeure's forthright presence made it abundantly clear: I was no longer an only child.

Ijeure was hungry and I was cooking. She watched, full of appreciation, as I chopped the onions. Then she called her husband via Skype and pointed the camera at the kitchen counter. 'My brother is cooking for me!' she shouted, and her husband, with his delicate features, looked on in amazement, almost tenderness, as I sliced a bell pepper. Not that he intended to follow my example in the future, but he was impressed – he had obviously assumed that men worked with their heads, rather than their hands.

The next morning I wanted to show Ijeure around Berlin. She had brought dozens of pairs of shoes with her, but they were all high heels – not exactly the ideal footwear for walking around the city. Ijeure didn't disagree, but she had assumed we would get around by car. And if I didn't have a car, we'd take a taxi. She glared at me, genuinely put out, when I told her we would be walking. 'Waka, waka,' she said in a strange, snippy tone. Waka, waka? What did that mean? It took me a moment to realise she was parodying Pidgin English. She presumably meant to suggest that it's only people who speak Pidgin English who walk anywhere. It was a social disgrace to go anywhere on foot. Had she come to affluent Germany to get around on her own two feet? Little did she know that, in Germany, walking and rambling was practically the national sport.

But her brother was adamant. You can't get to know a city hopping in and out of taxis, so off we went to buy her some trainers. They didn't exactly go with her lively, eye-catching outfits, but she would have to live with it.

The next evening, Ijeure lay exhausted on the sofa for a while ('You've dragged me through the entire city!'). Then, when she had recovered, she returned to the crucial question, this time slightly modified: if I didn't believe in God, why wasn't I a worse person?

I replied that you could behave decently even if there's no God.

'Why do you keep refusing to accept His existence?'

Trying to find a compromise, I added, 'Maybe there is a God, maybe not, we don't know.'

Oh yes, we did, she countered. We knew very well. Hadn't I read the Bible? It was full of evidence for His existence, full of proof and miracles that had happened to people.

Playing the devil's advocate with the classic art of subversion, I asked whether that then meant that everyone who didn't believe in Christianity was living in sin. Did that then mean that her African ancestors, who had lived before the first missionaries came from Europe, all awaited eternal damnation? As for the evidence in the Bible, had she not noticed that the four Gospels all told divergent and contradictory stories?

Ijeure's reaction was a loud laugh, as if it was impossible to know where to start with such wilful folly. I was just stubborn, she insisted. I always thought I knew better, that was my problem! God, she said with a chuckle, had unfortunately made me too smart to be able to see the truth; if I had a lower IQ, I wouldn't even think of doing such absurd mental pirouettes.

'Why,' she asked at last, 'do you wake up in the morning? Isn't it because God wakes you up?'

I thought of the lullaby with the line, 'Tomorrow you'll wake up again, if God wills it so,' which had given me the creeps as a child, and I softened a little.

If I just had more devout friends around me, everything would be different, Ijeure concluded.

Of course, that wasn't going to persuade me. 'I'm not going to become a believer out of peer pressure.' Again she laughed at my defiance. The unbeliever is always a stubborn ass who resists the obvious truth.

'According to the Book of Revelation, the world was supposed to have ended long ago, but it's still turning!'

'That's nonsense! Where does it say that?'

'You keep referring to the Bible, but you don't even know it – interesting!'

'Show me where it is! Show me exactly where it is, I want to see it with my own eyes!'

I picked up the Bible, but unfortunately I couldn't find the bit I wanted right away. Ijeure wasn't surprised in the slightest. The point went to her.

Now she switched from the God question back to the question of marriage. Neither of us backed down in the slightest. She maintained the line that the meaning of life was to have children. 'Otherwise nothing remains of you once you're dead.'

'Well,' I said smugly, 'perhaps a few things I've written will stick around. Books last a surprisingly long time. The Bible you swear by has been around for 2000 years!'

After a short pause, she went back on the offensive. I'm not yet married because I've been fixated on German women; that's not going to get me anywhere, because Nigerian women make better wives and would certainly appreciate me better. She had to say it again – some of her friends were pulling their hair out because they couldn't understand why Ijeure still hadn't set them up with her brother.

Then she took a short breather before carrying on in a slightly more conciliatory tone. 'You make things too complicated. You want the perfect woman! But nobody is perfect. You need to see that. Nobody is perfect!'

'I've never claimed they were!'

'Then why don't you want my friend?'

'I don't even know her!'

'She's very pretty.'

'It's not about being pretty! You need to have common interests.'

'What kind of common interests?'

'Books, for example.'

'She reads.'

'Ijeure, please! I've never once seen you with a book in your hand, yet what do you say about your friend? "She reads."'

'If you die without children, nothing of you will remain. You can have your wine and cigarettes every evening on the balcony, but everything is pointless.'

'Still, it wouldn't be bad if I found someone I got on with before I died, right?'

She sighed. Then was practically gushing as she described how she quarrelled with her husband every day of her God given life. It wasn't a criticism, it was part and parcel of married life!

She was right there.

When I had to go to work in the morning, there would be a theatrical outburst of 'No, don't go! I'll miss you! I'll die!'

'No need to exaggerate,' I'd reply.

'No need to be so insensitive.'

In short, we argued and we loved each other. I learned that it wasn't about avoiding conflict; on the contrary, it's friction that generates warmth. Sibling closeness burned a lot of energy, but there seemed to be no shortage of it.

Once, she went shopping by herself (did she think I secretly disapproved of her consumerist relationship with my homeland?), and she didn't come back that evening. Dinner was ready, it was 9 o'clock, and she wasn't answering her phone. I was starting to panic. It was extremely unlikely that anything had happened to her in the Mall of Berlin, and she had got the hang of the subway by now, but suddenly I was envisaging the worst possible scenarios. I knew it was ridiculous to call the police. Should I call Ikunna for advice? I would just worry her unnecessarily. I tried to concentrate, to focus on a harmless explanation as to why Ijeure wasn't home yet, but as much as I tried I couldn't find one. It turned 9.30 p.m., and I still couldn't get through to her. This had never happened before.

Then finally the long-awaited sound of the key in the lock of the front door! I threw my arms around Ijeure's neck in relief. 'Oh, I'm so glad you're back!'

Delighted with my reaction, she replied, 'You see! You were worried about me, so you do love me!'

Then came the first Sunday: time for church. Ijeure wanted to go to the Cathedral – Berliner Dom. Until then she had only seen it from the outside, but it had made an impression on her. The service started at 10.30. It would take us twenty minutes by tram, so I told her, 'We have to leave at ten. You need to be in the bathroom by eight.' It was nine when she finally headed into the bathroom. I gave her timekeeping updates every ten minutes. Of course, my worst character traits had long since taken hold of me; I knew we'd never make it to the service on time, and I couldn't help thinking, darkly, it serves her right.

'Ijeure, we have to leave in 15 minutes!'

'Ijeure, you do realise we need to leave in ten minutes...?'

'Ijeure, you're the one who wants to go to church, not me. It doesn't last three hours like back home, it's only 50 minutes. If we're late, we'll have missed half. You've got five minutes!'

It was 10.25 when she emerged from the bathroom. Now we could go, she announced cheerfully. There was no point in going now, I told her; by the time we get there the service would be almost finished. The only way we could get there more quickly would be by taxi. But I wasn't prepared to do that. Why should I pay for a taxi just because my sister couldn't get ready in time?

So we stayed home. That was a low point of tension between us. We didn't exchange a single word for two days. In our capacity to take offence, we truly were of the same blood, no question about it.

On the third day, weary of our protracted siege, we decided to declare a truce. The mood changed in a second. Ijeure declared that she would visit me every three years in future, but I needn't be alarmed, she would only stay two weeks at a time. And of course she would come to the wedding – it wasn't too late, but I should get a move on.

And then the following Sunday came. When we reached the steps of the cathedral, we were ten minutes late. Ijeure sat on the steps, pulled off her sneakers, slipped on her shimmering gold high heels, and together we set foot into the cathedral, under the gaze of the entire congregation. Seldom had God's creation been so colourful.

When I took Ijeure back to the airport after three weeks, it was clear that only siblings can argue like this and still make up. I have to accept it. Blood is indeed thicker than water, and it's pointless to continue to deny it.

Since Ijeure returned to Nigeria, I've been getting regular calls and emails from her. 'I miss you so much!' she tells me. Or: 'I miss you much more than you miss me!'

'That's not true, Ijeure,' I reply.

She wants to know if it's still raining constantly. And how 'our book' is coming on. Once she actually wrote 'How's our book?' Boy, oh boy.

When it comes to Nigeria, I thought, resistance is futile.

# Epilogue

As children we loved singing the seemingly senseless nursery rhyme 'Drei Chinesen mit dem Kontrabass'.

*Three Chinese men with a double bass*
*Sitting chatting on the street one day.*
*Along comes a policeman.*
*'What do we have here?'*
*Three Chinese men with a double bass.*

We revelled in the word play, the linguistic challenge it presented: every time you sang the verse again, you could only use one vowel sound throughout. We'd be in fits of laughter, as every time the bizarre vowels rendered it more and more absurd.

*Thre Chenes men weth e debble bess*
*Setting chetting en the stret wen dey.*
*Eleng cems e pelesmen.*
*'Whet de we hev her?'*
*Thre Chenes men weth e debble bess.*

Did that really happen I wonder? Were there ever actually three Chinese men sitting around in the street playing the double bass? Very curious. Not something you'd see every day. And chatting among themselves the whole time – that certainly would attract attention. Suspicion, even. Quite right for a copper to stop and enquire. All bonhomie like the slapstick gendarme Louis de Funès, because at the end of the day we need a little law and order on the streets. 'Well, well, well… what do we have here?'

And then soon enough we see that it really is just three Chinese men sitting around with a double bass having a chat. It might feel a little unfamiliar at first, but then you get used to it and realise that that is really all there is to it.

———•——

END

———•——